Instructor's Resource Manual

Instructor's Resource Manual
for Ronald J. Comer's

Abnormal Psychology

FOURTH EDITION

STEPHEN M. SAUNDERS
Marquette University

with Video Guide
by
Ronald J. Comer

Worth Publishers

Instructor's Resource Manual
by Stephen M. Saunders
to accompany
Abnormal Psychology, Fourth Edition

Printed in the United States of America

ISBN: 0-7167-3855-4

Printing: 5 4 3 2 1

Year: 04 03 02 01

Cover art by Wiktor Sadowski

Worth Publishers

41 Madison Avenue

New York, NY 10010

www.worthpublishers.com

Contents

Preface

To the Instructor

This manual is intended to be a resource for instructors to either develop an abnormal psychology course or improve an existing course. Each chapter of this manual includes the following sections.

Topic Overview: An outline of the chapter is provided for instructors as a quick reference to the material covered in the text.

Learning Objective: To enable instructors to coordinate lectures with the text, a list of the chapter's learning objectives is provided. These might be shared with students at the beginning of each chapter or prior to exams.

Key Terms: The key terms from the chapter, most of which are either in **bold** or in *italics,* are provided.

CD-ROM: Video Questions: Each chapter includes a list of video questions as they appear on the Abnormal Psychology CD-ROM, which accompanies each textbook. As a homework assignment, you can have your students watch the video clip, then answer these questions. Students can answer the questions directly into a text box appearing next to the video clip. When they have finished answering these questions, they can print out their assignments and hand them in for grading.

Comer Video Segments: A list of videos appropriate for the topics in the chapter is provided. Detailed descriptions of the videos are found in Appendix E.

Overhead Transparencies: The resources include a set of color overheads, and the transparencies pertinent to the chapter are listed.

Transparency Masters: Appendix C includes tables from the textbook that have been rendered in larger type. They can be reproduced onto transparency paper and used during the lectures. Some are intended for photocopying and distribution to students.

DSM-IV Masters: Appendix D includes the DSM-IV criteria for each disorder discussed in the textbook (as well as many not discussed in the text).

Class Demonstrations and Activities: Numerous demonstrations and activities that might prove useful in communicating the chapter's content to students are provided. These are intended to encourage students to interact with the material, to help them think critically about the topic being discussed, and to pique their interest in the facts relevant to the discussion. Finally, they are intended to generate discussion and ideas that complement the course and that can be seamlessly integrated into lecture material (e.g., "As one of the groups theorized, suicidal people often seem to be ambivalent about dying. A famous suicide researcher first wrote about this.").

Appendix A: Teaching References

Appendix B: Internet Sites

Appendix C: Transparency Masters

Appendix D: DSM-IV Masters

Appendix E: Video Guide

Supplements

The following ancillaries may be obtained by contacting your sales representative:

Video Segments for Abnormal Psychology (Tapes 1–3: ISBN 0-7167-5121-6; Tape 4: ISBN 0-7167-5157-7) Designed to bring an added dimension to lectures, this collection of four videotapes contains over 80 clips that depict disorders, show historical footage, and illustrate clinical topics, pathologies, treatments, laboratory experiments, and clinical dilemmas. Each clip runs from one to eight minutes. A fourth tape adds over 90 minutes of excerpts taken from *The Mind, Second Edition; The Brain, Second Edition;* and *The World of Abnormal Psychology.*

Test Bank (Printed: ISBN 0-7167-3856-2; CD-ROM: ISBN 0-7167-3857-0) by Debra and John Hull of Wheeling Jesuit University. This test bank offers more than 2,000 multiple-choice, fill-in-the-blank, and essay questions. Each question is rated by difficulty, identified as factual or applied, and keyed to the page in the text where the source information appears. The electronic version on a dual platform CD-ROM allows you to add, edit, and resequence questions. The CD is also the access point for online testing. With Diploma from Brownstone Research Group, instructors can create and administer secure exams over a network and over the Internet. The program allows you to restrict tests to specific computers or time blocks, and includes an impressive suite of gradebook and result-analysis features.

Instructor's Transparency Set (ISBN 0-7167-3858-9) Fifty full-color images, charts, photos, and graphs from the text are available for use in lectures.

Student Workbook (ISBN 0-7167-3853-8) by Katherine M. Nicolai of Rockhurst University. The Student Workbook and Study Guide actively involve students in the text material, using a variety of engaging exercises. Students who complete the exercises can better organize and apply what they have studied.

Abnormal Psychology Web Companion

www.worthpublishers.com/comerabnormalpsychology4e

This Web site offers an ever-expanding set of resources for both students and instructors. Features include flashcards for learning key vocabulary, multiple-choice practice tests for every chapter with built-in instructional feedback, Web links, and periodic newsletters that inform students of new research in the context of the book's coverage. The Web site is also the access point for online quizzing. Instructors can easily and securely quiz students online using prewritten, multiple-choice questions for each text chapter (not from the test bank). Students receive instant feedback and can take the quizzes many times. Instructors can review results by quiz, student, or even question, and can get weekly results via e-mail.

Study Habits

Students often come to instructors, especially after the first exam has been returned, wondering why their grades do not reflect their intense effort. Many times, of course, inquiry into their "intense" effort reveals obvious problems, such as not reading all of the chapters, reading the chapters the night before the exam, or not coming to class. Other times inquiry reveals that the student simply has poor study habits.

The following are recommendations that can be made to students, either individually or to the entire class, for improving study habits. Because studying is indeed a habit (a repetitive behavior that is overlearned to the point that active self-observation about performance is inhibited), these suggestions can be presented within the context of behavioral or cognitive models (see Chapter 3).

The Essentials of Good Study Habits

1. Set up a regular and practical schedule.
   - Study at a specific time at a specific place.
   - Don't try to study every day if that is impractical (which it usually is). Be wary of setting yourself up for failure.
   - Stick to your schedule, especially early in the semester. (Establish the habit.)
2. Find a place where you can concentrate.
3. Reward yourself for studying (operant conditioning).
   - Use specific rewards for specific achievements (e.g., after finishing the first half of a chapter, reward yourself with ice cream; after finishing reading the chapter, reward yourself with a CD).
   - Remember the Premack principle: David Premack demonstrated an extremely important principle of behaviorism. Activities that people enjoy are effective reinforcers for engaging in activities that people do not enjoy doing. In other words, rewards for

studying do not have to be material. To use the principle to reinforce studying, students should write an extensive list of activities they enjoy doing. This list can be generated, according to Premack, by simply observing what they spend a lot of free time doing. The principle maintains that they should engage in a specific enjoyable activity only after they have completed a less enjoyable task. A simple example, to which most students can relate, is studying their least favorite subject first (e.g., physics) and their most favorite subject last (e.g., psychology).

NOTE: It is important that students establish realistic and attainable goals for themselves and that they reward themselves after they achieve even the smallest goal. Rewarding themselves only after finishing a chapter will lead to infrequent rewards and, thus, an ineffective reinforcement schedule.

Improving Reading: The SQ3R Technique

SQ3R is a proven, five-step technique for improving the effectiveness of reading.

1. Survey: Preview the material. This is best done section by section (rather than an entire chapter).
2. Question: After you have a sense of what the reading will be about, ask yourself some questions about the topic.
3. Read: Read with an eye toward answering the questions you asked.
4. Recite: After finishing that particular section, recite to yourself, aloud, the answers to the questions, including supporting evidence based on research.
5. Review: After you have read the section, go back and review.

Test-Taking Strategies

1. It is a myth that one's initial hunch is likely to be correct. A research study of answer changes has shown that answer changes from wrong to correct are more common than answer changes from correct to wrong.
2. Use test time efficiently. First, preview the test and its various sections (e.g., the multiple-choice section, the short-answer section, the essay section). Anticipate how long each section will take to complete, especially the essay sections. During the test, keep track of the remaining time and where you are in the test. (Most instructors announce the remaining time at regular intervals.)
3. Don't spend too much time on a particular question if you are uncertain of the answer. It is better either to guess at the answer or to mark the question and come back to it. "Incubation" research has shown that spending extended time on a problem is less likely to generate the correct solution than leaving the problem (letting it incubate), then coming back to it.
4. Don't assume that questions are more difficult than they are. Most instructors are not trying to trick you. Most write a question with one best answer in mind.
5. Improving performance on multiple-choice questions can be achieved by following these strategies.
   a. Read the question, then try to anticipate the answer before reviewing the choices; if your answer is one of the choices, you are probably correct.
   b. Read the question completely. Be sure you understand it; reread it if necessary. Ask for clarification if you do not understand the question (if instructors didn't want you to do this, they wouldn't bother coming to class during testing time).
   c. Eliminate choices that you know are incorrect.
   d. Options that present broad, sweeping generalizations (e.g., "always" and "never") are usually incorrect.
   e. Options that are carefully qualified are often correct.
6. Improving performance on essay questions can only be accomplished if you know the answer. Improving performance when you definitely know the right answer depends on your ability to communicate your answer. This skill can be improved by practice.
7. Review the test if you have time.

Class Demonstrations and Activities

Some of the following activities relate directly to the chapter, but some are independent of it. Some relate to the videos provided with the instructor's manual and others to the Web pages. The activities can be used either in class or as homework assignments. All require direct student participation, and most are short enough to be incorporated in lectures.

The activities are based on the following assumptions:

1. Few students have read the material prior to class or to the particular discussion. That is, most students will have little or no exposure to the material being discussed.
2. Most students will have an opinion about the topic, even given the first assumption.
3. Abnormal psychology is an ongoing science. There are few facts or absolute truths, and it is essential that professionals and students in the field be able to think critically about information (i.e., to distinguish opinion from evidence). Mastery of the process of the scientific method is essential.

You will notice several recurrent ideas among these activities. General suggestions for implementing these activities are described in detail below.

Open (Class) Discussion

Many instructors desire to have occasional or even frequent discussion during classes. Discussion gives students the opportunity to interact with the material, which promotes learning, and to clarify problems, questions, or misunderstandings. However, generating discussions can be difficult. The following suggestions are ideas for encouraging students to participate in class discussions.

1. Establish discussion as a norm. If you want discussion throughout the semester, you must establish it from the very first class. Thus, it is important to get a discussion going the first class. It does not have to be lengthy or detailed, but there should be some discussion.
2. As the teacher, it is important to establish yourself as the expert or leader in the first class. Don't start with discussion. Rather, initiate a discussion activity about halfway into the class period.
3. Establish rules for discussion. The SOLER rules are useful for all interpersonal situations.
   a. S: Sit up straight and square to the other person.
   b. O: Sit openly; don't cross your arms or scowl.
   c. L: Lean in when speaking or being spoken to.
   d. E: Establish eye contact with the other person.
   e. R: Relax (smile, nod).
   f. Speak to each other respectfully; be aware of your tone and volume.
   g. Be aware of body language (e.g., grimaces, rolling eyes).
   h. Expect disagreement; listen to other people's ideas before forming an opinion.
4. In the first class of the semester, choose an example that cannot fail to create opinions and discussion.

   Example 1: It is likely that, before the first class, there will be a nationally publicized incident or example of mental illness (e.g., a murder by a mentally ill person or a celebrity's suicide or overdose). Ask students for some popular explanations, whether implicit or explicit, of what happened.

   Example 2: Describe a famous but perhaps unknown (to your students) example of the behavior of a mentally ill person (e.g., Charles Manson or John Hinckley). Ask students for ideas about the causes of such behavior.

Be careful when using a highly controversial example, as some students may become upset or feel attacked about their opinion. Also, never use a recent local example, because there may be students who are personally involved in the issue.

Group Work

Some students are often reluctant to talk, even if they have something to say, whereas others won't stop talking. An extremely effective way to involve all students—setting a norm or expectation that they will participate in the class—is to divide them into smaller groups of six to eight and give them a task to accomplish in the next eight minutes or so. Dividing the class into smaller groups and giving instructions to accomplish a task (e.g., creating a list of questions to ask a suicidal person) can help both types of students. The loquacious tendency of the talkative student will be easier to detect in a smaller group, and he or she will feel pressure to not dominate the conversation (although he or she may lead the discussion). The reserved student also will be more noticeable and will likewise feel pressure to contribute. The latter student may find it easier to speak up in a smaller group.

Some classes are fairly large, whereas others are fairly small. There may be anywhere from two to twenty divided groups in a class. If there are fewer groups, have them give a brief (e.g., two-minute) report to the class on their "findings." Have each group designate a spokesperson to discuss the group's findings with the class. This person usually misses some detail. When this happens, other group members may feel compelled to supplement the report, and the result is that all members of the group have an opportunity to speak up in the larger class. When there are a large number of groups, you may want them to produce a half-page report to be handed in immediately or at the end of the period.

Do not allow group members to adopt their own position: Force them to defend or promote a position (randomly assign the position). Forcing a debate position is a good way to help students to think about both sides of an argument. As social psychologists have shown, allowing group members to adopt their already established position encourages defensiveness and inhibits one's capacity to listen to others' arguments. Moreover, allowing a group to "vote" on their position can lead to arguments.

This activity works well even if more than one group promotes the same position, as different groups of students will often come up with very different conclusions about the same position, or different arguments defending similar conclusions.

Brainstorming as the Start of Science: Don't Ask for Recitations of Fact

The class will cover the findings uncovered by the scientific method. However, the scientific method always starts with an opinion or an idea (i.e., a hypothesis about the relationship between two variables or events). Students sometimes feel compelled to demonstrate that they know things. More commonly, students will be reluctant to talk if they are uncertain about the veracity of what they are saying. Encourage students to brainstorm to generate ideas. After generating ideas, the students will be more likely to attend to the presentation of research evaluating their opinions and ideas.

There are two elements of brainstorming: thinking and reporting. Essential thinking instruction is similar to psychoanalytic free-association instructions: Think freely, without editing your thoughts; no idea is bad. The second aspect is sharing your thoughts with others and writing or recording the thoughts.

If students brainstorm, they frequently will stumble across ideas, theories, and sometimes facts about mental illness and psychopathology, as many of these concepts are fairly intuitive. For example, eating disorders are related to pressures to be thin; depression is related to activity level; not exposing oneself to feared objects or situations will maintain those fears, whereas confronting an object or situation will result, eventually, in a reduction of that fear.

"Pretend, for a Moment, That You Are a"

Activities and discussions work best when students recognize their relevance to their own lives. Most students can easily imagine themselves in the following careers, jobs, or situations:

- A manager or supervisor of a group of people (e.g., a McDonald's manager or a director of a group of salespeople)
- A business owner (e.g., "Pretend you are the CEO of Impact Airlines")
- A grade school or high school teacher, principal, or counselor
- A close relative (e.g., a parent having difficulty with a child, a spouse having difficulty with a mate, or an adult having difficulty with an elderly parent)
- A doctor or nurse
- A mental health professional, such as a therapist or counselor (this is particularly useful after viewing some of the Comer videos; e.g., "Suppose you were this person's therapist")
- A friend
- A consultant to attorneys, the U.S. Congress, schools, etc. (e.g., "Thanks to this class, you are now an expert on the topic of depression. You and I are going to testify before Congress on funding for more biological research on the causes of depression.")

The Anonymous 5-Minute Essay

A useful tool for evaluating what students understand is the five-minute essay. Ask students to tear a sheet of paper from their notebook. Instruct them that they are *not* to put their name on the sheet. Give them a topic, then ask them to start writing. After five minutes, collect the papers either to share with the class or, more likely, to evaluate between classes.

1. Essays can emphasize points, such as "Explain why high school principals and counselors should be concerned about alcohol abuse among students."
2. Essays can permit students to ask questions that they are hesitant to bring up either in class or to you in person, such as "Take five minutes and write down what you'd like to know about the sexual disorders that we haven't yet discussed."
3. Essays can allow instructors and students to evaluate students' understanding of key issues, such as "In as much detail as possible, explain the cognitive theory of depression." There are two advantages to this particular essay: To evaluate understanding and to evaluate (and improve) students' capacity to answer essay questions on exams.

After this particular type of essay, you either can ask immediately for questions (e.g., "Okay, who needs the theory reexplained?") or review the sheets between classes to gauge students' understanding and to clear up misconceptions. This particular essay exercise is an excellent way to develop students' capacity to answer essay questions that may appear on exams. Many students complain that they understand what they are trying to write or communicate, but that they don't communicate it well, especially under time pressure (as with exams). A specific suggestion is to tell students to take their essay home and grade it as if they were the instructor. If they find that their essay is poor—that is, that it does not accurately reflect their understanding—then they should rewrite it. Then, they should compare their first essay with their revised essay.

"Here's $25,000 to Be Awarded to"

Most academics can relate to the grant-seeking process. Students can relate to competition for money or awards as well. Present the students with a problem (e.g., the stigma associated with seeking mental health treatment), then ask for ideas on how it might be solved. Tell them that the best idea will be awarded $25,000 for implementation, but that only one idea gets the award.

This exercise encourages creative and critical thinking. Creative ideas get attention, but they won't get funded unless they are also practical (able to be completed). This exercise is best done in group work (see above).

"Let's Write a Self-Help Bestseller"

This activity is an effective way to encourage students to integrate and organize the information presented to them on a particular topic or disorder. There are hundreds of self-help books on the market, and all tend to follow a simple outline:

I. Description of a common problem
II. Source of the problem
III. Possible solutions

These three points correspond to the themes of abnormal psychology courses (description, cause, and treatment). Students can write an outline of a self-help book or a draft of a chapter on the problem description (e.g., "How might this problem be influencing your life?"). Alternatively, they can generate self-help interventions to overcome the problem. Students should be encouraged to be as accurate as possible, that is, to have their work correspond to the descriptions and interventions presented in the textbook and lectures. Expressing this information in their own words is an excellent way to encourage students to assimilate the facts. This activity is especially helpful during discussions of disorders.

Stephen M. Saunders
Marquette University

Instructor's Resource Manual

CHAPTER

1 Abnormal Psychology: Past and Present

TOPIC OVERVIEW

What Is Psychological Abnormality?
- Deviance
- Distress
- Dysfunction
- Danger
- The Elusive Nature of Abnormality

What Is Treatment?

How Was Abnormality Viewed and Treated in the Past?
- Ancient Views and Treatments
- Greek and Roman Views and Treatments
- Europe in the Middle Ages: Demonology Returns
- The Renaissance and the Rise of Asylums
- The Nineteenth Century: Reform and Moral Treatment
- The Early Twentieth Century: The Somatogenic and Psychogenic Perspectives

Current Trends
- How Are People with Severe Disturbances Cared For?
- How Are People with Less Severe Disturbances Treated?
- What Are Today's Leading Theories and Professions?

Crossroads: A Work in Progress

LEARNING OBJECTIVES

1. Describe the different ways of defining abnormality from the perspectives of deviance, distress, dysfunction, and danger.
2. Discuss some of the difficulties of defining a person's behavior as abnormal.
3. Describe the main modern treatments of abnormality.
4. Describe the ways that ancient peoples, Greeks, Romans, and persons in the age of the Renaissance viewed and treated abnormal behavior.
5. Describe moral treatment.
6. Describe the somatogenic and psychogenic perspectives of the early 1900s.
7. Describe the current treatment of severely disturbed individuals. Contrast this to the current treatment of less severely disturbed individuals.
8. Compare and contrast the current dominant theories in abnormal psychology.
9. Compare and contrast the professions that study and treat abnormal behavior.

KEY TERMS

abnormal psychology
asylum
clinical practitioner
clinical psychologist
clinical scientist
community mental health approach
counseling psychologist
culture
dangerousness
deinstitutionalization
demonology
deviance
distress
dysfunction
eccentricity
educational psychologist
exorcism
family therapist
general paresis
humors
hypnotism
hysterical disorder
inpatient treatment
lycanthropy
marriage therapist
mass madness
moral treatment
norms
outpatient treatment
patient dumping
private psychotherapy
psychiatric nurse
psychiatric social worker
psychiatrist
psychoanalysis
psychogenic perspective
psychotropic medications
somatogenic perspective
state hospital
syphilis
tarantism
therapy
treatment
trephination

MEDIA RESOURCES

CD-ROM Video Questions

The following is a list of video questions as they appear on the Abnormal Psychology CD-ROM that accompanies each textbook. As a homework assignment, have your students watch the video clip, and then answer these questions. Students can answer the questions directly into a text box appearing next to the video clip. When they have finished answering these questions, they can print out their assignment and hand it in for grading.

Also use these CD-ROM segments as assignments to expose your students to material prior to your lectures.

Early Procedures in Mental Hospitals

1. The treatment procedures shown represent which perspective of abnormal behavior—somatogenic or psychogenic? Why?

   A: Psychogenic; the procedures indicate a belief that abnormal behavior has a physical cause.

2. What were the goals of the procedures shown?

   A: to correct underlying physical pathology

3. Who first used baths to treat abnormal behavior?

   A: Greek physicians

4. Which of the treatments shown would cause the least harm to the patient? Why?

   A: treatment involving baths and sheets because they were not invasive

5. Which treatments were the most risky? Why?

   A: ECT, lobotomy, and the coma therapy, because they involved surgery or were designed to cause brain seizures and/or comas

6. Which areas of the brain are "disconnected" as the result of a lobotomy?

   A: the frontal lobes and the brain's lower centers

7. What developments in the treatment of mental illness make it unlikely that those medical procedures will ever be resumed on a large-scale basis?

   A: (1) discovery of psychotropic medications, (2) deinstitutionalization, (3) managed care, and (4) the community mental health approach that involves outpatient treatment

Comer Video Segments

(See the Video Guide in Appendix E for detailed descriptions.)

Defining Psychological Abnormality

Segment 1 Deinstitutionalization and Jailing the Mentally Ill
Segment 11 Elevator Phobia
Segment 22 Survey of Dieting and Body Image Among 33,000 Women, by Drs. Susan Wooley and Wayne Wooley
Segment 28 Therapy Reaction Tapes
A. Elderly client questions value of therapy
G. Therapist questions termination
Segment 31 Sociocultural Overview of Opioid Dependence
Segment 40 Deinstitutionalization and Homelessness
Segment 41 Therapy Discussion Group: Patients with Severe Mental Disorders
Segments 49 and 50 Patients' Rights

History of Abnormal Psychology

Segment 1 Deinstitutionalization and Jailing the Mentally Ill
Segment 2 Medical Procedures Used in Mental Hospitals in the First Half of the Twentieth Century
Segment 8 Client Centered Therapy by Dr. Carl Rogers
Segment 19 Early Electroconvulsive Therapies
Segment 32 Methadone Treatment Program, 1973
Segment 40 Deinstitutionalization and Homelessness
Segment 42 Prefrontal Lobotomy Procedure, 1942
Segment 43 Patients Before and After Prefrontal Lobotomy, 1944
Segment 44 Lobotomized Persons at a State Hospital Today
Segment 45 Early Case of Multiple Personality Disorder

Current Trends in Abnormal Psychology

Segment 1 Deinstitutionalization and Jailing the Mentally Ill
Segment 3 Modern Day Mental Hospital Ward
Segment 4 PET Scan Procedure and Results: Comparison of Schizophrenic and Nonschizophrenic Twins
Segment 5 MRI Scan: Comparison of Schizophrenic and Nonschizophrenic Twins
Segment 10 Multimodal Therapy by Dr. Arnold Lazarus
Segment 11 Elevator Phobia
Segment 13 Anxiety Disorders
Segment 14 Fear of Airplane Travel: Clinical Features and Special Exposure Treatment
Segment 20 Modern Electroconvulsive Therapy by Dr. Max Fink
Segments 38 and 39 Antipsychotic Drugs
Segment 40 Deinstitutionalization and Homelessness
Segment 47 Dr. Ivar Lovaas Treats Young Autistic Child with Behavioral Intervention
Segments 49 and 50 Patients' Rights
Segment 55 PET Scans
Segment 58 Treatment for Pain Disorders

Overhead Transparencies

Transparency 1, Figure 1–1, p. 19, The impact of deinstitutionalization

CLASS DEMONSTRATIONS AND ACTIVITIES

Rosenhan's *On Being Sane in Insane Places*

To discuss the problem of "sticky" diagnostic labels and the manner in which they influence others' perceptions, describe Rosenhan's study, "On Being Sane in Insane Places" (*Science*, 1973, pp. 250–257). In this study, eight mentally healthy people, several of them psychologists and psychiatrists, complained of hearing voices that repeated "Empty," "Dull," and "Thud," and were admitted to mental hospitals. Once inside, they acted normally for the remainder of their stay. One of the pseudopatients was a professional artist, and the staff interpreted her work in terms of her illness and recovery. As the pseudopatients took notes about their experience, staff members referred to the note-taking as schizophrenic writing. Ask students for any other types of behavior that they can think of that would be misinterpreted in this situation. Ask students for other examples, which they have encountered or could imagine occurring, where a psychiatric label (such as depression, anxiety, or eating disorder) might "stick" and influence others' perceptions.

When discussing this study and students' reactions to it, it might be worthwhile to discuss criticisms of the study. For example, it will be important to emphasize that auditory hallucinations (such as those supposedly heard by the pseudopatients) are extremely rare and pathognomonic (indicate severe pathology), and that it might have been entirely appropriate for these persons to be hospitalized immediately. Also, the "patients" were discharged with the diagnosis "in remission," which means "without signs of the illness," a very rare diagnosis. Regarding the use of the study to criticize psychiatric diagnoses as unreliable or invalid, one author responded: "If I were to drink a quart of blood and, concealing what I had done, come to the emergency room of any hospital vomiting blood, the behavior of the staff would be quite predictable. If they labeled and treated me as having a bleeding peptic ulcer, I doubt that I could argue convincingly that medical science does not know how to diagnose that condition" (Kety, 1974, p. 959).

Mental Health and the Media

Ask students to find newspaper articles and magazine articles that deal with mental illness. They can also find videotapes of talk-show guests, television programs, and/or films with the same theme. Have them evaluate the quality of the coverage, the accuracy or inaccuracy of the information presented, and the assumptions made about mental illness. You can adapt this discussion as a written or extra-credit assignment.

Perceptions Portrayed by Self-Help Books

Ask students to visit local bookstores or libraries to examine self-help books. Have them evaluate the quantity and the quality of the books. Ask them to bring in examples of books that seem to be useful. You can facilitate this discussion during class.

Group Work: Positive and Negative Labeling

Ask small groups to develop lists of words used to label normal and abnormal behavior and persons. Typically, you should find that more words are listed for abnormal persons than for normal ones. Ask the class to explain the difference in the lengths of the lists. Discuss the positive and negative connotations of the lists.

Distress, Dysfunction, Danger, and Deviance

Maintain a file of newspaper clippings that depict the four criteria of abnormality: distress, dysfunction, danger, and deviance. You can use this file throughout the semester when attempting to make diagnoses of disorders.

Group Work *or* the Anonymous Five-Minute Essay *or* Open Discussion: This Place Makes Me Crazy

This can be done either in small groups or as a short essay or as an open discussion. The general theme is that not only individuals but also families, workplaces, occupations, and neighborhoods can be dysfunctional. (1) Ask small groups to come up with examples of workplaces or occupations that fit this description. (2) Ask for anonymous essays of dysfunctional groups that students are personally familiar with (e.g., "I once worked in a job where . . . "). (3) Lead a general discussion on this topic. Ask students to describe the features that were dysfunctional (e.g., vindictive personnel, chaotic management, rules that kept changing, confusion, blaming, unethical practices). Many students will be able to identify with these examples of how environment and stress can affect individual behavior.

Factors in Deinstitutionalization

A variety of factors led to the deinstitutionalization movement, including rising criticism of the inhumane treatment of mental patients and the discovery of powerful antipsychotic drugs. You can describe the dramatic reduction in the census of state mental hospitals in the United States from more than 500,000 in 1950 to about 100,000 in 1990. Ask students for their opinions on the pros and cons of this movement.

Rocks in My Head

Lead a discussion on material dealing with the Middle Ages, and ask students where they think the phrase "rocks in your head" originated. Explain that street vendors (quacks) performed pseudosurgery during the Middle Ages. A person troubled by negative emotions or other symptoms of mental illness could go to the vendor, who would make a minor incision in the scalp; an assistant would sneak the "surgeon" a few small stones, and the surgeon would pretend to have taken them from the patient's head. The stones, he claimed, were the cause of the person's problems and the patient was now "cured." Ask students for any modern-day examples of miracle cures. This is a useful way to dicuss the concept of the placebo effect—that is, the effectiveness of treatment is often due to the patient's belief that it will work.

Institutional Treatment of the Mentally Ill

Lead a discussion that points out that asylums in the early twentieth century grew so fast and were so underfunded and understaffed that they became filthy, degrading human warehouses. Although there are more well-trained professionals today, mental health care and research are still greatly underfunded. One result is that a significant number of the homeless in the United States are mentally ill and are not getting the help they need. Another is that in many states mentally ill persons are being housed in jails even though they have not committed crimes. Discuss these consequences.

Defining Normal

Ask students to define "normal," then ask how they personally determine when someone's behavior is abnormal and solicit relevant examples. Ask students to discuss how they arrived at their definitions. Use an overhead transparency to keep track of the different definitions. Compare the specific criteria for abnormality discussed in the text to formulate a class definition.

Distinguishing between Normal and Abnormal

Identify examples from literature or real life that exemplify the difficulty encountered when trying to draw clear distinctions between normal and abnormal behavior.

Example: Sometimes the distinction is obvious. A 32-year-old man complains that his thoughts are being repeated in public and on television and that he is being tortured by invisible rays. He claims that people living in the apartment above him are transmitting abusive messages through the heating system. At times he stares into the mirror, grimacing horribly. He often shouts nonsense words and phrases, seemingly from nowhere, and laughs loudly for no apparent reason. He screams at people walking by him on the street. His family takes him to the hospital after he begins pounding on the walls of his apartment, screaming nonstop.

Example: Joseph Heller's novel *Catch-22* tells the story of a bomber navigator (Yossarian) during World War II. His situation sounds unusual, at first: He is a 34-year-old flier who is terrified of flying. He has frequent nightmares and behavioral outbursts. He is known to threaten people and to drink too much. He begs to be let out of his current situation because he feels he is crazy. (The U.S. Army won't release him for reasons of insanity, however, because he obviously is sane if he wants to be released; if he were insane, he wouldn't ask to be released: "a perfect catch, Catch-22.") After explaining that he is terrified of being shot at, his drinking and other behavior suddenly seem "normal."

Example: Kurt Cobain, the lead singer for the alternative rock group Nirvana, had such chronic stomach problems that he had trouble eating. He awoke every morning starving and wanting food, but every time he ate, he would throw up and end up weeping. Doctors were unable to determine the cause of the problem. He despaired and became suicidal. Instead of committing suicide, he turned to drugs, becoming a heroin junkie. Is this normal? Was his drug use pathologic, even if it was understandable? (Cobain eventually did commit suicide.)

Why Should Students Care about Psychopathology? What Relevance Does It Have?

Discuss the relevance of mental illness and abnormal psychology. Beginning the course with this discussion is a useful way to set the "norm" for the rest of the semester (see the Preface).

Discuss the potential relevance of mental illness to those who work with the public (e.g., small business owners, salespeople, doctors, teachers, and lawyers). Emphasize that the issue of prevalence of psychological disorders is really a question of whether it would be beneficial to someone, in any of these situations, to be familiar with the existence and presentation of mental illnesses (e.g., to recognize depression or alcohol abuse). Frame the discussion by saying, "Pretend, for a moment, that you are a business owner (school principal, etc.). In any year, what impact will mental illness have on your business (school, etc.)?"

The ECA study conducted standardized household interviews of a random sample of 18,000 adults asking, among other things, about psychological symptoms and help-seeking behavior. Researchers found that, in any one-month period, 16 percent of persons are experiencing or suffering from a mental illness. This indicates an annual prevalence of over 25 percent, and a lifetime prevalence of over 30 percent. (Only 28.5 percent of the diagnosable mentally ill in the study sought any treatment.)

Group Work *or* Open Discussion: What Are the Risk Factors for Mental Illness?

Ask students to generate a list of what they presume are some of the risk factors for mental illness. Inform them that risk factors are associated with an increased likelihood of a mental illness being present or developing. This activity can lead to a discussion of assumptions (or myths) about mental illness and/or a discussion of the scientific study of mental illness.

The following are risk factors:

- Age: Young people have higher rates of mental illness than older people.
- Marital status: Separated, divorced, and never married individuals have higher rates of mental illness than married or widowed people.
- Education: Less educated individuals have higher rates of mental illness.
- Personal income: The lower the income, the higher the rate.
- Employment: Unemployed people have higher rates of mental illness.
- Contact with friends: Isolation is a risk factor; fewer contacts are associated with higher rates of mental illness.
- Satisfaction with relationships: Greater satisfaction is associated with lower rates.
- Marital happiness: Greater happiness is associated with lower rates.

The following are not risk factors:

- Gender: It used to be thought that women had higher rates of mental illness.
- Ethnicity or race
- Intelligence: Measured intelligence (e.g., IQ) doesn't prevent mental illness, although there is some evidence that more intelligent people have more difficulty admitting that they have a mental illness.

Diagnostic Categories: Criticisms and Advantages

Discuss the rationale and criticisms of diagnoses. Begin with criticisms of diagnoses, which are easier for students to generate. After generating criticisms, point out that diagnostic labels are necessary and solicit opinions why.

Criticisms:

- Diagnoses can give scientists and clinicians a false sense of having explained behavior. For example, a clinician might claim that his patient is highly suspicious because he has a paranoid disorder, but this tells us nothing about why the patient is paranoid. Likewise, to say that a patient is suicidal because of her depression does not aid in either understanding or helping the patient.
- Diagnoses can be used to rationalize or excuse certain undesirable behaviors.
- Diagnoses can stigmatize individuals, creating an "us versus them" sense, by promoting the idea that there is a clear-cut distinction between normal and abnormal behavior.
- Diagnoses can be "sticky," influencing others' perceptions of subsequent behavior, as exemplified in the Rosenhan study.

Advantages:

- Scientific: Science relies on a common language and categorization. Conventionalized categories or names for illnesses are necessary to facilitate research into their etiology and treatment. Agreeing on findings from studies of depression or schizophrenia would be very difficult if scientists did not agree on what these disorders are and are not.
- Clinical: The presence of an illness is indicated by providing a diagnosis. If there is no diagnosis, then the person has no illness. Thus, diagnoses tell clinicians when to initiate treatment and when treatment should be terminated (because the person is better). Likewise, diagnoses can tell us what treatment might be effective.
- Legal significance: Defining abnormal behavior helps determine when a person is responsible for his or her behavior. For example, on March 30, 1981, John Hinckley, Jr., shot and seriously

wounded President Ronald Reagan outside a hotel in Washington, D.C. In May 1982, a jury declared Hinckley innocent by reason of insanity.

How Do We Define "Abnormal Behavior"?

Discuss the limitations of each criterion for abnormal behavior if it were used as the sole criterion. This is an effective instructional technique to emphasize the complexity of the field and the danger of dismissing "incomplete" information. Follow this discussion with the DSM-IV criteria.

- Social norms or social deviancy: Social norms change; what is deviant in one era may not be in another. Ask students whether their parents think their musical taste is "normal," then instruct them to ask their parents about their tastes when they were younger.
- Danger criteria: Most mentally ill people are not dangerous to others.
- Maladaptiveness criterion: This criterion can be highly subjective and can change from situation to situation. For example, adaptive behavior on a Friday night at a fraternity party is not necessarily appropriate in a work situation.
- Personal distress criterion: Some mentally ill persons feel little distress.

Changing Explanations of Abnormal Behavior

Students often struggle with the changing explanations, over the years, of abnormal behavior. Lead a discussion of "the state of the world" as a way to understand these explanations. Explanations and ways of treating or controlling abnormal behavior are the result of the prevailing models or theories of humanity and human beings' relation to the world. Explanations also reflect the limits or the extent of knowledge. To understand how various historical cultures have viewed abnormal behavior, it is useful to examine what their world was like and what were the prevailing ideas for understanding that world.

- The Greeks explained insanity as the work of the gods. Treatment involved taking the afflicted to the temple of the god Asclepius, the god of healing.
- The Middle Ages (sixth to fourteenth centuries) were characterized by nearly constant warfare, the bubonic plague, and the ascendancy of the church, which rejected science and emphasized the activity of the devil. The mentally ill were "treated" for demonic possession.
- The Renaissance, the Enlightenment, and the Age of Reason marked the rise of science and the decline of demonology. The sixteenth-century German physician Johann Weyer concluded that many so-called witches were simply mentally imbalanced, and he argued successfully that the mentally ill needed to be cared for by the community and by the family.
- In the nineteenth and twentieth centuries, the discovery of biological causes of insanity led to the belief that mental illness is incurable (persuading some to commit patients permanently to state mental hospitals). The discovery of antipsychotics led to deinstitutionalization.

CHAPTER

2 Research in Abnormal Psychology

TOPIC OVERVIEW

LEARNING OBJECTIVES

1. Describe the role of clinical researchers in the field of abnormal psychology.
2. Describe the case study, including its uses and limitations (strengths and weaknesses).
3. Describe the correlational method. What is a positive versus a negative versus a null correlation? What are the uses and limitations of correlational research?
4. Describe the experiment. Describe the reasons that experimenters use control groups, random assignment, and blind design.
5. Describe the following experimental designs: quasi-experimental design; natural experiments; analogue experiments; single-subject experiments.

KEY TERMS

ABAB design
analogue experiment
baseline data
biased evidence
blind design
case study
clinical significance
confounds
control group
correlation
correlational coefficient
correlational method
dependent variable
epidemiological study
experiment
experimental group
experimental method
external validity
high-risk study
incidence
independent variable
internal validity
longitudinal study
magnitude of correlation
natural experiment
negative versus positive correlation
no (zero) correlation
nomothetic understanding
placebo
prevalence
quasi-experiment
random assignment
rights of subjects
scientific method
single-subject experiment
statistical significance

MEDIA RESOURCES

CD-ROM Video Questions

The following is a list of video questions as they appear on the Abnormal Psychology CD-ROM that accompanies each textbook. As a homework assignment, have your students watch the video clip, and then answer these questions. Students can answer the questions directly into a text box appearing next to the video clip. When they have finished answering these questions, they can print out their assignment and hand it in for grading.

Also use these CD-ROM segments as assignments to expose your students to material prior to your lectures.

Mood Disorders: Hereditary Factors

1. What type of research method did Dr. Egeland use in her search for causes of manic-depressive (bipolar) disorder?

   A: case studies of a close-knit old-order Amish community in eastern Pennsylvania

2. What was Dr. Egeland's research hypothesis?

   A: that there were genetic factors contributing to manic-depressive disorder

3. What was Dr. Egeland's rationale for searching for genetic causes of manic-depressive disorder?

A: If chromosomes carry the blueprint for our inherited physical traits, then perhaps the chromosomes influence our behavior as well.

4. Why did Dr. Egeland choose this group of people?

   A: They are a very homogenous population. They tend to marry within the community and spend their entire lives in the community.

5. What types of investigative procedure did she utilize to collect data on the subjects?

   A: She took blood and tissue samples, which allowed her to study the genetic makeup of the population.

6. Did Dr. Egeland find any genetic markers for the disorder among the Amish that she studied?

   A: Yes. She found a marker on the short arm of chromosome 11.

7. What was Dr. Egeland's research conclusion?

   A: that there was a hereditary factor involved in some forms of manic-depressive (bipolar) disorder

Comer Video Segments

(See the Video Guide in Appendix E for detailed descriptions.)

Segment 4 PET Scan Procedure and Results: Comparison of Schizophrenic and Nonschizophrenic Twins
Segment 5 MRI Scan: Comparison of Schizophrenic and Nonschizophrenic Twins
Segment 21 Experiment Linking Placebo Effects to Endorphins
Segment 25 Lateral Hypothalamus Stimulation Leads to Hunger and Eating Behavior
Segment 26 Subjects Get Pleasure from Experiencing Hunger and Food Thoughts
Segment 27 Medial Hypothalamus Anesthetization and Eating Behavior
Segment 201 Studies Link Mood Disorders to Hereditary Factors
Segment 202 Aggression, Violence, and the Brain
Segment 203 Craving for Cocaine: Triggers and Treatment
Segment 211 Man with History of Alcohol Dependence Is Tested for Genetic Predisposition
Segment 212 The Effects of Alcohol and Other Depressants on the Brain
Segment 215 Woman with Alzheimer's Disease
Segment 218 Temple Grandin, an Extremely High-Functioning and High-Achieving Person with Autism, and Research on Autism

Transparency Masters

TM–2, Table 2–1, p. 33, Relative Strengths and Weaknesses of Research Methods

CLASS DEMONSTRATIONS AND ACTIVITIES

Case Study

Present a case study to the class.

Correlational Study

Discuss a situation in which a correlational design is required, that is, where it is either practically or ethically impossible to conduct an experiment. Examples include the association between smoking and heart disease, sexual abuse and eating disorders, alcohol abuse and work problems, and high levels of expressed emotion and schizophrenia.

Autism and Emotionally Frigid Parenting: The Dangers of Concluding Causation from Correlation

Present the case of clinicians concluding that autism is due to parenting practices. Children with autism were taken by their parents to Leo Kanner, a child psychiatrist at Johns Hopkins University. Kanner observed the behavior exchanges between children and parents and found that these parents appeared to be less warm than other parents. He concluded that these parents were "emotional refrigerators" and that their detached, emotionally vacant child-rearing practices caused the autism; the children responded to this rejection by becoming defensive and rejecting themselves. Psychoanalyst Bruno Bettelheim reached the same conclusion, but he argued that their hostility was unconscious and unintended. Nonetheless, Bettelheim advocated placing the children in residential settings with more loving caregivers so that the children could learn to trust and to let down their defenses. Discuss the fact that Kanner and Bettelheim were sincere in their efforts to help, but that they had concluded causation based on correlation (the observation that two events—autism and emotional detachment—coincided). Discuss the effect such conclusions might have had on parents. Point out that the axiom "Correlation does not imply causation," if not followed, can cause serious problems.

Facilitated Communication: Strict Experimental Controls Debunk a Useless Intervention

Facilitated communication (FC) is a method for providing assistance to a nonverbal person—such as a child with autism—by using a keyboard to type messages and thus communicate with others. The procedure involves the "facilitator" or assistant supporting the patient's hand, making it easier for the patient to strike the keys he or she wishes to strike. Proponents of FC have asserted that previously uncommunicative persons, such as those with autism or profound mental retardation, can now communicate with others and, in fact, that many such patients have been found to be highly intelligent. In one study of FC, patients were asked how they felt. With the facilitator's help, patients described themselves, revealing their personalities. Patients exhibited unique spellings, or typographical errors, or unique word usages. They occasionally reported, via FC, that they had been sexually abused. A number of questions were raised about FC. The most important was whether the facilitators were unwittingly selecting the keys that spelled out the messages. What was needed was a controlled experiment. An article in *American Psychologist* summarized the findings as follows:

> Relevant controlled, peer-reviewed published studies repeatedly show that, under circumstances when access to information by facilitators is systematically and tightly manipulated, the ability to produce communication through FC varies predictably and in a manner that demonstrates that the content of the communication is being determined by the facilitator. (Jacobson, Mulick, and Schwartz, 1995, p. 754)

The following is from an abstract of a 1998 article in the journal *Focus on Autism and Other Developmental Disabilities:*

> The first author, a certified speech-language pathologist (SLP), served as the facilitator for two students with autism to assess pointing control during facilitated communication. The teacher instructed the students during typical classroom activities, and two classroom assistants collected data. We used a counterbalanced alternating treatments design with the SLP/facilitator being either blind or sighted. She wore sunglasses throughout the investigation with a cardboard cutout inserted for the blind condition. The alternating treatments data reveal that the students responded more accurately when the SLP/facilitator could see in spite of the fact that she did not think she was influencing their responding and did not intentionally do so.

Science and Society

The previous example clearly illustrates the sometimes dramatic tension between concrete experimental evidence and the human desire to believe certain things. In the FC example, there is great desire to help persons with autism, which can be a profoundly disabling disorder.

Double-Blind Research

Discuss the ethical dilemmas involved in the use of control groups in research. Double-blind research requires that both the subject and the experimenter not know who receives treatment and who is given a placebo. Discuss whether there is an ethical obligation to halt the research if it becomes clear that treatment subjects are benefiting significantly from the treatment that is not being received by control subjects.

CHAPTER

3 Models of Abnormality

TOPIC OVERVIEW

LEARNING OBJECTIVES

1. Define and describe the basic biological terminology, including parts of neurons, the brain, and types of neurotransmitters. Distinguish between organic mental disorders and functional mental disorders. Discuss the various therapies used by the biological model, including a discussion of drugs, electroconvulsive therapy, and psychosurgery.
2. Summarize the origins of Freud's theory. Describe Freud's explanation of abnormal functioning, including descriptions of the id, ego, superego, ego defense mechanisms, and psychosexual stages.
3. Summarize the behavioral model of abnormal functioning, including the main features of classical conditioning and operant conditioning and how they are used to explain abnormal behavior.
4. Summarize the cognitive model. Give examples of typical maladaptive assumptions, specific upsetting thoughts, and illogical thinking processes. Describe cognitive therapy.
5. Summarize Rogers's theory and therapy, including definitions of unconditional positive regard, unconditional self-regard, and conditions of worth. Describe Gestalt theory and therapy. Describe existential theories and therapies.
6. Summarize the sociocultural model. Describe the various sociocultural therapies.
7. Compare and contrast the various models of abnormal functioning. Describe the different ways of defining abnormality from the perspectives of deviance, distress, dysfunction, and danger.

KEY TERMS

accurate empathy
anal stage
antianxiety drug
antibipolar drug
antidepressant drug
antipsychotic drug
behavioral couple therapy
biopsychosocial theories
catharsis
classical conditioning
client-centered therapy
cognitive therapy
cognitive-behavioral theory
community mental health treatment
conditioned response
conditioned stimulus
conditioning
conditions of worth
conjoint family therapy
couple therapy
deterministic
diathesis-stress explanation
dream
ego
ego defense mechanism
ego theory
electroconvulsive therapy
endocrine system
existential therapy
experiencing
extrapyramidal effects
family systems theory
family therapy
fear hierarchy
fixation
free association
genes
genital stage
genuineness
Gestalt therapy
group therapy
hormone
humanist
id
latency stage
latent content
libido
lobotomy
manifest content
model
modeling
neuron
neurotransmitter
object relations theory
operant conditioning
oral stage
paradigm
phallic stage
pleasure principle
positive regard
primary prevention
psychoanalysis
psychodynamic model
psychosurgery
psychotropic medication
reality principle
receptor
reciprocal effects explanation
repression
resistance
role-play

secondary prevention
self theory
self-actualization
self-efficacy
self-help group
superego
synapse
systematic desensitization
tertiary prevention
transference
unconditional positive regard
unconditional self-regard
unconditioned response
unconditioned stimulus
unconscious
working through

MEDIA RESOURCES

CD-ROM Video Questions

The following is a list of video questions as they appear on the Abnormal Psychology CD-ROM that accompanies each textbook. As a homework assignment, have your students watch the video clip, and then answer these questions. Students can answer the questions directly into a text box appearing next to the video clip. When they have finished answering these questions, they can print out their assignment and hand it in for grading.

Also use these CD-ROM segments as assignments to expose your students to material prior to your lectures.

Electroconvulsive Therapy

1. Describe the procedure shown for administering electroconvulsive shock treatment.

   A: Electrodes are attached to a headband that is secured on the patient's head. Ninety to 120 volts of AC electricity are sent through the electrodes by means of a delayed activation treatment switch. The shock is administered for 0.10 to 0.15 second, to induce convulsions sufficient to cause lesions. In the second clip, the electrodes are dipped in water, the nurse puts a tongue depressor in the patient's mouth, and the patient is partially restrained. In the first clip, the patient does not receive a tongue depressor, nor is he restrained.

2. Describe the way in which the procedure shown on the video differs from the current procedures used, as described in your text.

   A: Sixty-five to 140 volts are used. ECT is administered for seven to nine sessions, spaced two or three days apart.

3. Does it surprise you that ECT is being used today to treat people with depression? Why or why not?

   A: It may surprise you because it seems so barbaric. Then again, it may not surprise you because biological treatments are paramount today.

4. According to your text, for what disorder is ECT used today?

   A: for depression, particularly for patients who fail to respond to other treatments

5. According to your text, what is the percentage of subjects who improve by receiving ECT?

   A: Approximately 60 percent of depressed subjects report mood improvement.

6. How would you feel about receiving ECT? Why?

   A: Individual answers given.

"Larry" Psychoanalytic Therapy Session

1. What appears to be the dynamic focus of Larry's therapy?

   A: Larry wants to deal with his lack of success in dating.

2. What mechanism appears to be at work when Larry appears not to have anything to talk about?

   A: resistance to dealing with dynamic focus of his therapy; his concern with lack of dating success, after he had a miserable date

3. What technique does the therapist use that leads Larry to recall his date?

   A: free association

4. When Larry is describing the appearance of the woman in his dream, he says to the therapist that he bets she (the therapist) will say that he (the client) is thinking that the woman in the dream looks like the therapist. What defense mechanism is Larry manifesting?

   A: projection; Larry is associating the therapist with the woman in the dream but is not consciously aware of this.

5. Larry appears to have "forgotten" that the therapist does indeed wear glasses. According to psychodynamic principles, what is he displaying?

   A: resistance

6. According to psychodynamic principles, what is Larry manifesting when he associates the woman in the dream with the therapist?

A: transference

7. In interpreting the meaning of the woman in his dream holding a white rose, Larry recalled that his date's name was Rose and that his mother had a rose garden. Using psychodynamic principles, these comments suggest that Larry is at what stage of Freudian ego development? Why?

   A: Oral stage, because he is associating the woman he dates with his mother. Perhaps his inability to have success with adult women stems from his being fixated at the child stage with his mother, never having achieved a more mature, adult relationship with her.

"Jim" Treating Drug Addiction: A Behavioral Approach

1. For what disorder is Jim receiving treatment?

   A: crack cocaine addiction

2. What type of treatment is he receiving?

   A: behavioral therapy

3. Jim's treatment provider expresses the behavioral perspective of how Jim became addicted. What is this perspective?

   A: Jim's body learned to be addicted and his body has to unlearn responses to the triggers that make him crave cocaine.

4. What is the goal of Jim's behavioral treatment?

   A: The goal is that Jim's body will unlearn its physiological responses to triggers that make his body crave drugs. When the physiological responses are unlearned, Jim will not crave the drug.

5. What form of behavioral conditioning has resulted in Jim's addiction—classical or operant?

   A: Both. Classical conditioning, because his body has learned a response to the drug and to the sights, sounds, and smells that precede drug use. His body craved cocaine to ward off withdrawal symptoms (lower body temperature, sweating, etc.). Operant conditioning, because when he smoked crack cocaine, he obtained the reward—being high—that he was seeking. He continued to use the drug so that he would receive the same result.

6. Compare the results of Jim's treatment with Pavlov's dogs ceasing to salivate to the sound of the bell.

   A: Pavlov's dogs salivated to the bell for a time after the meat powder was withdrawn because their bodies had associated the bell with receiving the meat powder. After a time, they no longer salivated to the bell alone, because no meat was forthcoming. Jim's body manifested physiological responses of craving for cocaine even after Jim was not using cocaine because his body associated certain sounds, sights, and smells with impending cocaine use. Eventually, Jim's body no longer had those physical responses because Jim was not ingesting cocaine.

7. How many treatments did Jim receive to enable him to prepare to smoke the crack without having strong physiological reactions?

   A: twenty treatments

8. Why is Jim's prognosis for staying off of cocaine hopeful?

   A: because his body has unlearned the physical responses that caused craving

Comer Video Segments

(See the Video Guide in Appendix E for detailed descriptions.)

Biological Model and Treatment

Segment 4 PET Scan Procedure and Results: Comparison of Schizophrenic and Nonschizophrenic Twins
Segment 5 MRI Scan: Comparison of Schizophrenic and Nonschizophrenic Twins
Segment 18 Person with Extreme Symptoms of Mania, Including Rushed Speech
Segment 19 Early Electroconvulsive Therapies
Segment 20 Modern Electroconvulsive Therapy, by Dr. Max Fink
Segment 21 Experiment Linking Placebo Effects to Endorphins
Segment 25 Lateral Hypothalamus Stimulation Leads to Hunger and Eating Behavior
Segment 26 Subjects Get Pleasure from Experiencing Hunger and Food Thoughts
Segment 27 Medial Hypothalamus Anesthetization and Eating Behavior
Segments 38 and 39 Antipsychotic Drugs
Segment 42 Prefrontal Lobotomy Procedure, 1942
Segment 43 Patients Before and After Prefrontal Lobotomy, 1944
Segment 44 Lobotomized Persons at a State Hospital Today
Segment 203 Craving for Cocaine: Triggers and Treatment
Segment 206 People with Bipolar Disorder
Segment 207 Woman with Major Depressive Disorder Improves with Electroconvulsive Therapy
Segment 208 Woman with Depression Receiving Antidepressant Drug Treatment

Segment 209 Patients with Mood Disorders Respond to Treatment
Segment 210 Woman Receives Treatment for Chronic Pain
Segment 211 Man with History of Alcohol Dependence Is Tested for Genetic Predisposition
Segment 212 The Effects of Alcohol and Other Depressants on the Brain
Segments 213 Man with Gender Identity Disorder Describes His Feelings and His Body Image
Segments 214 Young Man with Symptons of Schizophrenia
Segment 215 Woman with Alzheimer's Disease
Segment 216 Man with Severe Amnestic Disorder: Anterograde Amnesia
Segment 218 Temple Grandin, an Extremely High-functioning and High-Achieving Person with Autism, and Research on Autism

Psychodynamic Model and Treatment

Segment 9 Psychoanalytic Therapy Session
Segment 28 Therapy Reaction Tapes
- C. Client flatters therapist
- D. Teenage client expresses anger at therapist
- G. Therapist questions termination
- H. Therapist criticizes client
- I. Therapist flatters client

Behavioral Model and Treatment

Segment 11 Elevator Phobia
Segment 14 Fear of Airplane Travel: Clinical Features and Special Exposure Treatment Program
Segment 15 Informal Exposure Treatment for a Dog Phobia
Segment 47 Dr. Ivar Lovaas Treats Young Autistic Child with Behavioral Intervention
Segment 203 Craving Cocaine: Triggers and Treatment

Cognitive Model and Treatment

Segments 6 and 7 Dr. Aaron Beck Conducts Cognitive Therapy
Segment 23 Woman with Anorexia Nervosa

Humanistic-Existential Model and Treatment

Segment 8 Client Centered Therapy by Dr. Carl Rogers

Sociocultural Model

Segment 1 Deinstitutionalization and Jailing the Mentally Ill
Segment 22 Survey of Dieting and Body Image Among 33,000 Women, by Drs. Susan Wooley and Wayne Wooley
Segment 30 Onset and Etiology of Opioid Dependence
Segment 31 Sociocultural Overview of Opioid Dependence
Segment 32 Methadone Treatment Program, 1973
Segments 49 and 50 Patients' Rights
Segment 111 Sister's Reaction to Brother's Schizophrenia
Segment 114 Schizophrenia and Social Relationships
Segment 205 Stress on the Job: Psychological and Physical Effects
Segment 209 Patients with Mood Disorders Respond to Treatment
Segment 210 Woman Receives Treatment for Chronic Pain
Segment 216 Man with Severe Amnestic Disorder: Anterograde Amnesia

Family Theory

Segment 29 Family Dynamics Reaction Tape
Segment 30 Onset and Etiology of Opioid Dependence
Segment 36 Home Visit by Person with Schizophrenia
Segment 37 Parent's Reaction to Her Adult Child's Schizophrenia
Segment 110 Suicide's Impact on Family Members
Segment 111 Sister's Reaction to Brother's Schizophrenia
Segment 216 Man with Severe Amnestic Disorder: Anterograde Amnesia
Segment 217 Man with Multiple Personality Disorder (Dissociative Identity Disorder)

Eclectic Therapy, Group Therapy, Self-Help Groups, Residential Treatment

Segment 3 Modern Day Mental Hospital Ward
Segment 10 Multimodal Therapy by Dr. Arnold Lazarus
Segment 11 Elevator Phobia
Segment 33 Group Therapy for Substance Dependence
Segment 41 Therapy Discussion Group: Patients with Severe Mental Disorders
Segment 209 Patients with Mood Disorders Respond to Treatment
Segment 210 Woman Receives Treatment for Chronic Pain

Electroconvulsive Therapy

Segment 2 Medical Procedures Used in Mental Hospitals in the First Half of the Twentieth Century
Segments 16 and 17 Major Depressive Disorder
Segment 19 Early Electroconvulsive Therapies
Segment 20 Modern Electroconvulsive Therapy, by Dr. Max Fink
Segment 207 Woman with Major Depression Disorder Improves with Electroconvulsive Therapy

Deinstitutionalization and Community Mental Health

Segment 1 Deinstitutionalization and Jailing the Mentally Ill
Segments 38 and 39 Antipsychotic Drugs
Segment 40 Deinstitutionalization and Homelessness
Segment 112 Hallucinations by a Man with Schizophrenia
Segment 113 Recovery from Schizophrenia
Segment 114 Schizophrenia and Social Relationships

Overhead Transparencies

Transparency 2, Figure 3–1, p. 47, The human brain
Transparency 3, Figure 3–2, p. 48, A typical neuron
Transparency 4, Figure 3–3, p. 59, Theoretical orientation of today's clinicians

Transparency Masters

TM–2, Table 3–4, p. 79, Comparing the Models

CLASS DEMONSTRATIONS AND ACTIVITIES

Drug Treatment and the Revolving-Door Syndrome

Discuss the pros and cons of drug treatment with your students; list these on an overhead transparency. For which types of patients and mental disorders is drug treatment the most cost-efficient approach? Next, discuss the revolving-door syndrome in mental hospital admissions. The release of patients into the community without adequate support services has resulted in an increase in admissions to mental hospitals, with patients experiencing a greater frequency of admissions, though with shorter stays than in the past. A possible contributing factor is the use of drugs as a major outpatient treatment method. Individuals are admitted, stabilized with drugs and other therapy, then released with drug therapy. The symptoms diminish or disappear, the patient stops the drug treatment, the symptoms return, and the patient is readmitted.

Spontaneous Remission

An area of debate in therapy outcome research concerns the percentage of patients who improve over time without treatment. Eysenck suggested that the figure is about 2 out of 3, the same as those who improve with psychotherapy. How can therapists continue to provide therapy when many patients will spontaneously remit symptoms? Ask students to discuss this question.

Genetic Testing for Huntington's Disease

Discuss specific tests now available for genetic disorders using Huntington's disease as an example. With Huntington's, all individuals with the genetic marker develop this fatal degenerative disease in middle age; those who test free of the genetic marker never develop this disease. If a person does not undergo such testing and has a parent with Huntington's disease, he or she has a 50 percent chance of having the disease (i.e., testing takes the odds to 100 percent or to 0 percent). Family members can be tested before they make reproductive decisions to find out if they might pass this dominant-gene disease onto offspring. Discuss the human genome project and the likelihood that, in the future, the genetic markers of many such diseases (including mental disorders) will be identified. Have students discuss the pros and cons of having a genetic test done. Would the students want to be tested for these disorders? If not, why not?

Developing a Personal Perspective

Discuss how the theoretical model of behavior that a student adopts has an impact not just on the student's view of psychology but also on the student's view of himself or herself. Ask students if they think of their own behaviors as being caused by unconscious processes, by biological forces, by learning experiences, or by their environment. Lead a discussion on individual understanding of psychology based on the perspective. Ask students to identify their model and explain why they are influenced by this model.

Sociocultural Perspective

When addressing the sociocultural explanations of abnormal behavior, point out some of the major factors that are associated with this perspective, such as poverty, family structure and communications, societal stress, and class. Then ask students, if they were clinical psychologists, what kinds of clients they would like to serve. Where would they like to practice: a private practice or an inner-city agency for homeless individuals? Continue this discussion with input from the students on the best methods available to mediate sociocultural factors.

Role Playing

Using the sociocultural perspective, the techniques of role playing can be demonstrated to the class. Have the class form small groups and then ask one of the students in each group to assume the role of a patient and another the role of a therapist. You can suggest the disorders and perspectives that each group should use or let the students develop their own. The students can then attempt to role-play the respective parts. Observe the groups as they role-play. Select the best example and have them continue in front of the class.

Overview of Models of Abnormality I

Write the names of the various models (psychodynamic, behavioral, cognitive, humanistic-existential) on an overhead transparency. Then ask students to list words, ideas, and names that they associate with each of the models. This activity will reintroduce the concepts of these models to the students and help them realize how much they already know about these models.

Overview of Models of Abnormality II

Divide the class into six sections, and then have each section adopt one of the theoretical perspectives described in this chapter. Using a case from the text, or one from your own experience, have each group attempt to explain the "client's" behavior from their theoretical model. After each group has presented its perspective, continue with a discussion of how each model explains some behaviors better than other behaviors.

Overview of Models of Abnormality III

Asking students how they might react to someone's mental illness is an interesting and useful way to reveal to them their "working model" of the causes and treatments of mental illness.

Present the following or a similar scenario: A friend comes to you depressed and talks about how "lousy" a person she is. Your friend has a very negative view of herself. You've noticed that for the last several weeks she hasn't exercised, which she usually does, and hasn't gone out with friends. Your friend describes difficulty sleeping and studying and generally feels physically unwell. You also know that she has had a great deal of difficulty with her family, and you suspect she may have been emotionally abused. She tells you she's going nowhere, that she can't do anything, that she has no future, and that no one will ever love her.

What do you say to your friend?

Of the following list of issues, which is the most important?

- How your friend *thinks* about herself and her future (cognitive perspective)
- What she *does* and doesn't do (i.e., she is isolated and is not getting any exercise) (behavioral perspective)
- She might have a neurochemical imbalance or *physical* disorder of the brain. (biological perspective)
- Her problem might stem from her *past* and perhaps she is not even aware of it. (psychodynamic perspective)
- She should realize what a good person she is and that she has the *potential* to be anything. (humanistic perspective)

Based on your perspective what do you tell her to do?

Classical Conditioning: Taste Aversion

Discuss conditioned taste aversions within the context of classical conditioning. For example, discuss taste aversions associated with food poisoning or the flu. You can also describe Garcia's research on coyotes that avoided sheep after eating lithium-treated mutton. Ask students for other examples.

Classical Conditioning: Childhood (and Adult) Fears

Simple examples of classical conditioning abound, such as the child who is afraid of dogs after being bitten, or the student who is afraid of school after being bullied. Ask for examples of common fears and how they might develop.

Operant Conditioning: Maintaining Fears

A useful way to introduce the idea of operant conditioning is to ask students how they might help someone overcome a serious fear. This will almost always generate suggestions about exposure, such as, "Have the fearful child sit on your lap while someone else pets the dog." This is a useful way to introduce ideas related to operant conditioning.

"Here's $25,000 to Be Awarded to . . . ": Operant Conditioning and Classrooms

Present small groups with the challenge of using operant conditioning to manage unruly groups, such as schoolchildren. Ask the groups to come up with creative and nonaversive and practical solutions. Have the groups present their ideas, then have the class vote on which group receives the grant to implement their idea.

Cognitive Model

An excellent way to introduce cognitive theory and the idea of irrational ideas and cognitive errors is to generate a list of common cognitive mistakes that college students make. Develop an overhead transparency with these types of examples: "An A is the only grade worth earning" or "The teachers are out to fail us." You can use the following list from Freeman and DeWolf's *Woulda, Coulda, Shoulda* to help students develop relevant examples of incorrect thinking.

- All-or-nothing thinking: believing the world is all good or all bad, all gain or all loss.
- Catastrophizing: exaggerating the negative aspects of an event.
- Comparing: judging by others' rather than by one's own performance, feelings, and values.
- Emotion reasoning: letting emotions overwhelm common sense.
- Fortune-telling: being disappointed with oneself for not being able to predict the future.
- Mind reading: jumping to conclusions about what others think or what they think you are thinking.
- Overgeneralization: thinking that if something has happened once, it will always happen.
- Perfectionism: requiring oneself to perform flawlessly.
- Unquestioning acceptance of critics: letting others define one's self-worth.

Categories of Irrational Thinking or Cognitive Errors

Write a list of categories of irrational thinking on an overhead transparency or on the board. Give examples of statements that a person might make to himself or herself, and then ask students to categorize each statement. Discuss what kind of effects these thoughts might have on a person.

Example Statements

- "He didn't say 'Hi' when I passed him in the hall. He must be mad at me." (Could lead to social phobia.)
- "He doesn't seem to like me. Nobody likes me." (Could lead to depression.)
- "She made critical remarks about my favorite singer. I need to reconsider my musical taste." (Could lead to intense self-doubt and relying on opinions of others.)
- "She got upset when I asked about her family. I should have known she was going to react like that." (Could lead to fear of conversing with others.)
- "I look heavier than her. I need to lose weight." (Could lead to eating disorders.)
- "I did poorly on this test. I will do poorly in this class." (Could lead to intense exam anxiety.)

The Biological Model

Lead a discussion of the following topic. A tremendous amount of research on neurotransmitters in abnormal behavior has been conducted over the last 10 years. Although the exact causal relationships have not been determined, there is mounting evidence that neurotransmitters play a significant role in various abnormal behaviors. Some research areas have emphasized deficiencies of dopamine and its link to Parkinson's disease. Other findings have shown that excesses in dopamine reactivity are found in schizophrenia. Antipsychotic drugs are thought to alleviate the symptoms of schizophrenia by blocking or masking the action of dopamine. Many of the disorders that were best explained by other models are now being better explained by the biological model. Ask students for their input and examples.

Role-Playing a Therapist

Assign small groups of students a theoretical model. Have some students role-play the client while others interview the client from the assigned perspective. Psychoanalytic and behavioral therapists are good choices.

Evil as the Cause of Mental Illness

Joan Houghton spent five weeks in a hospital following a psychotic episode. She recovered completely and took a job at the National Institute of Mental Health. In 1980 she wrote about her experiences, including her return home after being hospitalized:

> One Sunday I went to church alone after being absent for several weeks. The minister (who knew of my history, faith, and strong belief in God) began his sermon with reference to the devil. He said, "If you ever want to be convinced of the existence of the devil, you should visit a mental institution." To illustrate his point, he described people who had lost control of their bodily functions, who screamed out obscenities. I . . . drove home vowing to never return . . . but maybe I had misunderstood. [I invited the minister to my home.] His visit was our last encounter. Not only did he see evil in mental illness, but he conveyed an unforgiving attitude to those who have the misfortune of residing in mental hospitals.

Discuss how some people believe that mental illness is God's punishment, or the result of evil. Ask students what they think of that belief.

CHAPTER

4 Clinical Assessment, Diagnosis, and Treatment

TOPIC OVERVIEW

Clinical Assessment: How and Why Does the Client Behave Abnormally?
- Characteristics of Assessment Tools
- Clinical Interviews
- Clinical Tests
- Clinical Observations

Diagnosis: Does the Client's Syndrome Match a Known Disorder?
- Classification Systems
- DSM-IV
- Are Classifications Reliable and Valid?
- Can Diagnosis and Labeling Cause Harm?

Treatment: How Might the Client Be Helped?
- Treatment Decisions
- The Effectiveness of Treatment

Crossroads: Renewed Respect for Assessment and Diagnosis

LEARNING OBJECTIVES

1. Define clinical assessment and discuss the roles of the clinical interview, tests, and observations.

2. Summarize the axis approach of the DSM series and describe the general features of DSM-IV.
3. List the major classification of disorders from Axis I of the DSM-IV.
4. Discuss the dangers of diagnosing and labeling in classifying mental disorders.
5. Discuss types and effectiveness of treatments for mental disorders.

KEY TERMS

affective inventory
assessment battery
Bender Visual-Motor Gestalt Test
biofeedback
CAT scan
classification system
clinical interview
clinical test
cognitive inventory
comorbidity
concurrent validity
cross-situational validity
diagnosis
Draw-a-Person (DAP) Test
DSM-IV
EEG
face validity
field trial
ICD
idiographic
intelligence quotient (IQ)
intelligence test
interrater reliability
interview schedule
mental status exam
Minnesota Multiphasic Personality Inventory (MMPI)
MMPI-A
MMPI-2
MRI
naturalistic observation
neurological test
neuropsychological test
observer bias
observer drift
observer overload
participant observer
personality inventory
PET scan
predictive validity
profile
projective test
psychopharmacologist (pharmacotherapist)
psychophysiological test
rapprochement movement
reactivity
reliability
response inventory
response set
Rorschach test
self-monitoring
sentence-completion test
social skill inventory
standardization
structured interview
structured observation
syndrome
test battery
test-retest reliability
Thematic Apperception Test (TAT)
therapy outcome study
uniformity myth
unstructured interview
validity

MEDIA RESOURCES

CD-ROM Video Questions

The following is a list of video questions as they appear on the Abnormal Psychology CD-ROM that accompanies each textbook. As a homework assignment, have your students watch the video clip and then answer these questions. Students can answer the questions directly into a text box appearing next to the video clip. When they have finished answering these questions, they can print out their assignment and hand it in for grading.

Also use these CD-ROM segments as assignments to expose your students to material prior to your lectures.

Mark

1. What types of tests were used to assess the nature of Mark's aggression?

   A: neurological tests
2. Why were neurological tests indicated?

A: Mark manifested a gradual change in personality and temperament. He lost control of his temper more and more as time went on, until the day he attacked his girlfriend's daughter.

3. What was Mark's reaction to his violent assault on the girl?

   A: He did not know why he did it. He had never reacted that way before, and he was accustomed to dealing with young children, as he had a daughter of his own.

4. What did the first series of tests indicate?

   A: that Mark had a tumor

5. Additional tests were needed to see if the tumor had any effect on his aggression and violence. What type of test was used? What technique?

   A: The type of test was neuroimaging. The actual technique used was computerized axial tomography (CAT scan or CT scan).

6. According to your text, what does a CAT scan do?

   A: A CAT scan takes X rays of the brain at different angles.

7. What effect was the tumor having on Mark's brain?

   A: The tumor was located in an area of the brain that exerted pressure through the amygdala against the hypothalamus.

8. Why did this tumor cause Mark to be aggressive and violent?

   A: The parts of the brain affected by the tumor are those involved with aggression.

9. How did Mark's behavior change after the tumor was surgically removed?

   A: He could control his temper even better than before. He had no further outbreaks of violence.

10. Do you find it hard to believe that a brain tumor can cause someone to be violent? Why or why not?

    A: no answer provided

The Mind of the Psychopath

1. What is the nature of the test that Dr. Hare developed?

   A: It is an unstructured interview.

2. What is the name of the test?

   A: the Hare Psychopathy Checklist-Revised (PCL-R)

3. What is the test designed to assess?

   A: whether the client has a syndrome or clinical construct of behaviors known as psychopathy

4. What three types of characteristics does psychopathy consist of?

   A: interpersonal, affective, and behavioral

5. What are some specific characteristics that describe psychopaths?

   A: lacking in empathy, an emotional affect; egocentric; grandiose; predatory; callous; impulsive, manipulative, and glib

6. The narrator says that the Hare PCL-R is a standardized measure of psychopathy. Explain what standardization is and why the PCL-R is considered to be standardized.

   A: Standardization means that the assessment instrument has common steps to be followed whenever it is administered and established procedures for scoring and interpretation. A trained clinician, who integrates information from the client's file and other sources, gives the PCL-R. It is a 20-item scale with possible scores ranging from 0 to 40. The typical "normal" person has a score of 5. A score of 30 or above indicates psychopathy.

7. What behaviors does the PCL-R measure?

   A: glibness and superficial charm, conning and manipulative behavior, lack of remorse and guilt, and impulsiveness

8. The narrator says that the test is reliable and valid in predicting violent behavior. Define reliability and validity.

   A: Reliability refers to the consistency of multiple administrations of an assessment measure, meaning that the test will yield the same results in the same situation. For example, it should yield the same result every time it is given to the same people (known as test-retest reliability). Different people should also agree on how to score and interpret the results (known as interrater reliability). Validity means that the test accurately measures what it is supposed to measure.

9. Why is the PCL-R valid for predicting violent behavior?

   A: The assessment is designed to measure psychopathy. Among incarcerated persons, those who are deemed psychopaths according to the test are three times more likely to reoffend and four times more likely to violently reoffend. Twenty percent of inmates serving time for violent crime score high on the PCL-R.

10. If a prisoner were seeking parole from prison and administration of the PCL-R indicated that the individual was a psychopath, would that diagnosis help or hurt his chances for parole? Why?

    A: It would hurt. Statistics indicate that incarcerated persons who score high on the checklist are three times more likely to break the law again and four times more likely to commit another violent crime than those who do not score high on the test.

11. What percent of the general population is believed to have psychopathic characteristics?

    A: 1 percent

Comer Video Segments

(See the Video Guide in Appendix E for detailed descriptions.)

Segment 4 PET Scan Procedure and Results: Comparison of Schizophrenic and Nonschizophrenic Twins
Segment 5 MRI Scan: Comparison of Schizophrenic and Nonschizophrenic Twins
Segment 23 Woman with Anorexia Nervosa
Segment 37 Parent's Reaction to Her Adult Child's Schizophrenia
Segment 101 Postpartum Psychological Disorder
Segment 103 Compulsive Hoarding and Compulsive Symmetry, Order, and Balance
Segment 104 Perfectionism: Obsessive Compulsive Disorder versus Obsessive Compulsive Personality Disorder
Segment 115 Children with Attention-Deficit Hyperactivity Disorder (ADHD)
Segment 122 Adapting to One's Symptoms
Segment 202 Aggression, Violence, and the Brain
Segment 204 Assessing Psychopathy
Segment 208 Woman with Depression Receiving Antidepressant Drug Treatment
Segment 211 Man with History of Alcohol Dependence Is Tested for Genetic Predisposition
Segment 213 Man with Gender Identity Disorder Describes His Feelings and His Body Image
Segment 215 Woman with Alzheimer's Disease
Segment 219 Psychopathy

Overhead Transparencies

Transparency 6, Figure 4–3, p. 93, An MMPI Profile
Transparency 7, Figure 4–4, p. 97, The Bender Visual-Motor Gestalt Test
Transparency 8, Figure 4–5, p. 104, How Many People in the United States Qualify for a DSM Diagnosis During Their Lives?
Transparency 9, Figure 4–6, p. 111, Does Therapy Help?

Transparency Masters

TM–5, Table 4–1, p. 94, Sample Items from the Beck Depression Inventory

DSM-IV Masters

E–3 Axis I Disorders
E–4 Axis I Disorders
E–5 Global Assessment of Functioning (GAF)
E–6 Global Assessment of Functioning (GAF)
E–7 New Categories and Changes in DSM-IV
E–8 New Categories and Changes in DSM-IV
E–9 New Categories and Changes in DSM-IV

CLASS DEMONSTRATIONS AND ACTIVITIES

Personality Inventories

Bring to class examples of personality inventories, projective tests, and intelligence tests. Discuss the most important aspects of each test. Try to include items from the tests mentioned in this chapter, such as the MMPI, Rorschach Inkblot, and TAT. Elicit student reactions to the content of the tests. Ask the question, Are these tests valid today? Request suggestions from the class on how to improve these specific examples you have presented.

"Pretend, for a moment, that you are a . . . ": DSM-IV Multiaxial Assessment

Multiaxial assessment can be confusing to students who do not understand its relevance. Students can realize the importance of multiple axes when discovering for themselves the importance of Axes III and IV in particular. Present yourself as a patient seeking psychotherapy for depression or anxiety. Tell students that you recently have had medical problems and that you have experienced some stressful life events. Present fairly severe instances of both, and ask which is more relevant to the treatment being planned by them. A disagreement will likely ensue about which is more important, leading to a general consensus that both are important. Discuss Axes III and IV within this context.

Role-playing an Interviewer

Divide students into small groups and tell them to role-play as counselors. Each student is to develop a list of things he or she would most want to know about a client at the end of the first session together. Next, have the students share their lists and develop one master list. Discuss what their impressions of the important information are and why.

Validity

Ask students for examples of each of the following kinds of validity they have experienced in college: face validity, predictive validity, content validity, and construct validity. Ask them to provide examples of situations in which proper validity standards were not met.

Diagnostic Categories: Criticisms and Advantages

It is useful to have a discussion of the rationale and criticisms of diagnoses. This activity works best by starting with criticisms of diagnoses, which are easier for students to generate. After generating criticisms, point out that diagnostic labels are necessary and request guesses as to why.

Criticisms

- Diagnoses can give scientists and clinicians a false sense of having explained behavior. For example, a clinician might claim that his patient is highly suspicious because he has a paranoid disorder, but this tells us nothing about why the patient is paranoid. Likewise, to say that a patient is suicidal because of her depression does not aid in either understanding or helping the patient.
- Diagnoses can be used to rationalize or excuse certain undesirable behaviors. For example, this instructor's manual was late to the publisher because I have a disorder (procrastination superstratus).
- Diagnoses can and sometimes do stigmatize persons, creating an "us vs. them" sense, that is, by promoting the idea that there is a clearcut distinction between normal and abnormal behavior.
- Diagnoses may be "sticky," influencing others' perceptions of subsequent behavior, as exemplified in the Rosenhan study.

Advantages

- Scientific: Science relies upon a common language and categorization. Agreed-upon categories or names for illnesses are necessary to facilitate research into their etiology and treatment. Agreeing on findings from studies of depression or schizophrenia would be very difficult if scientists did not agree on what these disorders are and are not.
- Clinical: The presence of an illness is indicated by giving someone a diagnosis. If there is no diagnosis, then the person has no illness. Thus, diagnoses tell clinicians when to initiate treatment and when treatment should be terminated (because the person is better). Likewise, diagnoses can tell us what treatment might be effective.
- Legal significance: Defining abnormal behavior helps us determine when a person is responsible for his or her behavior. On March 30, 1981, John Hinckley, Jr. shot and seriously wounded President Ronald Reagan outside a hotel in Washington, D.C. In May 1982 a jury declared Hinckley innocent by reason of insanity.

Media and Personality Test

Have students collect questionnaires from popular magazines or self-help books (definitely give a deadline, and consider giving extra credit). On an overhead transparency, compare these items with the more standardized, classical personality inventories, such as the MMPI.

The Importance of Standardization

All tests must be standardized if a person is to be compared to others. This means giving the same test in the same fashion to all who take it; it also means comparing a person's scores to an appropriate comparison group. The importance of these can be demonstrated easily.

Ask for four volunteers to do the following. Hand each of them a sheet with several multiplication problems (e.g., 325 × 27). The numbers should be the same, but some should be presented in a row and others in column format (the manner in which they need to be written to do the problem). Ask each student to do the problems. Collect the sheet after 15 seconds for the first student, after 30 seconds for the second, and after completion for the other two students. Compare the results and ask the first two for their reaction (they will complain that they weren't given as much time). With the latter two, state this: "You [point to student] did very well when compared to a group of fifth-grade kids I gave these problems to; you are very smart" [give student a "Very Smart"certificate]. "You [point to other student] did not do so well. The advanced college math students down the hall did much better" [don't give student a "Very Smart" certificate]. Ask their reactions.

This activity can be used to introduce the standardization of administration necessary for the WAIS, the Rorschach, and the MMPI.

Neuropsychological Testing

A growing area of assessment in the past two decades is neuropsychological testing. Several simple neuropsych tests can be brought to class (or created), such as the Trail-Making Tests (two tests: in the first, the patient draws lines through a series of numbers in circles in consecutive order; in the second, numbers and letters are alternated, i.e., 1-A-2-B-, etc.). The Finger-Tapping Test is also easy to demonstrate (i.e., how many times can a person tap his or her index finger in a set amount of time, usually one minute). Simple tests such as these, when administered to many people, can reveal whether the parts of the brain are working well together (e.g., the part of the brain that alternates numbers and letters). Persons with neurological problems (such as injuries) may have difficulty with these tasks, depending on whether that part of the brain is being tested.

Personality Tests and Job Screening

A trend that appears to be increasing in recent years is the tendency of companies to use personality tests in the application screening process for prospective hires. Ask students to share such experiences. Explore the types of questions asked and what the students thought of the tests. Ask the class to discuss the pros and cons of using personality tests in this situation.

Evaluating the DSM Series

Show the lists of disorders from DSM, DSM-II, DSM-III, DSM-III-R, and DSM-IV. The increase in material since the DSM-I is quite dramatic and worth discussing. Ask students to discuss why each edition has more material than the prior editions. One explanation is that our society is becoming more disordered. An alternative explanation is that the mental health profession has become more specific and inclusive of true problems. A third is that the profession "wants" more problems to increase business. An interesting disorder to trace through the series is schizophrenia.

CHAPTER

5 Generalized Anxiety Disorder and Phobias

TOPIC OVERVIEW

Stress, Coping, and the Anxiety Response

Generalized Anxiety Disorder

The Sociocultural Perspective
The Psychodynamic Perspective
The Humanistic and Existential Perspectives
The Cognitive Perspective
The Biological Perspective

Phobias

Specific Phobias
Social Phobias
What Causes Phobias?
How Are Phobias Treated?

Crossroads: Diathesis-Stress in Action

LEARNING OBJECTIVES

1. Distinguish between fear and anxiety and describe the anxiety disorders and how common these disorders are.
2. Define phobia; then describe agoraphobia, social phobia, and specific phobia.
3. Discuss treatments for generalized anxiety disorder and phobias.
4. Discuss the current state of the field in relation to generalized anxiety disorder and phobias.

KEY TERMS

acute stress disorder
adrenal glands
agoraphobia
antianxiety drug
anxiety
anxiety disorder
assertiveness training group
autonomic nervous system (ANS)
barbiturate
basic irrational assumption
benzodiazepine
beta blocker
biofeedback
buspirone
central nervous system
classical conditioning
client-centered therapy
cognitive therapy
conditioned response
conditioned stimulus
conditions of worth
confederate
coping self-statements
corticosteroids
covert desensitization
displacement
electromyograph (EMG)
endocrine glands
existential anxiety
exposure therapy
exposure treatments
family pedigree study
fear
fear hierarchy
flooding
free-floating anxiety
gamma-aminobutyric acid (GABA)
generalized anxiety disorder
hormone
in vivo desensitization
modeling
moral anxiety
negative self-statements
neurotic anxiety
obsessive-compulsive disorder
panic disorder
panic disorder with agoraphobia
parasympathetic nervous system
participant modeling
phobia
posttraumatic stress disorder
preparedness
rational-emotive therapy
realistic anxiety
relaxation training
repression
sedative-hypnotic drugs
self-help exposure therapy
self-instruction training
situation anxiety
social phobia
social skills training
social skills training group
specific phobia
stimulus generalization
stress
stress management program
stress response
stressor
support group
sympathetic nervous system
systematic desensitization
trait anxiety
unconditional positive regard
unconditioned response
unconditioned stimulus
unpredictable negative events

MEDIA RESOURCES

CD-ROM Video Questions

The following is a list of video questions as they appear on the Abnormal Psychology CD-ROM that accompanies each textbook. As a homework assignment, have your students watch the video clip and then answer these questions. Students can answer the questions directly into a text box appearing next to the video clip. When they have finished answering these questions, they can print out their assignment and hand it in for grading.

Also use these CD-ROM segments as assignments to expose your students to material prior to your lectures.

"Claude & Claude" Emotion, Stress, and Health

1. Claude has two layers of conflict that cause stress on his job. What are they?

   A: 1. The conflict between his personality (he is a loner) and the job routine (he works with a large number of people in a windowless room). 2. The on-the-job conflict with his younger boss, the constantly bombarding communications from his boss (by memo and in person), other air traffic controllers (by phone and in person), and the planes (radio communications).

2. What is the nature of the occupational stress?

   A: Keeping the planes from colliding in the air, dealing with his boss, handling the constant bombardment of information from planes and other controllers, communicating in both French and English, relying on technology to avert disaster, and dealing with stress of technology failures, when he has to keep the planes separated by means of radio communication

3. Explain the nature of the "fight-or-flight" signals from the brain. What purpose do they serve?

   A: 1. When the brain senses that the organism is in danger, neurons in the locus coeruleus send their axons toward the cerebral cortex and release norepinephrine, regulating arousal and vigilance in response to the environmental stimuli. 2. The purpose of the fight-or-flight signals are to warn the organism to "fight" or "flee" for self-protection. 3. The constant bombardment of these messages causes physiological responses that can lead to heart disease, ulcers, and cancer, for the body is in an ever ready state to fight or flee. 4. If stress is prolonged, the body can no longer adapt to the physiological responses and becomes exhausted. 5. In addition to physical exhaustion, the messages upset the balance between the limbic system (the emotional center of the brain) and the frontal cortex (the thinking and planning portion of the brain), leading to erratic behavior.

4. Why are the "fight-or-flight" signals that the air traffic controllers receive from their brains counterproductive in their work setting?

   A: because they can't fight with their boss or flee from their jobs

5. What could be the ultimate effect of relentless stress responses on the air traffic controllers' judgment and decision-making?

   A: They may make errors in judgment as a result of not being able to think clearly.

6. What part of their daily routine helps them cope with on-the-job stressors?

   A: They work an hour on and then an hour off, drink coffee, and smoke cigarettes.

7. What personal stressors does each man have in addition to his job?

   A: Both are married with two children. One has another child on the way.

8. Both men are 40. Assuming they have been working as air traffic controllers for most of their adult lives, what might the ultimate effects of the job stresses be?

   A: gastrointestinal problems, such as ulcers and gastritis (one controller, Claude, already has this), heart disease, and cancer

Comer Video Segments

(See the Video Guide in Appendix E for detailed descriptions.)

Segment 11 Elevator Phobia
Segments 12 and 13 Anxiety Disorders
Segment 14 Fear of Airplane Travel: Clinical Features and Special Exposure Treatment Program
Segment 15 Informal Exposure Treatment for a Dog Phobia
Segment 205 Stress on the Job: Psychological and Physical Effects

Overhead Transparencies

Transparency 10, Figure 5–1, p. 119, Does Anxiety Beget Anxiety?
Transparency 11, Figure 5–2, p. 120, The Autonomic Nervous System (ANS)
Transparency 12, Figure 5–3, p. 124, Poverty, Race, and Anxiety
Transparency 13, Figure 5–4, p. 130, What Do People Do to Relieve Stress?
Transparency 15, Figure 5–6, p. 145, How Common Are the Specific Phobias?

Transparency Masters

TM–6, Table 5–2, p. 122, Anxiety Disorders Profile

DSM-IV Masters

E–10 DSM-IV Criteria for Agoraphobia
E–11 DSM-IV Diagnostic Criteria for Specific Phobia
E–12 DSM-IV Diagnostic Criteria for Social Phobia
E–13 DSM-IV Diagnostic Criteria for Generalized Anxiety Disorder

CLASS DEMONSTRATIONS AND ACTIVITIES

Open Discussion: How Fears Change with Age

Lead a discussion of how an individual's fears change with age. Many fears increase or decrease during certain stages of life. Cite examples such as the young child's fear of the dark and the college student's fear of academic failure. What are some major fears of college students? Discuss how certain fears increase with age, whereas other fears decrease.

Group Work or Open Discussion: Rational and Irrational Fears (Phobias)

Phobia was the Greek god of fear. The scary face of Phobia was painted on the shields of Greek warriors to strike fear into the hearts of their opponents. Either lead a class discussion about the difference between rational and irrational fears or, alternatively, ask different groups of students to generate lists of rational and irrational fears. Either the open discussion or a comparison of the lists will generate disagreement. Inevitably, an irrational fear on one list will appear on the rational fear list of another group. Discuss how mental health professionals distinguish irrational from rational fears, given that there is no easy agreement. Phobias evoke intense anxiety and avoidant behaviors that interfere greatly with everyday living and usually require professional treatment.

Open Discussion: Student Phobias

Make an overhead transparency of Box 5–3 and discuss the list. State that students should mention only phobias that "friends" have. Have students speculate on why phobias were given such technical and complicated labels. One clever explanation is that when professionals can't treat and understand something, they give it an unpronounceable name so that the patient can understand why progress is slow. Until behavioral therapy techniques proved successful, phobias were resistant to change.

Group Work: Common Student Phobias

Before dividing into groups, ask the whole class to generate a list of typical situations that make students anxious. Next, divide the class into small groups, then ask each group to develop a strategy for coping with one of the situations. This is a good method to create a discussion and solicit suggestions to change behaviors without embarrassing students.

A complementary exercise is to tally the fears of class members (you can ask students to write them down to preserve anonymity), then discuss the most common fears. If the class is typical of the American population, public speaking will rank very high. It is beneficial to have the class determine which of the fears are specific and which are social phobias. Sometimes this is easy (e.g., fear of storms, fear of spiders, fear of bats), but social phobias may be mislabeled as specific (e.g., fear of eating in restaurants, fear of blushing).

Anxiety Disorders on Television and in the Movies

To emphasize the idea that disorders have specific criteria, have students report on diagnosable mental illnesses they encounter on television or in the movies. Students should document the specific behaviors or experiences that a character is exhibiting that fulfills the diagnostic criteria. This assignment helps emphasize the difference between the appearance of a disorder and meeting criteria for a disorder, that is, the difference between popular and professional conceptions of mental illness. If assignments are turned in prior to the lecture on particular disorders, you can use the information generated to enhance your lecture and to give these disorders a more personal touch.

Let's Write a Self-Help Bestseller (see Preface instructions for doing this activity)

Ask students for ideas on how to write a self-help manual on overcoming severe shyness (which might be diagnosable as social phobia), a traumatic experience (such as childhood abuse), or panic. Ideas for self-help interventions should include a rationale for why it might work.

CHAPTER

6 Panic, Obsessive-Compulsive, and Stress Disorders

TOPIC OVERVIEW

Panic Disorder
- The Biological Perspective
- The Cognitive Perspective

Obsessive-Compulsive Disorder
- What are the Features of Obsessions and Compulsions?
- The Psychodynamic Perspective
- The Behavioral Perspective
- The Cognitive Perspective
- The Biological Perspective

Stress Disorders
- What Triggers Stress Disorders?
- Explanations of Stress Disorders
- How Do Clinicians Treat Stress Disorders?

Crossroads: Lessons to Be Learned

LEARNING OBJECTIVES

1. Describe the features of panic disorder, and discuss the biological and cognitive explanations and therapies of this disorder.
2. Distinguish between obsessions and compulsions.
3. Define stress disorder and posttraumatic stress disorder, list typical symptoms, and provide psychological explanations and treatments for these disorders.
4. Discuss abuse and victimization in terms of stress disorders.

KEY TERMS

acute stress disorder
aggressive id impulses
agoraphobia
alprazolam
anal stage
antidepressant drugs
anxiety sensitivity
basal ganglia
behavioral inhibition system (BIS)
biological challenge test
caudate nuclei
checking compulsion
cleaning compulsion
clomipramine
compulsion
compulsive ritual
counting compulsion
covert-response prevention
critical incident stress debriefing
Disaster Response Network
dissociation
exposure and response prevention
eye movement desensitization and reprocessing
flashback
fluoxetine
habituation training
hippocampus
isolation
locus ceruleus
neutralizing
norepinephrine
obsession
obsessive-compulsive disorder
orbital frontal cortex
panic attack
panic disorder
panic disorder with agoraphobia
panic disorder without agoraphobia
posttraumatic stress disorder
rap group
rape
reaction formation
serotonin
thalamus
touching compulsion
undoing
verbal ritual
Veteran Outreach Center
yohimbine

MEDIA RESOURCES

CD-ROM Video Questions

The following is a list of video questions as they appear on the Abnormal Psychology CD-ROM that accompanies each textbook. As a homework assignment, have your students watch the video clip and then answer these questions. Students can answer the questions directly into a text box appearing next to the video clip. When they have finished answering these questions, they can print out their assignment and hand it in for grading.

Also use these CD-ROM segments as assignments to expose your students to material prior to your lectures.

"Jennifer" Obsessive-Compulsive Disorder

1. What are Jennifer's compulsions?

   A: checking herself in the mirror; banging her teeth against a glass; moving objects back to where they were moved from

2. What are Jennifer's obsessions that are associated with each of her compulsive behaviors?

   A: Worrying that some aspect of her appearance is not just right leads her to check herself in each mirror she sees; concern about how a glass "feels" leads her to bang her teeth against the glass until the glass "feels" just right; thinking that everything has a place leads her to move things back to where they were moved from.

3. How do Jennifer's obsessions and compulsions meet the DSM-IV criteria for obsessive-compulsive disorder?

   A: Jennifer recognizes that they are excessive and unreasonable. They cause her significant distress. For instance, she breaks her teeth on drinking glasses.

4. What form do Jennifer's obsessions take?

   A: impulses to take certain actions

5. What form do her compulsions take?

   A: constantly striving for symmetry, order, and balance in her activities, her appearance, and her surroundings

6. What is the common theme of Jennifer's obsessions and compulsions?

   A: orderliness and checking

7. Jennifer has adopted a compulsion to help her deal with one of her obsessive-compulsive behaviors. Describe this.

   A: Jennifer tries to always drink out of a Styrofoam cup or a glass with a straw or both a Styrofoam cup and a straw because she often breaks her teeth when she bangs them against a glass. Using a Styrofoam cup and a straw help defend her against her teeth-banging compulsion.

8. How do Jennifer's behaviors reduce her anxiety?

   A: Checking in the mirror allows her to fix anything about her appearance that she does not like, momentarily assuring her that her appearance is fine. Moving objects back to where they came from makes her feel as if everything is in its proper place.

9. Examine the research on the correlations of obsessive-compulsive disorder with certain traits and thoughts. Which of the correlations might Jennifer express? Give a brief research citation for your answers.

   A: (1) Jennifer may have an exceptionally high standard of conduct (Rachman, 1993; Rachman and Hodgson, 1980). (2) Jennifer may think that she must have perfect control over her thoughts and behaviors (Bouchard, Rheaume, and Ladouceur, 1999).

"Bill" Obsessive-Compulsive Disorder

1. What are Bill's compulsions?

   A: (1) taking napkins; (2) picking up and saving rubber bands; (3) picking up pennies; (4) arranging french fries before eating them

2. How are Bill's compulsions related?

   A: They are all related to order and touching (picking things up).

3. What reasons does he give for the compulsion of picking up pennies?

   A: (1) The penny seems to be calling out to him to pick it up. (2) He seems to believe in the maxim that if he passes up the penny, he will have bad luck for the rest of the day, whereas if he picks it up, he will have good luck. (3) If he does not pick up the penny, the thought that he did not will "haunt" him for the rest of the day. He won't be able to think of anything else.

4. How do Bill's obsessions and compulsions meet the DSM-IV criteria for obsessive-compulsive disorder?

   A: He believes that they are unreasonable and cause him distress.

5. What technique might a behavioral therapist suggest to help Bill overcome his compulsions?

   A: Exposure and response prevention. When he has the compulsion to pick up pennies or napkins or arrange french fries, he should refrain from doing so.

6. What cognitive techniques might a cognitive therapist suggest to help Bill overcome his compulsions?

   A: (1) Neutralizing the thoughts (a) that if he did not pick up the penny, he would have bad luck for the rest of the day and (b) that his french fries won't taste good if he doesn't put them in order before he eats them. (2) Covert-response prevention (similar to the behavioral technique of exposure and response prevention)—Distract his thoughts with something else when the penny "calls out" to him and not engage in the acts that his obsessive thoughts are encouraging (arranging french fries, picking up napkins or pennies).

Comer Video Segments

(See the Video Guide in Appendix E for detailed descriptions.)

Segment 14 Fear of Airplane Travel: Clinical Features and Special Exposure Treatment Program
Segment 15 Informal Exposure Treatment for a Dog Phobia
Segment 101 Postpartum Psychological Disorder
Segment 102 Obsessive-Compulsive Disorder in Childhood and Adolescence
Segment 103 Compulsive Hoarding and Compulsive Symmetry, Order, and Balance
Segment 104 Perfectionism: Obsessive-Compulsive Disorder versus Obsessive-Compulsive Personality Disorder
Segment 105 Compulsive Vocalizations (Noise Making) by a Child with Obsessive-Compulsive Disorder
Segment 106 Treatment for Obsessive-Compulsive Disorder

Overhead Transparencies

Transparency 15, Figure 6–1, p. 159, The Biology of Panic
Transparency 16, Figure 6–2, p. 162, Normal Routines
Transparency 17, Figure 6–3, p. 169, Successful Treatment for Cleaning Compulsions
Transparency 18, Figure 6–4, p. 171, The Biology of Obsessive-Compulsive Disorder

Transparency Masters

TM–7, Table 6–3, p. 159, Anxiety Disorders Profile

DSM-IV Masters

E–14 DSM-IV Criteria for Panic Attack

E–15 DSM-IV Diagnostic Criteria for Obsessive-Compulsive Disorder

E–16 DSM-IV Diagnostic Criteria for Posttraumatic Stress Disorder

CLASS DEMONSTRATIONS AND ACTIVITIES

Diathesis-Stress Model

Direct genetic causation of illness and abnormal behavior is rare. Recent research has indicated that many illnesses are now understood in terms of the interaction of hereditary and environmental factors, the diathesis-stress model. According to this theory, certain genes or hereditary vulnerability give rise to a diathesis or a constitutional predisposition. When an individual's predisposition is then combined with certain kinds of environmental stress, illness may result. With diseases like heart disease, high blood pressure, and cancer, both hereditary and environmental factors play a role. A major effort in abnormal research and clinical practice is to identify specific risk factors in a given individual, including both family history and personal lifestyle, then predict the onset of a mental disorder.

Howard Hughes and Obsessive-Compulsive Disorder

The following list provides an interesting look at Howard Hughes's obsessive-compulsive behavior. You can display this information about his odd behavior in the form of an overhead transparency. Use this list to start a discussion of any relative's or friend's behaviors that might also be considered obsessive-compulsive. Be certain the students do not become too personal in their discussions.

- Hughes would not touch any object unless he first picked up a tissue (which he called "insulation") so that he would never directly touch an object that might expose him to germs.
- Hughes saved his own urine in mason jars; hundreds of them were stored in his apartment. From time to time a staff member would covertly empty some of the filled jars.
- Hughes saved his newspapers in high stacks—so many of them that visitors sometimes had to weave carefully through a room to avoid toppling them.
- Hughes sometimes watched one film (his favorite was *Ice Station Zero*) more than a hundred times before switching to another. Similarly, he might have gone for days eating the same food (e.g., chicken noodle soup and one flavor of Baskin-Robbins ice cream) and no others.
- Hughes used heroin and other drugs.

Brainstorming Session: Reducing Stress

Ask students to volunteer something that students could do to alleviate stress. This generally evokes a wide variety of suggestions, illustrating how personal the experience of stress can be.

Psychology and Medical Health

The major causes of morbidity (illness) and mortality (death) have changed in the last century. In the early 1900s, viruses and bacteria were the leading causes of death. Ask students what happened to change this. (Medical and scientific advances such as antibiotics, vaccinations, and improvements in sanitation helped stamp out these causes of death.) Presently, leading causes of death include heart disease (related to smoking, eating, not exercising, being overweight, drinking too much), cancer, motor vehicle accidents, and suicide. Ask students what these causes have in common (all are related to behavior). Psychology is thus becoming increasingly important in overall health care. In particular, the field of health psychology is emerging as an important area of the health care system.

"Here's $25,000 to be awarded to . . . "

Divide students into groups, then ask each group to propose a method to reduce the occurrence of one of the causes of heart disease, such as smoking, drinking, and being overweight. Have the groups present their ideas, then have a class vote to see which group receives the grant to implement the group's idea.

Open Discussion: Stress and Appraisal

The Holmes and Rahe Social Readjustment Rating Scale attempted to quantify stressful events. Researchers have found a relationship between total score (adding up the events) and the likelihood of medical illness. The relationship is complex, however. Not everyone who is stressed gets sick, although being stressed clearly puts one at greater risk for being sick. An important issue is the person's appraisal of the event, which has two parts. During primary appraisal, the person decides whether the event is threatening or not (e.g., not all events are perceived as bad by everyone—a divorce might be a wonderful thing from a certain perspective). During secondary appraisal, the person decides whether he or she has the capacity to cope with the event. Discuss potentially stressful events in the lives of college students, such as midterm exams and term papers. Frame the events in terms of primary and secondary appraisal, then discuss what events are particularly stressful. Typically, these will be events that are both threatening (to good grades) and difficult to cope with (e.g., "impossible midterms," a confluence of deadlines).

"Pretend, for a moment, that you are a victim of a terrible trauma."

The symptoms of posttraumatic stress disorder (PTSD) are fairly well known and intuitively obvious to most people. To emphasize this, ask students to pretend that they went through some trauma, such as a motor vehicle accident in which someone died, or war combat, or being assaulted. Ask them to imagine what they would go through over the next few days and weeks. It is likely that students will generate the concepts of reexperiencing the trauma (e.g., dreams, intrusive recollections) and avoiding stimuli that might remind them of the trauma. It is unlikely that they will realize, intuitively, that there is a general numbing of responsiveness to the external world as well.

Open Discussion: Coping with Stress and the Vietnam War

The Vietnam War is a useful vehicle for discussing PTSD. Walker and Cavenar (1982) found that 20 to 25 percent of those who served in Vietnam suffered from PTSD. In comparison, it has been estimated that about 1 in 10 World War II veterans suffered PTSD. The events of the war were traumatic and stressful, but World War II is a particularly good example of the effect of the absence of coping factors.

Seeking social support among one's peers is an excellent coping strategy.

- In Vietnam, soldiers were transported (put into and taken out of combat) via jet plane, sometimes overnight. In previous wars, groups of soldiers would be put in and taken out of combat together—ships took soldiers in and out of combat, and the return home would take months, during which experiences could be shared with other combat veterans, catharsis could occur, and a general adjustment could be made.
- During the Vietnam War, it was standard procedure to replace individual soldiers who were killed or wounded with new recruits—rookies who were shunned by more experienced soldiers because, as rookies, they were more likely to do something reckless or dangerous.
- Every soldier had his own DEROS (date of expected return from overseas), which also tended to discourage a sense of being in the war as a group, but rather encouraged an individual's attempts to keep himself alive.

Another effective way to cope with a traumatic incident is to reappraise it, that is, to reexamine one's initial perceptions of it and try to convert a negative appraisal to a positive one.

- In previous wars, soldiers came home—after having done terrible things—to parades and encouragement that they did what needed to be done.
- In contrast, soldiers in Vietnam came home to parades protesting the war and belittling those who served in it. It was just as honorable, in some people's eyes, to refuse to serve as it was to serve. The combat veterans may have felt they were doing the right thing, going to risk life and limb for one's country, but they came home and were told over and over again that the war was wrong and that they were wrong to go.

"Pretend, for a moment, that you just had a panic attack."

Using an overhead, show the symptoms of panic attacks. Ask students to pretend that they have just experienced one (be aware that some have actually had panic attacks). Ask students what their reaction to these symptoms might be. Students likely will suggest that they would go to a hospital emergency room or assume that there was something seriously wrong. Encourage them to imagine that the panic attack was the worst experience of their life. Lead them to see that they would be intensely fearful of another panic attack. Using the process of questioning, help them to see how panic disorder (fear of more panic attacks, leading to misinterpretation of otherwise benign somatic experiences) can lead to more panic attacks.

CHAPTER

7 Mood Disorders

TOPIC OVERVIEW

Unipolar Depression

How Common Is Unipolar Depression?
What Are the Symptoms of Depression?
Diagnosing Unipolar Depression
What Causes Unipolar Depression?
The Biological View
Psychological Views
The Sociocultural View

Bipolar Disorders

What Are the Symptoms of Mania?
Diagnosing Bipolar Disorders
What Causes Bipolar Disorders?

Crossroads: Making Sense of All That Is Known

LEARNING OBJECTIVES

1. Compare depression and mania while discussing the symptoms of each.
2. Contrast unipolar depression and bipolar disorders while discussing the symptoms of each.
3. Discuss the role of recent life events in unipolar depression.
4. Describe the biological, psychological, and sociocultural perspectives of depression.
5. Describe the possible roles of the neurotransmitters in unipolar depression.

KEY TERMS

adoption study
anaclitic depression
arbitrary inference
attribution
automatic thoughts
bipolar disorder
bipolar I disorder
bipolar II disorder
catecholamine theory
cognitive triad
convulsion
cortisol
cyclothymic disorder
delusion
depression
double depression
dysthymic disorder
endocrine system
endogenous depression
errors in thinking
family pedigree study
genetic linkage study
hallucination
hopelessness
hypomanic episode
indoleamine theory
interpersonal deficits
interpersonal loss
interpersonal role dispute
interpersonal role transition
learned helplessness
lithium
magnification
major depressive disorder
major depressive episode
maladaptive attitudes
mania
manic episode
minimization
molecular biology
negative thinking
norepinephrine
phosphoinositides
reactive (exogenous) depression
second messenger
serotonin
shuttle box
sodium ion
symbolic loss
twin study
tyramine
unipolar depression

MEDIA RESOURCES

CD-ROM Video Questions

The following is a list of video questions as they appear on the Abnormal Psychology CD-ROM that accompanies each textbook. As a homework assignment, have your students watch the video clip and then answer these questions. Students can answer the questions directly into a text box appearing next to the video clip. When they have finished answering these questions, they can print out their assignment and hand it in for grading.

Also use these CD-ROM segments as assignments to expose your students to material prior to your lectures.

"Derrick" Hamilton Depression Scale

1. What does Derrick say that indicates that he is caught in what Aaron Beck calls the "cognitive triad"?

   A: I won't ever get better; I am getting older and may never have another job.

2. Name the stressors that preceded Derrick's two bouts of serious depression, and discuss why, in view of these triggers, he might be a good candidate for interpersonal therapy.

   A: The stressors are the breakdown of his marriage and the loss of his union job. Both are interpersonal losses that involve interpersonal role transitions and thus are appropriate for interpersonal therapy.

3. Based on the events that Derrick said led to episodes of serious depression, why would psychodynamic therapy likely not be a viable treatment option?

   A: He did not mention any childhood loss.

4. Name the conditions under which electroconvulsive shock therapy would be an appropriate treatment modality for unipolar depression, and state whether or not ECT would be indicated in Derrick's case.

   A: ECT would be indicated for severe depression with accompanying delusions. Try medications first, since they have worked for Derrick.

5. What in Derrick's background suggests that he would be an appropriate candidate for long-

term treatment with antidepressant medication?

A: He is prone to depression between major episodes, medication has helped before, and he has felt "almost normal."

6. Rank the following treatment modalities in order of their appropriateness for this individual, given the facts you learned in the video (1 for most likely to be successful to 6 for inappropriate). After each modality named, state the reason for your choice.
   a. ECT
   b. Antidepressant medication
   c. Psychodynamic therapy
   d. Behavioral therapy
   e. Cognitive therapy
   f. Interpersonal therapy

   A: Antidepressant medication and cognitive therapy should be ranked 1 and/or 2; followed by (3) interpersonal therapy, (4) behavioral therapy, (5) psychodynamic therapy, and (6) ECT (an inappropriate modality).

7. Assume that you are Derrick's case manager at a community mental health treatment center. You have been told that you may structure a multimodal treatment program for him, choosing three out of the following five possible treatments. However, you must back up your choices with evidence from treatment outcome studies. Apply the summary of the outcome studies found in the text to these modalities and state why you think there is empirical evidence for or against recommending each treatment for Derrick. If appropriate, you may also mention support for which modalities might be most effective when used together. Based upon your answers, which three modalities would you choose?
   a. psychodynamic
   b. behavioral
   c. cognitive
   d. interpersonal
   e. antidepressant medication

   A: There is strong support for cognitive therapy, interpersonal therapy, and antidepressant medication, less support for behavioral therapy, no support for psychodynamic therapy, and the strongest support for a combination of antidepressant medication and cognitive therapy.

8. Assume that you are a therapist specializing in Aaron Beck's paradigm of cognitive therapy. Outline a specialized treatment plan for Derrick that would cover all four phases of Beck's approach.

   A: (1) Increase activities and elevate mood—Schedule activities, emphasis on the "active." Look for a job. Be with people. (2) Challenge automatic thoughts—I will never get better; I won't get another job. (3) Identify negative thinking and biases—I am getting older and will end up homeless and on the street. (4) Change primary attitudes—Defeatist, fails to recognize he got better in the past.

Comer Video Segments

(See the Video Guide in Appendix E for detailed descriptions.)

Segments 16 and 17 Major Depressive Disorder
Segment 18 Person with Extreme Symptoms of Mania, Including Rushed Speech
Segment 101 Postpartum Psychological Disorder
Segment 108 Assessment Interview with Depressed Man, by Dr. Max Hamilton
Segment 109 Woman Discusses a Suicide Attempt and Her Present Positive State of Mind
Segment 110 Suicide's Impact on Family Members
Segment 201 Studies Link Mood Disorders to Hereditary Factors
Segment 206 People with Bipolar Disorder
Segment 207 Woman with Major Depressive Disorder Improves with Electroconvulsive Therapy
Segment 208 Woman with Depression Receiving Antidepressant Drug Treatment
Segment 209 Patients with Mood Disorders Respond to Treatment

Overhead Transparencies

Transparency 19, Figure 7–1, p. 193, What Makes People Feel Ashamed?
Transparency 21, Figure 7–2, p. 205, How Depressed Parents and Their Children Interact
Transparency 20, Figure 7–4, p. 212, Marital Status and Major Depressive Disorder

Transparency Masters

TM–8, Table 7–2, p. 199, Mood Disorders Profile
TM–9, Table 7–3, p. 209, Internal and External Attributions

DSM-IV Masters

E–17 DSM-IV Criteria for Major Depressive Disorder

E–18 DSM-IV Criteria for Manic Episode
E–19 DSM-IV Diagnostic Criteria for Dysthymic Disorder
E–20 DSM-IV Diagnostic Criteria for Bipolar I Disorder, Single Manic Episode, and Bipolar II Disorder
E–21 DSM-IV Diagnostic Criteria for Cyclothymic Disorder

CLASS DEMONSTRATIONS AND ACTIVITIES

Depression Inventories

Bring in depression inventories. Discuss why these inventories are useful in both therapy and research. Ask students to suggest changes or modifications that could improve these instruments.

"Pretend, for a moment, that you are a . . . "

Divide students into groups and assign each group a task similar to the following. Pretend they are a business owner who is interested in alleviating the negative (and costly) effects of depression on workplace productivity. Ask them to come up with creative and practical solutions to identifying and intervening with workers suffering from mood disorders. Similar roles are a high school principal, a medical doctor, a fraternity or sorority president, a college instructor, and a baseball team manager.

Open Discussion: Manic Episodes

Discuss the idea that manic episodes can be extraordinarily pleasant. Encourage students to imagine aloud why such episodes might be enjoyable (more cheerful, more productive, more outgoing).

"Let's Write a Self-Help Bestseller"

Discuss the stigma associated with mood disorders. Many persons implicitly (and sometimes explicitly) presume that mood disorders occur only in persons who are weak or who "enjoy being sad." Discuss the effect such attitudes might have on persons with mood disorders (reluctance to admit they have a problem or to seek help). Ask for ideas about how to educate the public about causes of these disorders, thus alleviating the stigma associated with them.

The Anonymous Five-Minute Essay

It is useful to ask students to take five minutes to explain the biological model of depression. Reviewing these answers can alert instructors to misconceptions and poor communication of important ideas. This can be done for the cognitive, behavioral, and psychodynamic models as well.

Open Discussion: Learned Helplessness

Martin Seligman and his colleagues suggested that depression is the result of learned helplessness. They proposed that depression, like learned helplessness, is the result of inescapable trauma or negative situations. The person learns that he or she has no control over these negative events and stops trying to respond in an efficient, adaptive manner. The individual thus learns to be helpless. Ask students for examples of how such a model of depression might apply.

Open Discussion: Beck's Cognitive Theory

According to Aaron Beck and his colleagues, depression is caused by an individual's tendency to think or reason in a certain fashion. In particular, people become depressed because of their personal schema about themselves, their world, and their future. Introduce the notion of perceptual sets and bias, which influence the manner in which a person perceives things. Perceptual sets cause distortions and selective attention that support the negative schema. An interesting exercise is to provide such a set of assumptions (personal schema) and then present a series of experiences and ask students for "congruent" (with the schema) interpretations of the event. For example, a woman may have a schema of herself as a terrible person. Her daughter is caught smoking at school. Another example: A young man believes that he is unlovable. His girlfriend breaks up with him. (These two people will take one event and distort it, then ignore or minimize contrary evidence, such as the fact that the daughter is a straight-A student or, in the case of the young man, that he acted in a way that encouraged his girlfriend to break up with him.)

CHAPTER

8 Treatments for Mood Disorders

TOPIC OVERVIEW

LEARNING OBJECTIVES

1. Describe the major psychological approaches to treatment of unipolar depression. That is, compare and contrast the psychodynamic, behavioral, and cognitive approaches to treatment.
2. Describe interpersonal psychotherapy and couples therapy.
3. What are the major biological approaches to unipolar depression? Describe ECT. Compare and contrast early antidepressants to currently used antidepressants.
4. How do the various psychotherapeutic approaches to treating depression compare?
5. Describe lithium therapy for bipolar disorder, including issues related to its use and its mechanism of action.
6. Describe adjunctive psychotherapy for bipolar disorder. What is it and why is it important?

KEY TERMS

adjunctive psychotherapy
antidepressant drug
behavioral marital therapy
bilateral ECT
carbamazepine (Tegretol)
couples therapy
electroconvulsive therapy (ECT)
fluoxetine (Prozac)
imipramine
insulin coma therapy
interpersonal psychotherapy (IPT)
iproniazid
lithium
MAO inhibitor
melatonin
metrazol
monoamine oxidase
second-generation antidepressant
second messenger
selective serotonin reuptake inhibitor (SSRI)
serotonin
sertraline (Zoloft)
tricyclic
unilateral ECT
valproate (Depakote)

MEDIA RESOURCES

CD-ROM Video Questions

The following is a list of video questions as they appear on the Abnormal Psychology CD-ROM that accompanies each textbook. As a homework assignment, have your students watch the video clip and then answer these questions. Students can answer the questions directly into a text box appearing next to the video clip. When they have finished answering these questions, they can print out their assignment and hand it in for grading.

Also use these CD-ROM segments as assignments to expose your students to material prior to your lectures.

"Meredith" Mood Disorders: Medication and Talk Therapy

1. Why did the psychiatrist prescribe antidepressants for Meredith?

   A: primarily because she has trouble sleeping

2. The medication was not sleeping pills. How did it help Meredith sleep better?

   A: According to the psychiatrist, it had a sedating effect.

3. If Meredith had had trouble getting out of bed in the morning, instead of trouble sleeping, would the psychiatrist have prescribed a different kind of antidepressant?

   A: Yes, one with an "activating" effect.

4. What effect did the medication have after three weeks?

   A: Meredith had no more problems sleeping, although she was experiencing the side effect of weight gain.

5. The psychiatrist cautions Meredith to keep an eye on her weight gain, and if it gets to be a problem he says he will change medications. What does this tell you about antidepressants?

   A: They have different effects on different people. If one causes side effects, others can be prescribed until the best medication for that particular patient is found.

6. Her psychiatrist referred her to Dr. Westcott, a psychologist. What was the most likely reason for his doing this?

   A: to deal with the psychological and emotional issues contributing to her depression

7. How has Meredith improved after six months of medication and talk therapy?

   A: She looks much better, she has no more sleeping problems, and her energy level is all that she wants it to be. She canceled an appointment with her psychiatrist to help out her daughter at school, a sign of improvement, according to the psychiatrist.

Electroconvulsive Therapy

1. Describe the procedure shown for administering electroconvulsive shock treatment.

   A: Large electrodes were attached to a headband that was placed on the head. Ninety to 120 volts of AC electricity was sent to the head through the electrodes, by means of a delayed activation treatment switch. The shock was administered for 0.10 to 0.15 second to induce convulsions sufficient to cause lesions. In the second clip, the electrodes were dipped in water, the nurse put a tongue depressor in the patient's mouth, and the patient was partially restrained. In the first clip, the patient was not given a tongue depressor, nor was he restrained.

2. Describe the way in which the procedure shown on the video differs from the current procedures used.

   A: Today patients receive strong muscle relaxants to minimize convulsions, thus eliminating the danger of fractures or dislocations. They also receive barbiturates to put them to sleep during the procedure, reducing their terror. Today's procedures are much more complex, but also less dangerous and disturbing.

3. Does it surprise you that ECT is being used today to treat people with depression? Why or why not?

   A: It may surprise you because it seems so barbaric. Then again, it may not surprise you, since biological treatments are paramount today.

4. For what type of mood disorder is ECT used today?

   A: It is used to treat unipolar depression, for severe cases that include delusions.

5. According to your text, for what percentage of subjects does receiving ECT yield improvement?

   A: Sixty to 70 percent of ECT patients improve.

6. What effect does ECT have on the brain?

   A: It delivers a broad, electrical disturbance to the brain that causes neurons to fire and neurotransmitters to be released. It affects many other systems of the body as well.

7. What is the main negative side effect of ECT?

   A: Patients who receive ECT, particularly bilateral ECT, typically have difficulty remembering the event prior to and immediately after their treatments. In most cases, this memory loss clears up within a few months. Some patients, however, have more long-term memory loss.

"Doug" Mood Disorders: Medication and Talk Therapy

1. What is the biological basis for Doug's depression?

   A: reduced levels of serotonin and norepinephrine in his brain

2. How do Doug's antidepressants work in his brain?

   A: The medication he is taking increases the amount of serotonin and norepinephrine in the synapses of the neurons in his brain.

3. For what types of depression should antidepressant medication be prescribed?

   A: depression that has a biological basis in abnormal neurotransmitter levels

4. What medication is used for people with mania?

   A: lithium

5. According to the video, it is not known how lithium works. What does your text say about this?

   A: The text says that it is not fully understood how lithium works. However, it is believed that lithium affects the synapse through a second-messenger system, rather than directly. It has also been suggested that lithium corrects bipolar functioning by directly changing sodium and potassium ion activity in the neurons.

6. According to the narrator in the video clip, how effective is lithium? According to the text, how effective is lithium in treating bipolar disorder?

   A: The narrator says that lithium eliminates or dampens symptoms of mania in 80 percent of the people who take it. The text says that 60 percent improve.

Comer Video Segments

(See the Video Guide in Appendix E for detailed descriptions.)

Segments 6 and 7 Dr. Aaron Beck Conducts Cognitive Therapy
Segment 8 Client-Centered Therapy by Dr. Carl Rogers
Segments 16 and 17 Major Depressive Disorder
Segment 19 Early Electroconvulsive Therapies
Segment 20 Modern Electroconvulsive Therapy, by Dr. Max Fink
Segment 28 Therapy Reaction Tapes A and E
Segment 207 Woman with Major Depressive Disorder Improves with Electroconvulsive Therapy
Segment 208 Woman with Depression Receiving Drug Treatment
Segment 209 Patients with Mood Disorders Respond to Treatment

Overhead Transparencies

Transparency 22, Figure 8–1, p. 224, Where Do College Students Turn When They Feel Depressed?
Transparency 23, Figure 8–3, p. 238, Reuptake and Antidepressants

Transparency Masters

TM–10, Table 8–1, p. 229, Mood Disorders and Treatment

CLASS DEMONSTRATIONS AND ACTIVITIES

Losing Mild Depression

Ask students what they do to get rid of the "blues." Everyone has an occasional down day. Ask students to share the types of strategies that they use to alter their mood level. Everyone has something that makes them happier—playing golf, seeing a movie, swimming, or talking to a friend, for example. How successful are these strategies? Develop a list on an overhead transparency to see if there is a common thread.

The Relationship between Exercise and Depression

Research has shown a link between regular physical exercise and the alleviation of depression. People who exercise regularly are less depressed. But could it be that people who are depressed just exercise less? Ask students to volunteer experiences when they or their friends used exercise as a way to feel better.

Group Work: Drugs versus Psychotherapy

Divide students into groups, then assign each group a position in the following debate: the effectiveness of drug therapy versus psychotherapy in the treatment of major depression. Instruct each side that group members must promote or defend the position assigned to them. Instruct them to appoint a recorder and a reporter who will make a 60-second statement about the group's conclusions.

"Here's $25,000 to be awarded to . . . "

Discuss the idea that manic episodes (e.g., a husband's emptying the bank account to buy cuckoo clocks) can have devastating effects on the trust between spouses. Point out that many impulsive and perhaps silly decisions are made without the influence of a manic episode, but that couples (especially the nonbipolar spouse) have difficulty distinguishing them. The result is a profound lack of trust. Divide students into groups to compete for an award to be given by an organization interested in bipolar disorder research. The assignment is to design a contract or an agreement between a patient with bipolar disorder and his or her spouse that will enable them to distinguish correctly between "normal" impulsive and perhaps irrational decisions or ideas and the onset of another manic episode. Have the groups present their ideas, then have a class vote to see which group receives the grant to implement the idea.

"Pretend, for a moment, that you are a counselor."

Divide students into groups. Ask them to imagine that they are a counselor seeing a patient with fairly severe depression. Ask them to assume a cognitive stance in therapy. How would they proceed? The groups likely will come up with ideas that are extremely similar to the manner in which Beck recommends that cognitive therapy proceed (e.g., "Ask the patient to write down his thoughts for the week"). Use this as a lead-in to a discussion of cognitive therapy.

The Anonymous Five-Minute Essay

Ask students to turn in an anonymous essay describing a personal experience they had with a friend or a loved one with a serious episode of depression. Some students will not have had such an experience, but most will have. Ask them to describe the situation and anything particularly memorable about it, such as talking to (or intervening with) a friend about suicide. You can expect that at least half the class will have had an experience with depression, which emphasizes the ubiquity of the disorder.

CHAPTER

9 Suicide

TOPIC OVERVIEW

LEARNING OBJECTIVES

1. Define suicide and know how common it is.
2. Describe each of the four kinds of people who intentionally end their lives: death seekers, death initiators, death ignorers, and death darers. Also describe the category of subintentional death.
3. Know the effects of cultural factors, race, and sex on suicide rates.
4. Understand the common precipitating factors in suicide.
5. Discuss how mood changes, hopelessness, and dichotomous thinking are related to suicide.
6. Describe the common predictors of suicide.
7. Give the psychodynamic view for suicide, including the role of Thanatos.
8. Explain the role of biological factors in suicide, including the role of serotonin.
9. Explain the role of sociocultural factors while comparing and contrasting Durkheim's three categories of suicide: egoistic, altruistic, anomic.
10. Discuss the characteristics of suicide prevention programs.

KEY TERMS

altruistic suicide
anomic suicide
anomie
crisis intervention
death darer
death ignorer
death initiator
death seeker
demoralization
devoutness
dichotomous thinking
egoistic suicide
hopelessness
lethality scale
modeling
mood disorder
paraprofessional
parasuicide
retrospective analysis
schizophrenia
serotonin
subintentional death
substance-related disorder
suicide
suicide education
suicide hotline
suicide prevention program
Thanatos

MEDIA RESOURCES

CD-ROM Video Questions

The following is a list of video questions as they appear on the Abnormal Psychology CD-ROM that accompanies each textbook. As a homework assignment, have your students watch the video clip and then answer these questions. Students can answer the questions directly into a text box appearing next to the video clip. When they have finished answering these questions, they can print out their assignment and hand it in for grading.

Also use these CD-ROM segments as assignments to expose your students to material prior to your lectures.

"Andy" Suicide

1. List all of the reasons Andy gave for deciding to jump from the bridge.

   A: 1. He'd let everybody down. 2. He felt as bad as the weather—cold and bleak. 3. He had bought whiskey and was walking and drinking.

4. As he got to the bridge, the thought came to him that "this" was the solution. 5. He wanted to die and be at peace, so he did not have to feel the constant pain.

2. What DSM-IV diagnoses might be appropriate for Andy?

   A: depression and alcohol abuse or dependence

3. Why was Andy afraid to talk to a doctor after his suicide attempt? Was Andy's postsuicide fear of talking to a doctor justified? Why or why not?

   A: Andy was afraid he would be locked up. Justified: If Andy told the doctor that he would try to kill himself again, the doctor may have had him committed to a hospital. Not justified: If Andy agreed, he might realize he was no longer actively planning to end his life.

4. Andy says he feels as if he will be in therapy for the rest of his life. What problem needs to be the focus of his therapy?

   A: His alcohol problem has to be the focus of treatment.

5. Do you think that Andy is still a suicide risk? Why or why not?

   A: Probably not at this time, because he is in therapy and resigned to being there. He feels loneliness, emptiness, and sadness, but the comment that he would like to resolve all of his issues and be happy is promising.

6. Which of Shneidman's four categories does Andy represent? Support your choice with facts.

   A: Death darer. He had not planned his attempt. Jumping off the bridge seemed like a good idea at the time. He also wanted to talk to someone after he survived.

"Sue" Suicide

1. Does Sue manifest any indications that she is suffering from any DSM-IV diagnosis?

   A: no

2. What led to Sue's suicide attempt?

   A: She does not recall planning to attempt suicide that night after she came home from work. The idea came up, and she said it seemed like a good way to deal with her personal problems and the problems she was causing others.

3. How does the presence of a gun in the home increase the risk of suicide lethality?

   A: The suicide attempt can be more spontaneous and requires less planning.

4. Which of Shneidman's four categories does Sue fit?

   A: She is probably a death seeker, because she used a gun and says she pointed it at her heart.

5. What are the similarities and differences in the issues and factors that led to Andy and Sue's suicide attempts?

   A: Similarities: Both of their attempts were not planned, but spontaneous. Both felt that they had let down other people. Neither appeared to be married or have children, and they appear to be living alone. Both are white Americans. Both appear to be in the same age group—early adulthood. Neither of them had experienced any immediate stress. Differences: Although both attempts were not planned, Andy speaks of suffering psychological pain for a long time, and his reason for suicide is to be free from the pain. Sue's attempt arises from what appears to her to be an easy way to deal with her problems with herself and others. Andy does not seem to have any present social supports. He talks about a lack of friends and family. Sue has friends and family who may be there for her. Andy has a substance abuse problem and a history of depression. We don't have any indication that Sue has a history of depression or substance abuse or dependence. Andy seems committed to being in therapy to overcome his pain. We don't know if Sue is going to be staying in therapy (no mention is made).

6. What aspect of Sue's attempt places her outside the statistical norm?

   A: She used a gun. Forty percent of female suicides involve guns, whereas two-thirds of male suicides use guns.

7. What factors concern you the most about Andy or Sue's ability to refrain from suicidal acts in the future? What factors make you feel optimistic that they won't attempt suicide again?

   A: Andy: Concerns: His alcohol problem, continuing depression, and lack of social and family support. Optimism: He is in therapy and he wants to resolve his problems. Sue: Concerns: Not sure she is in therapy; having a gun in the house. Optimism: No history of depression, her family and social support, and her feelings of shame for what she did (concern for parents and also perhaps shame for herself).

"Bonnie" Suicide

1. What immediate stressor could have led to Bonnie's suicide?

A: She was recently divorced. She also may have been about to lose her home and children.

2. Which of Shneidman's categories does Bonnie fit? List the facts that support your answer.

   A: Death seeker. She left notes around the house, and she used a rifle.

3. What were the family dynamics in Bonnie's immediate family at the time of her death?

   A: Bonnie had no contact with anyone but her younger brother, and perhaps her father. Her family appeared to have been disconnected for a long time.

4. Bonnie, like Sue, was outside the statistical norm for female suicides in one factor. What was this?

   A: Both Bonnie and Sue used guns.

5. Compare the reactions of Bonnie's mother and two sisters.

   A: Mother: Feels that she let her daughter down at some point; feels at fault; denies being angry with Bonnie, but is angry at "others"; will carry guilt forever. One sister: Shock and anger that Bonnie could do this to herself. Other sister: Anger at what Bonnie put family through.

"Jed" Suicide

1. What Shneidman category did Jed fall into? Support your answer with facts.

   A: Death seeker. He probably planned his suicide because he hanged himself.

2. What suicide high-risk group was Jed a member of?

   A: adolescent male

3. What was apparently going on between Jed and his mother at the time of his suicide?

   A: There was a high degree of conflict over his rebellion. His mother appeared to have made it into a "big deal."

4. What are Jed's mother's primary feelings in response to Jed's suicide?

   A: She is angry because she won't have any other children, and won't have grandchildren. She is also angry with Jed for wasting his life.

5. Jed's mother describes a thought process that Jed, Andy, and Sue all obviously manifest, and that Bonnie may have experienced as well. What was this attitude that they all seemed to share, and what is the term for it in the text?

   A: The term is dichotomous thinking. The faulty thinking is that the only choices are suicide or having to endure unsolvable problems. Jed's mother describes it as looking down a tube and not being able to see beyond "then." Jed's mother admits that she also engaged in this type of faulty thinking. She did not see that Jed's rebellion would ever let up.

6. What did Andy, Sue, Jed, and Bonnie all have in common?

   A: All of them had some sort of problem with or disconnection from their families. Not only was Bonnie disconnected from most of her family of origin, but her marriage had just ended. Andy talks of disappointing his family and not being the good "Lutheran." Sue might not have felt her parents' love. Jed was in a state of active conflict with his mother.

Comer Video Segments

(See the Video Guide in Appendix E for detailed descriptions.)

Segments 16 and 17 Major Depressive Disorder
Segment 28 Therapy Reaction Tape E
Segment 109 Woman Discusses a Suicide Attempt and Her Present Positive State of Mind
Segment 110 Suicide's Impact on Family Members
Segment 206 People with Bipolar Disorder
Segment 207 Woman with Major Depressive Disorder Improves with Electroconvulsive Therapy
Segment 208 Woman with Depression Receiving Antidepressant Drug Treatment

Overhead Transparencies

Transparency 24, Figure 9–1, p. 258, Suicide and Marital Status
Transparency 25, Figure 9–2, p. 259, Current U.S. Suicide Rates
Transparency 26, Figure 9–4, p. 271, Changing Suicide Rates

Transparency Masters

TM–11, Table 9–1, p. 252, Most Common Causes of Death in the U.S.
TM–12, Table 9–2, p. 262, Common Predictors of Suicide

CLASS DEMONSTRATIONS AND ACTIVITIES

Statistics and Suicide

Discuss the accuracy of statistics on suicide. For example, might some national statistics be adjusted to account for cultural beliefs and values? Ask students for cultural or religious examples. How often are deaths listed as accidents instead of suicides to spare mourners? May accidents sometimes be called intentional suicides?

Women at Risk for Suicide

The chapter mentions that men are more likely than women to kill themselves, but that women make three to four times as many attempts. What factors are involved in the risk of suicide among women? Lead a discussion of the following factors related to suicide.

- A history of physical and/or sexual abuse
- Major depression
- Borderline personality disorder (all personality disorders increase the risk for men)
- Loss of the father through death or desertion before age 20 (this factor is found in 50 percent of women who commit suicide but in only 20 percent of other women)
- European ancestry (twice the suicide rate of African Americans and other ethnic groups)
- Age at the middle of the life span (youngest and oldest groups have the lowest rates)
- Unemployment
- Impulsiveness and emotionality, moodiness, unhappiness, and lack of self-confidence
- An IQ above 135 (the Terman Genetic Studies of Genius found that the rate of suicide among gifted women was nearly 250 times that of the general population of women)

Contrast the list to the following, which are *not* indicators:

- Any particular phase of the menstrual cycle
- Pregnancy (actually associated with lower risk)
- Loss of the mother through death or desertion before age 20
- Chronic stress in the family of origin, parental conflict, and conflict in a woman's relationship with her parents

Group Work: Examples of "Suicidal Messages"

Divide students into groups, then ask each group to come up with an example of either a popular song or a movie that might influence someone to commit suicide. Discuss the examples with the whole class. After several recognizable examples are generated, lead a discussion on whether this could actually happen and whether a music group or movie producer could be held responsible for a suicide.

Group Work: Who Decides?

Divide students into groups, then assign one of the following positions: (1) It should be legal (or illegal) for doctors to help patients kill themselves. (2) It is a personal decision about whether an individual chooses to die. (This can lead to heated opinions, so warn students about group work rules, such as respecting others' opinions and defending positions.)

Open Discussion or Group Work: Suicide and the Media

Research suggests that suicide rates increase following depictions or descriptions of suicides in the media (e.g., in newscasts and movies). Many of these incidents have been well documented. Lead an open discussion on why this might happen. Alternatively, assign groups to take a position on whether there should be oversight (censorship) of such media accounts.

CHAPTER

10 Psychosocial Factors in Physical Disorders

TOPIC OVERVIEW

Factitious Disorder

Somatoform Disorders

What Are Hysterical Somatoform Disorders?
What Are Preoccupation Somatoform Disorders?
What Causes Somatoform Disorders?
How Are Somatoform Disorders Treated?

Psychophysiological Disorders

Traditional Psychophysiological Disorders
New Psychophysiological Disorders

Psychological Treatments for Physical Disorders

Crossroads: Expanding the Boundaries of Abnormal Psychology

LEARNING OBJECTIVES

1. Describe the criteria for diagnosing factitious disorder; include in this discussion Munchausen syndrome and the Munchausen syndrome by proxy.
2. Define somatoform disorders, including conversion disorders, somatization disorders, and pain disorders.
3. Explain how physicians distinguish between hysterical somatoform disorders and true medical problems.

4. Compare and contrast hypochondriasis and body dysmorphic disorders.
5. Compare and contrast the psychodynamic, cognitive, and behavioral views of somatoform disorders.
6. Describe the traditional psychophysiological disorders: ulcers, asthma, chronic headaches, hypertension, coronary heart disease.
7. Discuss how perceptions of control, personality, mood, and social support affect immune system functioning.
8. Discuss typical psychological treatments for psychophysiological disorders.

KEY TERMS

antibody
antigen
asthma
atrophy
aura
autonomic nervous system (ANS)
baroreceptors
B-cell
behavioral medicine
biofeedback training
body dysmorphic disorder
Briquet's syndrome
chronic headache
conversion disorder
coronary artery
coronary heart disease
corticosteroid
disregulation model
dysmorphophobia
Electra complex
electromyograph (EMG)
essential hypertension
exposure and response prevention
factitious disorder
glove anesthesia
"hardy" personality style
helper T-cell
hormones
hypertension
hypnosis
hypochondriasis
hysterical somatoform disorders
immune system
individual biological reactions
insomnia
life change units
local biological weakness
lymphocyte
malingering
mantra
meditation
migraine headache
mind-body dualism
Munchausen syndrome
Munchausen syndrome by proxy
muscle contraction, or tension, headache
myocardial infarction
natural killer T-cell
negative feedback loop
norepinephrine
pain disorder associated with psychological features
parasympathetic nervous system
phallic stage
preoccupation disorder
preoccupation somatoform disorders
primary gain
psychological factors affecting medical condition
psychoneuroimmunology
psychophysiological
psychosocial
psychosomatic
relaxation training
repressive coping style
secondary gain
self-hypnosis
self-instruction training
Social Adjustment Rating Scale
somatization disorder
somatoform disorder
sympathetic nervous system
Type A personality style
Type B personality style
UCLA Loneliness Scale
ulcer

MEDIA RESOURCES

CD-ROM Video Questions

The following is a list of video questions as they appear on the Abnormal Psychology CD-ROM that accompanies each textbook. As a homework assignment, have your students watch the video clip and then answer these questions. Students can answer the questions directly into a text box appearing next to the video clip. When they have finished answering these questions, they can print out their assignment and hand it in for grading.

Also use these CD-ROM segments as assignments to expose your students to material prior to your lectures.

"Fran" Treating Chronic Pain

1. Given what you saw of Fran, and what Dr. Fordyce said about her, what DSM-IV diagnosis would be appropriate?

   A: pain disorder associated with psychological factors

2. Dr. Fordyce does not deny that Fran's pain is real, meaning that it has a physical basis (that you do not see in the video). This statement would allow a psychologist to rule out what other type of pain-related disorder?

   A: Somatization disorder. Because Fran's pain had an actual cause, she would not be diagnosable with somatization disorder, the appropriate diagnosis when there is no physical or medical basis for the pain.

3. According to Dr. Fordyce, how does chronic pain develop?

   A: 1. Patients suffer an injury and overprotect themselves. 2. People around the patient see that they are moving carefully and are hurting and warn them to be careful. 3. As a result, the sufferers' cautious behaviors are reinforced.

4. In addition to people around Fran "rewarding" her behavior, Dr. Fordyce mentions a larger sociocultural factor that makes Fran's behavior possible. What is this?

   A: Our highly industrialized society allows human beings to survive without being able to take care of themselves.

5. What type of assessment did Fran undergo and for what purpose?

   A: The speed-walking test was done at the beginning, end, and during intervals of treatment to measure her progress.

6. What aspect of behavioral treatment is indicated by the use of the speed-walking test? *Hint:* Refer back to Chapters 3 and 4 of your text.

   A: Behavioral treatment employs quantifiable measurement of actual behavior to indicate the baseline of behaviors at the beginning of treatment and to track improvements in behavior attributable to treatment.

7. Why, according to Dr. Fordyce, is Fran at high risk for chronic pain?

   A: She is anxious, fearful, high-strung, thin-skinned, and depressed, and she compounds those symptoms with the pain. In effect, she suffers more because she is worried more.

8. What does the connection between Fran's physical and psychological symptoms suggest about the connection between the mind and the body?

   A: As Dr. Fordyce states, the mind influences how we feel.

9. The narrator states that Fran is receiving behavioral and physical therapy. Yet Dr. Fordyce's statement about the mind-body connection suggests what about the nature of the behavioral therapy? *Hint:* It might include some other type of therapy.

   A: The behavioral therapy she is receiving would be more accurately referred to as cognitive-behavioral therapy, because her mental state is being taken into account. In pure behavioral therapy, what or how one thinks is not an issue.

Comer Video Segments

(See the Video Guide in Appendix E for detailed descriptions.)

Segment 21 Experiment Linking Placebo Effects to Endorphins
Segment 52 Self-Stimulation, Learning, and Behavior
Segment 57 Links between the Brain and the Body: Acupuncture, Pain, and Far Eastern Theories
Segment 58 Treatment for Pain Disorders
Segment 60 Biofeedback Training by Dr. Neal Miller
Segment 205 Stress on the Job: Psychological and Physical Effects
Segment 210 Woman Receives Treatment for Chronic Pain

Overhead Transparencies

Transparency 27, Figure 10–2, p. 295, "Mirror Mirror on the Wall . . ."
Transparency 28, Figure 10–3, p. 303, Negative Feedback Loop
Transparency 29, Figure 10–5, p. 311, Warning: Psychological Disorders May Be Dangerous to Your Health

Transparency Masters

TM–13, Table 10–4, p. 298, Disorders That Have Physical Symptoms
TM–14, Table 10–6, p. 306, Most Stressful Life Events

DSM-IV Masters

E–22, DSM-IV Diagnostic Criteria for Somatization Disorder

E–23, DSM-IV Diagnostic Criteria for Conversion Disorder

E–24, DSM-IV Diagnostic Criteria for Pain Disorder and Hypochondriasis

E–25, DSM-IV Diagnostic Criteria for Body Dysmorphic Disorder and Factitious Disorder

CLASS DEMONSTRATIONS AND ACTIVITIES

The Anonymous Five-Minute Essay: Type A Personality

Ask for anonymous descriptions of individuals with whom students are familiar that fit the description of the Type A personality. Likely examples will be Little League coaches, teachers, parents, and even some friends. Inform students that you may select their example for reading to the class.

The Anonymous Five-Minute Essay: "I can't go to school today."

An amusing exercise is to have students write down their most creative excuse for not attending school (related to faking illness). It should be an episode "in which they probably could have qualified for some acting award, and of which, to this day, they are proud." Inform students that you may select their example for reading to the class.

"Here's $25,000 to be awarded to . . . "

Type A personality styles are sometimes displayed by children. Researchers suggest that children as young as 3 can exhibit a marked pattern of impatience and restlessness, expectation of meeting high standards, and above-average competitiveness. Children may carry these personality styles, with their potential impact on health, with them into adulthood. Ask groups to develop a school-based program for encouraging these children to develop healthier personality patterns or styles. Have the groups present their ideas, then have the class vote on which group receives the grant to implement their idea.

Munchausen Syndrome versus Munchausen Syndrome by Proxy

Lead a discussion of these disorders. Munchausen syndrome is an extreme and long-term form of factitious disorder in which a person feigns symptoms to gain admission to a hospital and receive treatment. Munchausen syndrome by proxy is a factitious disorder in which parents feign or produce physical illnesses in their children. In both instances, the motivation appears to be attention from doctors (either because one is sick or because one's child is sick).

Distinguishing Disorders

The differences among factitious disorder, conversion disorder, somatization disorder, pain disorder, hypochondriasis, and body dysmorphic disorder can be difficult to understand. Pointing out the important distinction (such as the voluntary nature of symptoms in factitious disorder) is very helpful. Displaying the DSM criteria for these disorders simultaneously while leading a discussion of the differences also can be helpful.

Open Discussion: Too Healthy?

Ask students whether there should be a DSM category for people who are overly concerned with good health. They can be people who are overly concerned about eating habits or exercise. Should these types of behaviors be considered abnormal?

Open Discussion: Holmes and Rahe Scale

Hand out or display the Holmes and Rahe Scale. What are the most common and least common stressors experienced by students in the class? Alternatively, point to specific examples on the list and ask for a show of hands regarding whether such an event would be (or was) stressful. Discuss why or why not. This emphasizes the subjective nature of stress and the importance of appraisal.

Open Discussion: Student Health

Conduct a class discussion on the relationship between health and academic stress. Ask students whether health problems fit a semester pattern. Discuss students' beliefs about their own role in health and sickness. Can they affect the course of a disease?

Can they do things that prevent diseases? Is the patient to blame for being ill?

"Here's $25,000 to be awarded to . . . "

Discuss how optimism or fatalism affects the chances of eventually recovering from cancer. Recent research indicates that the state of mind concerning recovery is a powerful influence on the recovery rates of cancer patients. The more optimistic and positive the person is, the more likely he or she is to recover. Divide the class into groups, then have them create programs, to be used at hospitals or other sites, to encourage optimism in cancer patients. Have the groups present their ideas, then have the class vote on which group receives the grant to implement their idea.

CHAPTER

11 Eating Disorders

TOPIC OVERVIEW

Anorexia Nervosa
The Clinical Picture
Medical Problems

Bulimia Nervosa
Binges
Compensatory Behaviors
Bulimia Nervosa vs. Anorexia Nervosa

What Causes Eating Disorders?
Societal Pressures
Family Environment
Ego Deficiencies and Cognitive Disturbances
Mood Disorders
Biological Factors

Treatments for Eating Disorders
Treatments for Anorexia Nervosa
Treatments for Bulimia Nervosa

Crossroads: A Standard for Integrating Perspectives

LEARNING OBJECTIVES

1. List the central features of anorexia nervosa and bulimia, then discuss the age groups in which anorexia and bulimia are most common.
2. Compare and contrast the various behavioral patterns of anorexia and bulimia.
3. Compare and contrast ways in which bulimics and anorexics perceive their eating disorders.
4. Describe medical problems that can be caused by eating disorders.

5. Explain how each of the following factors can place a person at risk for an eating disorder: societal pressures, family environment, ego deficiencies and cognitive disturbances, mood disorders, and biological factors.
6. Describe treatments for anorexia nervosa, including weight restoration and resumption of eating, then discuss broader psychological changes and the aftermath of this disorder.
7. Describe treatments for bulimia nervosa, including individual insight therapy, group therapy, behavioral therapy, and antidepressant drugs, then discuss the aftermath of this disorder.

KEY TERMS

amenorrhea
anorexia nervosa
binge
binge-eating disorder
binge-purge syndrome
bulimia nervosa
compensatory behavior
enmeshed family pattern
exposure and response prevention
glucagon-like peptide-1 (GLP-1)
hypothalamus
ineffective parents
lateral hypothalamus (LH)
metabolic rate
multidimensional risk perspective
nonpurging-type bulimia nervosa
purging-type anorexia nervosa
restricting-type anorexia nervosa
supportive nursing care
tube and intravenous feeding
ventromedial hypothalamus (VMH)
weight set point

MEDIA RESOURCES

CD-ROM Video Questions

The following is a list of video questions as they appear on the Abnormal Psychology CD-ROM that accompanies each textbook. As a homework assignment, have your students watch the video clip and then answer these questions. Students can answer the questions directly into a text box appearing next to the video clip. When they have finished answering these questions, they can print out their assignment and hand it in for grading.

Also use these CD-ROM segments as assignments to expose your students to material prior to your lectures.

"Liz" Bulimia Nervosa

1. What are the DSM-IV criteria for bulimia nervosa?

   A: The DSM-IV criteria are (1) recurrent episodes of binge eating, (2) recurrent inappropriate compensatory behavior in order to prevent weight gain, (3) symptoms continuing, on average, at least twice a week for 3 months, and (4) undue influence of weight or shape on self-evaluation.

2. Which DSM-IV criteria of bulimia nervosa does Liz meet? Support your answer with examples of her past and present behaviors.

   A: 1. Liz has been binging for at least 3 years. 2. She had been starving and dieting since the age of 15 (she was 24 at the time of the movie clip). She had been purging for 3 years in order to get rid of all food that she ingested. 3. Her symptoms of binging and purging had been going on for 3 years, sometimes as many as 6 to 10 hours a day. 4. She felt guilt if she left any food in her system. 5. After a large meal, she described herself as looking as if she were pregnant and having gained 10 pounds. After she purged for the first time, she felt great and thought she had lost the weight immediately.

3. How does Liz's history fit the clinical pattern of bulimia nervosa discussed in the text?

A: It appears mainly in females; it lasts for several years; weight stays within normal range (Liz did not appear to be too thin); it began after a period of dieting (her teen years); she felt great tension and guilt before she first purged; she felt relaxed after she purged; she felt good that she could control her weight gain by purging.

4. Although Liz was hospitalized for 5 months, she does not tell us about her hospital treatment. According to the text, what types of treatment might she have received?

   A: behavioral therapy that encouraged her to eat and not purge (exposure and response prevention); supportive nursing care; individual insight therapy; group therapy; antidepressant medications

5. Has Liz relapsed?

   A: Liz has relapsed. She has been hospitalized twice. She indicates that she has continuing bouts of binging and purging.

6. What is the prognosis that Liz will have a full recovery?

   A: Her prognosis for a full recovery is guarded for several reasons. She has a long history of bulimia and exhibited extreme dieting practices before she developed bulimia. She has spent a great amount of time binging and purging. Although we don't have the specifics, her doctor characterized her as "psychotic" at the beginning of her 5-month hospitalization, suggesting that she had another mental diagnosis, perhaps major depression. She also is wary of her own ability to control her harmful impulses, and her attitude may cloud her prospects for a full recovery.

Comer Video Segments

(See the Video Guide in Appendix E for detailed descriptions.)

Segment 22 Survey of Dieting and Body Image Among 33,000 Women, by Drs. Susan Wooley and Wayne Wooley
Segment 23 Woman with Anorexia Nervosa
Segment 24 Woman with Bulimia Nervosa
Segment 25 Lateral Hypothalamus Stimulation Leads to Hunger and Eating Behavior
Segment 26 Subjects Get Pleasure from Experiencing Hunger and Food Thoughts
Segment 27 Medial Hypothalamus Anesthetization and Eating Behavior

Overhead Transparencies

Transparency 30, Figure 11–1, p. 322, Body Dissatisfaction on the Rise
Transparency 31, Figure 11–2, p. 327, Overlapping Patterns of Anorexia Nervosa, Bulimia Nervosa, and Obesity
Transparency 32, Figure 11–3, p. 333, Dangerous Shortcuts

Transparency Masters

TM–15, Table 11–3, p. 331, Anorexia Nervosa vs. Bulimia Nervosa
TM–16, Table 11–4, p. 341, Sample Items from the Eating Disorder Inventory II

DSM-IV Masters

E–26, DSM-IV Diagnostic Criteria for Anorexia Nervosa
E–27, DSM-IV Diagnostic Criteria for Bulimia Nervosa

CLASS DEMONSTRATIONS AND ACTIVITIES

Open Discussion: Twin Studies and Weight

A recent study analyzed weight and height records from a Swedish sample of 247 identical twin pairs and 426 fraternal twin pairs. The investigators found that identical twin siblings ended up with similar body weights whether or not they were raised in the same home, whereas childhood environment did not strongly affect body weight. Lead a discussion on the implications of this study. What does it say about dieting and trying to lose weight? Point out that many persons are well over their set weight and should attempt to lose weight, but that deciding what one's body should look like without regard to what one's body "wants" may set one up for extreme frustration and eating disordered behavior.

Group Work: Cultural Attitudes and Food

Have the class form small groups and develop an example of contradictory cultural or familial attitudes with respect to food and eating behavior. That is, ask groups to come up with extreme or dramatic differences in attitudes between two cultures or families. Have groups present their findings. Discuss how these may influence eating disordered behavior.

Food and the Media

In preparation for the next class, ask students to analyze messages (implicit and explicit) from television, popular magazines, newspapers, and tabloids about food. Some students can contrast food ads on prime-time TV and on children's TV shows. Others can evaluate whether food is sold as a biological necessity or as a reward, a status symbol, or as a way to fulfill a psychological need. Others can evaluate types of manipulations used to lure the potential customer into buying specific foods. Lead an open discussion on the findings during the next class.

Calculating BMI

The best way to determine whether weight is reasonable is to calculate the body mass index (BMI). BMI equals one's weight in kilograms divided by one's height in meters squared (kg/m^2). Allow the students some time to calculate their own BMI. It will be necessary to provide conversion formulas for pounds to kilograms and inches to meters. Write the following on the board:

BMI	Classification
17.5	cutoff for anorexia nervosa
<18	severely underweight
18–20	slightly underweight
20–25	optimal for health
25–27	slightly overweight
>30	obese

The typical reaction to these figures, which are based on scientific, longitudinal research, is skepticism. Students are often skeptical that a BMI can be considered healthy, given that the person "looks fat." This is an extremely useful way to jump-start a discussion on the attitudes of Americans toward weight; that is, Americans are more concerned about weight with respect to appearance than about weight with respect to health.

Ideal Female Body

To emphasize the changes in the ideal female body image, you can bring in pictures of women considered to embody the ideal in various eras. Good examples are a painting by Reubens; any screen idol of the 1950s (e.g., Marilyn Monroe), whose bust and hips swelled from a tiny waist; the emaciated model Twiggy of the 1960s; and Kate Moss today.

Diets

Ask students to collect diet articles in popular magazines. Additionally, ask them to find some very old examples; these might be found in your school library. On an overhead transparency analyze the advice, the quality, and the emotional tone of current and older diets. Ask students to discuss the differences between the two types as listed on the overhead. Do the students think the current approach is more effective?

The Anonymous 5-Minute Essay

Ask students to develop a list of assumptions they make when they see a thin person or a fat person. What do the students assume about the person based solely on body type? Read some of these stereotypes and open the class to discussion. Be careful not to offend anyone in the class.

Advertising

The message implicit in all advertising is "never be satisfied." If consumers can be convinced that the way they look or the way they are is inadequate, then they will be more likely to buy products that help them be the way they want to be. It has been estimated that the average person sees between 400 and 600 ads per day, and it is estimated that 1 in 11 ads include a direct message about beauty. Ask the class whether these might have anything to do with the finding that most young women in the United States are dissatisfied with their body (i.e., consider themselves overweight).

What Effect Does Dieting Have?

Dieting makes one hungry and predisposes one to binge eat, which predisposes one to feel guilty and either try to purge the food (e.g., vomit) or expunge it through even more dieting, setting up a vicious cycle. In short, dieting declares war on food, a biological necessity, and encourages one to conclude that food is the enemy and must be avoided at all costs (e.g., anorexia nervosa) or that any admission of food into the body must be counteracted (e.g., purging). While leading a general discussion on the effects of dieting, bring up the following two studies. A sample of 15-year-old schoolgirls in London was divided into dieters and nondieters; of the dieters, 21% developed an eating disorder within the subsequent year, compared to about 3% of the nondieters. In a different study of 1033 twins, researchers found that dieting status predicted subsequent diagnosis of bulimia nervosa over a 3-year follow-up period.

Open Discussion or Group Work: Why More Women than Men?

Judith Rodin coined the term "normative discontent" to describe women's pervasive dissatisfaction with their bodies. Forty-five percent of U.S. households have someone currently on a diet; 55% of females between the ages of 25 and 54 are currently "dieting," and a study in California found that 80% of fourth-grade girls are currently dieting or have in the past dieted. Most (63%) females say their weight affects how they feel about themselves. Ask groups or the whole class to discuss why women are particularly vulnerable to eating disorders (e.g., beauty ideals apply more to women than to men; boys are praised for doing and excelling, whereas girls are praised for how they look).

"Here's $25,000 to be awarded to . . . "

Related to the previous activity, divide the class into groups and have them create school-based programs to encourage girls to resist the messages they are exposed to every day that are pressuring them to be thin and to dislike their bodies. Have the groups present their ideas, then have a class vote to see which group receives the grant to implement their idea.

"Pretend, for a moment, that you are a counselor."

Divide students into groups. Ask them to imagine that they are a counselor seeing a patient with anorexia nervosa. Ask them to develop an effective therapy. How would they proceed? After five minutes or so, change the presenting problem to bulimia nervosa. Now how would they proceed? Do groups favor cognitive or behavioral approaches? Do the disorders require similar or different approaches? Why? Use this as a lead-in to a discussion of therapies and treatments for these disorders, pointing out that forced feeding is often necessary with anorexia nervosa; that is, reasoning with the person simply does not work.

CHAPTER

12 Substance-Related Disorders

TOPIC OVERVIEW

Depressants
- Alcohol
- Sedative-Hypnotic Drugs
- Opioids

Stimulants
- Cocaine
- Amphetamines
- Caffeine

Hallucinogens

Cannabis

Combinations of Substances

What Causes Substance-Related Disorders?
- The Sociocultural View
- The Psychodynamic View
- The Behavioral View
- The Biological View

How Are Substance-Related Disorders Treated?
- Psychodynamic Therapies
- Behavioral Therapies
- Cognitive-Behavioral Therapies
- Biological Treatments
- Sociocultural Treatments

Crossroads: New Wrinkles to a Familiar Story

LEARNING OBJECTIVES

1. Explain the terms "tolerance" and "withdrawal symptoms" and give examples.
2. Name some commonly used depressants, including alcohol, and explain their effects on the central nervous system.
3. Distinguish between two major sedative-hypnotic drugs—antianxiety drugs and barbiturates—and explain why barbiturate abuse is dangerous.
4. Know which drugs are opioids and be able to explain the effects of these drugs, including heroin.
5. Describe the typical effects of cocaine and contrast these with the effects of the other major stimulant, amphetamines.
6. Describe the general effects of the hallucinogen LSD.
7. Describe the current short-term and long-term effects of cannabis use.
8. Describe, compare, and contrast the psychodynamic, behavioral, biological, and sociocultural explanation of substance abuse, then discuss the therapies of each view.

KEY TERMS

addiction
alcohol
alcohol dehydrogenase
alcohol withdrawal delirium
Alcoholics Anonymous (AA)
alcoholism
alternative behaviors
amphetamine
antagonist drug
aversion therapy
barbiturate
behavioral self-control training (BSCT)
benzodiazepine
caffeine
cannabis
cannabis sativa
cirrhosis
classical conditioning
cocaine
codeine
community prevention program
confabulation
covert sensitization
crack
crashing
cross-tolerance
culture-sensitive program
delirium tremens ("the DT's")
depressant
detoxification
disulfiram (Antabuse)
dopamine
dopamine-2 (D2) receptor gene
drug
endorphin
ergot alkaloids
ethyl alcohol
fetal alcohol syndrome
fetal cocaine syndrome
flashback
free-basing
GABA
hallucinogen
hallucinosis
hashish
heroin
intoxication
Korsakoff's syndrome
lysergic acid diethylamide (LSD)
marijuana
metabolize
methadone
methadone maintenance program
morphine
naloxone
naltrexone
narcotic
narcotic antagonist
opioid
opium
partial antagonist
polysubstance use
polysubstance-related disorder
psychedelic drugs
receptor gene
reinforcement
relapse-prevention training
residential treatment center
reticular formation
reward center
reward-deficiency syndrome
rush
sedative-hypnotic drug
serotonin
stimulant
substance

substance abuse
substance-abuse personality
substance dependence
synergistic effect
synesthesia
tetrahydrocannabinol (THC)
therapeutic community
tolerance
withdrawal

MEDIA RESOURCES

CD-ROM Video Questions

The following is a list of video questions as they appear on the Abnormal Psychology CD-ROM that accompanies each textbook. As a homework assignment, have your students watch the video clip and then answer these questions. Students can answer the questions directly into a text box appearing next to the video clip. When they have finished answering these questions, they can print out their assignment and hand it in for grading.

Also use these CD-ROM segments as assignments to expose your students to material prior to your lectures.

"Al" Alcohol Disorders: Hereditary Factors

1. In recounting his drinking history, when does Al think he started drinking like an alcoholic?

   A: He felt that he started out drinking like an alcoholic.

2. What does he mean by the fact that he drank "alcoholically"?

   A: He drank a lot from the beginning, despite becoming physically ill and despite his son's commenting on how much he was drinking.

3. Describe the type and nature of the test Dr. Begleiter used to see if Al's brain was "different" from the brain of a nondrinking person.

   A: Dr. Begleiter used a neurophysiological instrument to assess Al's P3 brain waves in response to unexpected stimuli. Brain waves were measured by the placement of the electrodes on the scalp. These electrodes picked up brain wave activity. A computer generated color pictures of brain wave activity.

4. How was Al's brain different from that of a nondrinking person?

   A: Al's brain scan indicated the absence of P3 waves when he was presented with unexpected stimuli.

5. What does the absence of P3 brain waves indicate about brain functioning?

   A: There are cognitive and sensory deficits deep in the brain, including the area of the brain stem.

6. Why did Dr. Begleiter and his colleagues need to perform the P3 assessment on children? What two groups of children did they study?

   A: They needed to ascertain first if Al's brain was different because of his alcoholism or if his brain difference contributed to his alcoholism. By examining the brains of young boys with and without alcoholic fathers, researchers could begin to ascertain the direction of effect on the brain (i.e., which came first, alcoholism or P3 deficits?).

7. What did the study of children's brains indicate?

   A: Children of alcoholic fathers had the same deficits in P3 waves as men who had been longtime drinkers. Children without alcoholic fathers had no such deficits.

8. How will knowing that some forms of alcoholism are hereditary help future generations?

   A: Children, especially boys, will know that if they drink, they are at high risk for addiction.

"Jim" Treating Drug Addiction: A Behavioral Approach

1. For what disorder is Jim receiving treatment?

   A: crack cocaine addiction

2. What type of treatment is he receiving?

   A: behavioral therapy

3. Using the behavioral perspective, Jim's treatment provider discusses how Jim became addicted. What is this perspective?

   A: Jim's body learned to be addicted, and his body has to unlearn responses to the triggers that make him crave cocaine.

4. What is the goal of Jim's behavioral treatment?

   A: Jim's body will unlearn its physiological responses to triggers that make his body crave drugs. When the physiological responses are unlearned, Jim will not crave the drug.

5. What form of behavioral conditioning has resulted in Jim's addiction—classical or operant?

   A: Both. Classical conditioning, because his body has learned a response to the drug and to the sights, sounds, and smells that precede drug use. His body craved cocaine so as to ward off withdrawal symptoms (lower body temperature, sweating, etc.). Operant conditioning, because when he smoked crack cocaine he obtained the reward—being high—that he was seeking. He continued to use the drug so he would receive the same result.

6. Compare the results of Jim's treatment with Pavlov's dogs ceasing to salivate at the sound of the bell.

   A: Pavlov's dogs salivated at the sound of the bell for a time after the meat powder was withdrawn because their bodies had associated the bell with receiving the meat powder. After a time, they no longer salivated to the bell alone, because no meat was forthcoming. Jim's body manifests physiological responses of craving for cocaine even after Jim was not using cocaine, because his body associated certain sounds, sights, and smells with impending cocaine use. Eventually, Jim's body no longer had those physical responses because Jim was not ingesting cocaine.

7. How many treatments did Jim receive to enable him to prepare to smoke the crack without having strong physiological reactions?

   A: 20 treatments

8. Why is Jim's prognosis for staying off of cocaine hopeful?

   A: His body has unlearned the physical responses that caused craving.

"Greg" Treating Drug Addiction: A Behavioral Approach

1. What was Greg's life like before he went into treatment?

   A: He says his life was in shambles. He had abandoned his family, was unemployed and unemployable, and was on welfare. He has resorted to committing crimes to get money for drugs.

2. How serious was Greg's substance abuse?

   A: It was a serious addiction. Before treatment, craving and using were one, meaning that when he craved the drug, he used the drug.

3. What techniques had Greg learned to stay sober?

   A: He employed a combination of behavioral (relaxation) and cognitive (imagining the dire consequences of using the drug again) techniques, what the text refers to as *behavioral self-control training (BSCT)* and *relapse prevention training.*

4. How seriously did Greg take his addiction?

   A: Very seriously. He felt that if he used crack again, he would either die or be in prison.

5. Why did Greg want to tell his story?

   A: He wanted other people to see that it was possible to get better—to give people hope.

Comer Video Segments

(See the Video Guide in Appendix E for detailed descriptions.)

Segment 30 Onset and Etiology of Opioid Dependence
Segment 31 Sociocultural Overview of Opioid Dependence
Segment 32 Methadone Treatment Program, 1973
Segment 33 Group Therapy for Substance Dependence
Segment 34 Persons After Recovery from Substance Dependence
Segment 203 Craving for Cocaine: Triggers and Treatment
Segment 211 Man with History of Alcohol Dependence Is Tested for Genetic Predisposition
Segment 212 The Effects of Alcohol and other Depressants on the Brain

Overhead Transparencies

Transparency 33, Figure 12–1, p. 354, Teenagers and Substance Use
Transparency 34, Figure 12–3, p. 368, How Easy Is It for Teenagers to Acquire Substances?

Transparency Masters

TM–13, Table 12–2, p. 353, Relationships Between Sex, Weight, Oral Alcohol Consumption, and Blood Alcohol Level
TM–18, Table 12–3, p. 359, Risks and Consequences of Drug Misuse

DSM-IV Masters

E–28, DSM-IV Diagnoses Associated with Class of Substances
E–29, DSM-IV Criteria for Substance Dependence
E–30, DSM-IV Criteria for Substance Abuse

CLASS DEMONSTRATIONS AND ACTIVITIES

Group Work: Drug Searches and Drug Testing

Present yourself as a school district superintendent who must decide whether to allow random drug searches and mandatory drug testing in your schools. Arkansas has used blood tests, Breathalyzer tests, and polygraph tests on high school students. New Jersey conducts spot searches of lockers, gym bags, and purses, even though the Fourth Amendment outlaws "searches and seizures" without a warrant issued upon "probable cause." You are seeking the informed opinion of experts. One side is for such activities, the other is against it. Divide students into groups, then assign each group one of these two positions. Tell students to prepare their arguments.

Open Discussion or Group Work: Pregnancy and Drugs

Either lead the class in a discussion or assign groups to discuss whether pregnant women who use drugs should face criminal prosecution. Do students think facing charges would cut down on a pregnant woman's drug abuse, or would it keep such women away from professionals who provide prenatal care because they might get arrested? Is fetal abuse the equivalent of child abuse? Can you think of alternatives to criminal charges? Because parents who smoke increase their young children's risk of asthma, should smokers also be liable? Because a man's sperm count can remain low for more than 2 years after he stops using cocaine, should a wife who is unable to become pregnant be able to sue her husband if he had used cocaine? This is not just an abstract discussion, as several states have enacted laws that punish the mother for endangering the fetus.

Open Discussion: Alcohol Use or Abuse?

Ask students where they draw the line between the use and abuse of alcohol. Do their answers focus more on the amount or type of alcohol used? Ask for examples of friends' behavior that are clearly abuse.

Abuse versus Dependence

The difference between these diagnoses can be confusing to students. Display the criteria for each side by side, and point out the differences. Abuse involves maladaptive behavior, whereas dependence involves not just maladaptive behavior but also physical symptoms and apparent lack of control. Of course, the former is the precursor of the latter.

Media and Drug Use

Use an overhead transparency to develop a list of the drug behaviors that are currently portrayed in the media, particularly the movies. Ask students for examples from the most current movies. Ask if drug-related behaviors are changing in the movies. If yes, in what manner? Are drugs becoming more accepted in our society?

Does DARE Work?

Discuss the effectiveness of drug education today. How effective have current efforts, such as DARE (Drug Abuse Resistance and Education) been in preventing children from becoming drug abusers? Recent data indicate that this program is less successful than originally hoped. Ask your students to discuss what they would do to improve the DARE program.

Presume You Are an Expert . . .

Tell the students that you received a phone call from your senator last night at home. He or she recognized that you are doing a fine job instructing students on the issue of substance abuse. Your senator wants you and several students to come to Washington, D.C., to testify before a Senate subcommittee on a proposed change in drug enforcement laws. Ask students to prepare a 5-minute presentation outlining the most important aspects of illegal drug usage. Remind them that their testimony will influence law. Also remind them that their testimony is "expert" and that the validity of their statements may be challenged.

Open Discussion: Alcohol versus Drugs

Drug use and interdiction is a major focus of activity of the U.S. government, but its effects pale in comparison to the negative effects of alcohol. Ask students which is more of a problem for the country, alcohol or drugs? (Alcohol accounts for 20% of all national expenditures on health care, costs the United States $90 billion or more annually, is a factor in one-third to one-half of all suicides, homicides, assaults, rapes, and accidental deaths, accounts for 40% of all fatal car accidents, 50% of deaths from falls, 52% of deaths from fires, and 38% of deaths by drowning.) Lead a discussion of why the country focuses on drugs and generally ignores alcohol.

CHAPTER

13 Sexual Disorders and Gender Identity Disorder

TOPIC OVERVIEW

Sexual Dysfunctions
- Disorders of Desire
- Disorders of Excitement
- Disorders of Orgasm
- Disorders of Sexual Pain
- Treatments for Sexual Dysfunctions

Paraphilias
- Fetishism
- Transvestic Fetishism
- Exhibitionism
- Voyeurism
- Frotteurism
- Pedophilia
- Sexual Masochism
- Sexual Sadism

Gender Identity Disorder

Crossroads: A Private Topic Draws Public Attention

LEARNING OBJECTIVES

1. Describe each of the four phases of the sexual response cycle: desire, arousal, orgasm, and resolution.
2. Explain the two most common dysfunctions of the desire phase, hypoactive sexual desire and

sexual aversion, then describe dysfunctions of the arousal phase, male erectile disorder and female arousal disorder.

3. Discuss the orgasmic sexual dysfunctions of premature ejaculation, male orgasmic disorder, and female orgasmic disorder.
4. Define paraphilias and fetishism and describe behavioral treatment for them.
5. Define, compare, and contrast transvestic fetishism, exhibitionism, voyeurism, frotteurism, and pedophilia.
6. Compare and contrast sexual masochism and sexual sadism.
7. Define and discuss gender identity disorder.
8. Discuss the new directions in therapy for sexual dysfunction.

KEY TERMS

affectual awareness
aphrodisiac
autoerotic asphyxia
aversion therapy
bed nucleus of stria terminalis (BST)
cross-dressing
desire phase
directed masturbation training
dyspareunia
erectile disorder
estrogen
excitement phase
exhibitionism
female orgasmic disorder
female sexual arousal disorder
fetishism
frotteurism
gender identity disorder
hormone treatments
hypoactive sexual desire
hypoxyphilia
male erectile disorder
male orgasmic disorder
masturbatory satiation
mutual responsibility
nocturnal penile tumescence (NPT)
nondemand pleasuring
orgasm phase
orgasmic reorientation
paraphilia
pedophilia
penile prosthesis
performance anxiety
phalloplasty
premature ejaculation
prolactin
relapse-prevention training
sensate focus
sex therapy
sex-change surgery
sexual addiction
sexual arousal disorder
sexual aversion
sexual dysfunction
sexual masochism
sexual response cycle
sexual sadism
spectator role
stop-start technique
tease technique
testosterone
transsexualism
transvestic fetishism
transvestism
vacuum erection device (VED)
vaginismus
voyeurism

MEDIA RESOURCES

CD-ROM Video Questions

The following is a list of video questions as they appear on the Abnormal Psychology CD-ROM that accompanies each textbook. As a homework assignment, have your students watch the video clip and then answer these questions. Students can answer the questions directly into a text box appearing next to the video clip. When they have finished answering these questions, they can print out their assignment and hand it in for grading.

Also use these CD-ROM segments as assignments to expose your students to material prior to your lectures.

"Brad"

1. Brad calls his condition "transsexualism." What is another name for it?

   A: The textbook also calls it gender identity disorder. The doctor in the film referred to it as gender dysphoria.

2. What was the essence of Brad's problem prior to sex reassignment surgery?

   A: Biologically, he was a girl, but he felt that he was a boy.

3. How did this disorder affect Brad's sense of himself?

   A: He felt as if he was two people—the girl others thought he was and the boy that he thought he was.

4. How did this disorder affect Brad socially?

   A: He did not know how to relate to others.

5. What did Brad think was wrong with him?

   A: He thought he was crazy. He had never heard of transsexualism.

6. What was his reaction when his mother told him that he needed to wear a bra?

   A: At first, he said he would cut off his breasts. He thought better of it after he realized he might bleed to death.

7. How has Brad's emotional state changed since he received sex-change surgery?

   A: He says he feels like he is one person.

8. Why do surgeons who perform sex-change surgery want the client to resolve other psychological problems prior to undergoing the surgery?

   A: The doctor indicated that people with gender identity disorder often have a lot of problems as a result of the disorder. If they don't resolve these issues first, they might expect the surgery to resolve all of those problems.

Comer Video Segments

(See the Video Guide in Appendix E for detailed descriptions.)

Segment 213 Man with Gender Identity Disorder Describes His Feelings and His Body Image

Overhead Transparencies

Transparency 35, Figure 13–6, p. 402, Sexual Behavior and Gender

DSM-IV Masters

E–31, DSM-IV Diagnostic Criteria for Hypoactive Sexual Disorder and Sexual Aversion Disorder

E–32, DSM-IV Diagnostic Criteria for Female Sexual Arousal Disorder and Male Erectile Disorder

E–33, DSM-IV Diagnostic Criteria for Female Orgasmic Disorder and Male Orgasmic Disorder

E–34, DSM-IV Diagnostic Criteria for Premature Ejaculation, Dyspareunia, and Vaginismus

E–35, DSM-IV Diagnostic Criteria for Exhibitionism, Fetishism, Frotteurism, and Pedophilia

E–36, DSM-IV Diagnostic Criteria for Sexual Masochism, Sexual Sadism, Transvestic Fetishism, Voyeurism

E–37, DSM-IV Diagnostic Criteria for Gender Identity Disorder

CLASS DEMONSTRATIONS AND ACTIVITIES

The Anonymous 5-Minute Essay

Take 5 minutes and permit students to write any concerns or questions they might have about sexuality, including variations of sexual behavior. Review the responses and answer them (or as many as you can) in the next class period.

Open Discussion: Cultural and Sexual Behavior

Point out how cultural norms, beliefs, and values influence what is considered healthy sexuality. For example, homosexual intercourse is not only permitted but encouraged in some cultures. Discuss how cultural norms change. For example, homosexuality was considered a mental illness in early versions of the DSM (students are fascinated by overheads of these particular pages from the manual). Outmoded terms such as "nymphomania" (which in the Victorian era applied to women who were regularly orgasmic and enjoyed sex) and "masturbatory insanity" (in the 1930s physicians believed that masturbation could cause fatigue, physical illness, and mental illness) can be used for illustration. Some of these ideas persist today without scientific evidence to support them. For example, many varsity coaches insist that college players not have sex prior to a game because having it will reduce their athletic ability.

Group Work: Childhood Misconceptions

Have the class form small groups to create lists of sexual messages and misconceptions they were exposed to during childhood. Have each group develop a list and elect a spokesperson to discuss their list. Have class members listen for themes or common misconceptions. Ask them how such misinformation might influence someone's sexual behavior as an adult.

Open Discussion: Sexual Fantasies

Ask students to define "sexual fantasy." Ask them to then determine at what point normal fantasy becomes abnormal.

Childhood Sexual Abuse Controversies

Introduce students to some of the controversies surrounding the evaluation of possible victims of sexual abuse of children (some of whom are evaluated as adults). Have the students discuss the controversies and suggest solutions. Some of the difficulties include the following:

A. Discrepancies

Discrepancies are often noted between the stories told by children and those told by their accused offenders. Although denial or minimization can play a role in the offender's account, differences are also found in the types of sexual behavior described in events and their sequences, as well as in timing. One big problem is that young children's sequencing abilities are not adequate to enable them to encode some facts accurately. The feelings they express are likely to reflect their experiences more accurately than the details of the events they describe.

B. Leading Questions

Leading questions, such as "Did he touch your private parts?" can influence what children say and come to believe. Such questions are inadmissible as evidence in the courtroom, and they are ill-advised in therapy, too.

C. Anatomically Correct Dolls

Some clinicians believe that anatomically correct dolls are leading questions in another form. Indeed, they increase the probability of a sexual response, whether or not it is accurate (nonvictimized children also may play at pseudosexual behavior with these dolls). They are more useful as a facilitative tool in therapy than as an investigative tool.

Open Discussion: False Memory Syndrome

Some people believe that therapists have helped clients create false memories of childhood abuse in some patients. Whereas, unfortunately, many people have been sexually abused as children, it is also true that memories can be forgotten, distorted, and created (i.e., generated from nothing).

CHAPTER

14 Schizophrenia

TOPIC OVERVIEW

LEARNING OBJECTIVES

1. Describe the positive symptoms of schizophrenia: delusions, disorganized thinking, heightened perceptions and hallucinations, and inappropriate affect.
2. Compare and describe delusions of persecution, reference, grandeur, and control.
3. Discuss the negative symptoms of schizophrenia, that is, poverty of speech, blunted and flat affect, and social withdrawal.
4. Describe the psychomotor symptoms of schizophrenia.
5. Summarize the characteristics of the prodromal, active, and residual phases of schizophrenia.
6. Compare and contrast disorganized (hebephrenic), catatonic, paranoid, and undifferentiated schizophrenia.
7. Describe residual schizophrenia.
8. Distinguish between Type I and Type II schizophrenia.
9. Discuss the sociocultural view of schizophrenia.

10. Summarize evidence from twin and adoption studies that supports the genetic view of schizophrenia.
11. Discuss the dopamine hypothesis and evidence that both supports and fails to support it.
12. Describe the abnormal brain structures of schizophrenic people.
13. Discuss the psychodynamic, behavioral, existential, and cognitive views of schizophrenia.

KEY TERMS

active phase of schizophrenia
alogia
amphetamine psychosis
antihistamine
antipsychotic drug
atypical antipsychotics
avolition
blunted and flat affect
catatonia
catatonic type of schizophrenia
clang
delusion
derailment
diathesis-stress
disorganized type of schizophrenia
dopamine hypothesis
double-blind hypothesis
downward drift theory
enlarged ventricle
expressed emotion
flat affect
formal thought disorder
genetic linkage
hallucination
inappropriate affect
L-dopa
loose association
mentally ill chemical abuser (MICA)
negative symptom
neologism
neuroleptic drug
neuroleptic malignant syndrome
paranoid type of schizophrenia
paraprofessional
Parkinsonian symptoms
perseveration
pestivirus
phenothiazine
positive symptom
poverty of content
poverty of speech
premorbid functioning
prodromal phase of schizophrenia
psychomotor symptom
psychosis
regression
residual phase of schizophrenia
residual type of schizophrenia
schizophrenia
schizophrenogenic mother
social withdrawal
Type I schizophrenia
Type II schizophrenia
undifferentiated type of schizophrenia

MEDIA RESOURCES

CD-ROM Video Questions

The following is a list of video questions as they appear on the Abnormal Psychology CD-ROM that accompanies each textbook. As a homework assignment, have your students watch the video clip and then answer these questions. Students can answer the questions directly into a text box appearing next to the video clip. When they have finished answering these questions, they can print out their assignment and hand it in for grading.

Also use these CD-ROM segments as assignments to expose your students to material prior to your lectures.

"Steve" Schizophrenia

1. What evidence is there that Steve is suffering from schizophrenia?

   A: He experiences psychosis, loss of contact with reality.

2. What specific schizophrenia symptoms does Steve have? Are they positive, negative, or psychomotor?

   A: Steve has positive symptoms of hallucinations and delusions.

3. What are the themes of Steve's visual hallucinations and delusions?

A: They seem to be related to his mother and sister. Although he sometimes sees a man's face, he says his visual hallucinations often begin with the vision of his deceased mother. He then often sees the face of a girl who resembles both his sister and a girl he once met. Voices suggest that he has to marry this female image, which Steve takes to mean his sister.

4. Are Steve's psychotic experiences related to having sex with his sister hallucinations or delusions? Explain your answer.

   A: He specifically states that he does not see himself having sex with her; thus they would not be considered hallucinations. He seems to be thinking about or imagining having sex with her, a thought that disgusts him. They would appear to be delusions.

5. What kind of voices does Steve hear? What do the voices say?

   A: He hears various kinds of voices. Sometimes it is like the voice of God; other times it is like a "fake" girl's voice, perhaps a male voice trying to sound like a female. He mentioned nonsense syllables ("whittleyhoop") and the word "misery."

6. Steve says he does not look like a person with schizophrenia. What symptoms might a person have that made them look like a person suffering from schizophrenia?

   A: psychomotor symptoms, such as awkward movements, repeated grimaces, and odd gestures

7. What is the most extreme form of psychomotor symptom? What are the three types of this symptom? What would a person look like who had these symptoms?

   A: The most extreme forms of psychomotor symptoms are collectively called catatonia. People may display a rigid upright posture for hours and resist efforts to being moved (catatonic rigidity); they may stop responding to their environment, remaining motionless and silent for long stretches of time (catatonic stupor); they may remain in a bizarre position for a long time (catatonic posturing); they may display waxy flexibility, indefinitely maintaining postures into which they have been placed by someone else; or they may display catatonic excitement, wildly waving their arms and legs.

8. What medication is Steve taking?

   A: Melaril

9. Based upon your text, what neurotransmitter system does this drug likely affect? Note: Treatment of schizophrenia is the topic of Chapter 15.

   A: the dopamine system

10. With what Steve has told us about his symptoms, what theories of the origins of schizophrenia (other than the biological perspective) might be useful in understanding how and why Steve became schizophrenic? Support your answers with specifics from the video.

    A: Because Steve's hallucinations and delusions have a recurring mother/sister theme, the psychodynamic perspective and family dynamics aspect of the sociocultural perspective may hold clues. The delusion of having sex with his sister and the fake female voice saying "misery" may relate to Steve's efforts to reestablish ego control and may indicate that he was in some sort of conflict with his family. Although he does not mention hearing a voice or seeing an image of his father, the voice of God may represent his father. Or perhaps his father was weak or absent, a factor that fits with the family dynamics perspective.

11. Do you think that Steve was fabricating the fact that he was hearing voices? Why or why not?

    A: He was not making them up. He likely heard something in his head. Research suggests that people reporting auditory hallucination have activity in the auditory areas of the brain, an indication that neural activity is taking place. However, the individual places his or her own interpretations on these signals.

Comer Video Segments

(See the Video Guide in Appendix E for detailed descriptions.)

Segment 1 Deinstitutionalization and Jailing the Mentally Ill

Segment 4 PET Scan Procedure and Results: Comparison of Schizophrenic and Nonschizophrenic Twins

Segment 5 MRI Scan: Comparison of Schizophrenic and Nonschizophrenic Twins

Segment 35 Person with Hallucinations

Segment 36 Home Visit by Person with Schizophrenia

Segment 37 Parent's Reaction to Her Adult Child's Schizophrenia

Segment 41 Therapy Discussion Group: Patients with Severe Mental Disorders

Segment 111 Sister's Reaction to Brother's Schizophrenia

Segment 112 Hallucinations by a Man with Schizophrenia
Segment 114 Schizophrenia and Social Relationships
Segment 214 Young Man with Symptoms of Schizophrenia

Overhead Transparencies

Transparency 36, Figure 14–1, p. 424, Socioeconomic Class and Schizophrenia
Transparency 37, Figure 14–2, p. 436, Family Links
Transparency 38, Figure 14–3, p. 441, Seasonality and Schizophrenia

Transparency Masters

TM–19, Table 14–2, p. 435, Type I vs. Type II Schizophrenia
TM–20, Table 14–3, p. 437, An Array of Psychotic Disorders

DSM-IV Masters

E–38, DSM-IV Diagnostic Criteria for Schizophrenia
E–39, DSM-IV Diagnostic Criteria for Paranoid Type, Disorganized Type, and Catatonic Type Schizophrenia
E–40, DSM-IV Diagnostic Criteria for Undifferentiated Type and Residual Type
E–41, DSM-IV Diagnostic Criteria for Schizoaffective Disorder
E–42, DSM-IV Diagnostic Criteria for Delusional Disorder

CLASS DEMONSTRATIONS AND ACTIVITIES

Differential Diagnosis for Schizophrenia

Schizophrenia was once a wastebasket category for many individuals who did not fit the criteria of other disorders. Discuss the sometimes difficult task of differentiating schizophrenia from other disorders. Ask students to generate possible scenarios or situations wherein delusions or even hallucinations might be "normal" even in the absence of a schizophrenic process. Possibilities include posttraumatic stress, borderline personality disorder, and substance effects.

Szasz and Schizophrenia

According to Thomas Szasz, the idea of mental illness, including schizophrenia, is a myth. Szasz believes that schizophrenia should be properly regarded as problems of living in a society that mistreats individuals who are different. Do your students believe this assertion? Have them discuss the pros and cons of this proposition.

"Pretend, for a moment, that you are a . . . "

Ask students to imagine that they are a health professional confronted by a person experiencing paranoid delusions. What questions would they have for the person? Would they want to interview others who know the person? What difficulties might they encounter interviewing this individual?

The Anonymous 5-Minute Essay

Ask students to take 5 minutes to write down everything they believe about schizophrenia, whether they know it to be true or not. Many students admit that they are under the impression that schizophrenia is impossible to treat, that schizophrenia is a disorder from which no one recovers, and that schizophrenia is associated with severe dangerousness. Subsequent to this, ask students the source of these impressions.

Distinguishing Delusions

Students often have difficulty distinguishing the various types of delusions, and a simple exercise can reinforce the distinctions. Present an overhead with various statements representing different delusions and ask students to identify them (silently, on a sheet of paper). For example, put the following on an overhead: "They are talking about me" (persecution or grandeur, depending on what they are saying), "The radio is sending me a special message" (reference), and "The man who lives above me is stealing my thoughts" (control or thought broadcasting).

CHAPTER

15 Treatments for Schizophrenia

TOPIC OVERVIEW

Institutional Care in the Past

Institutional Care Takes a Turn for the Better
- Milieu Therapy
- The Token Economy

Antipsychotic Drugs
- How Effective Are Antipsychotic Drugs?
- What Are the Unwanted Effects of Antipsychotic Drugs?
- New Antipsychotic Drugs

Psychotherapy
- Insight Therapy
- Family Therapy
- Social Therapy

The Community Approach
- What Are the Features of Effective Community Care?
- How Has Community Treatment Failed?
- The Promise of Community Treatment

Crossroads: An Important Lesson

LEARNING OBJECTIVES

1. Summarize past institutional care and the improved institutional care of the milieu therapy and token economy programs.
2. Discuss the effectiveness of antipsychotic drugs.

3. Discuss the side effects of antipsychotic drugs: Parkinsonian and related symptoms, neuroleptic malignant syndrome, and tardive dyskinesia.
4. Discuss new antipsychotic drugs, such as Clozapine.
5. Discuss the effects of psychotherapy on schizophrenia, including insight, social, and family therapies.
6. Describe effective community care of schizophrenic patients.

KEY TERMS

aftercare
agranulocytosis
antihistamine
antipsychotic medication
atypical antipsychotic drug
back wards
case managers
chlorpromazine
clang
clozapine
community approach
community mental health center
day center
deinstitutionalization
extrapyramidal effect
halfway house
institutionalization
milieu therapy
national interest group
neuroleptic drug
olanzapine
operant conditioning
paraprofessional
perseveration
pestivirus
phenothiazines
psychoeducation
quetiapine
risperidone
sheltered workshop
social therapy
state hospital
tardive dyskinesia
token economy program

MEDIA RESOURCES

CD-ROM Video Questions

The following is a list of video questions as they appear on the Abnormal Psychology CD-ROM that accompanies each textbook. As a homework assignment, have your students watch the video clip and then answer these questions. Students can answer the questions directly into a text box appearing next to the video clip. When they have finished answering these questions, they can print out their assignment and hand it in for grading.

Also use these CD-ROM segments as assignments to expose your students to material prior to your lectures.

"Augustine" Schizophrenia: Pharmacological Treatment

1. What has made it possible for people with schizophrenia to live somewhat independently?

   A: the discovery of antipsychotic medication

2. How were antipsychotic medications discovered?

   A: They were discovered by accident. Dr. Henri Laborit, from France, discovered that a group of antihistamines calmed patients before surgery without causing a loss in consciousness. French psychiatrists tried one of the drugs, chlorpromazine, on their patients with psychotic symptoms. Their patients' symptoms were sharply reduced.

3. What symptoms of schizophrenia do we see in Augustine before he is taking medication? Refer to Chapter 14 of the text.

   A: The negative symptom of alogia (poverty of speech). The only psychomotor symptom is his pulling at his hair. Mostly he does nothing. He does not respond to Dr. Bigelow's questions unless prompted.

4. How do antipsychotic drugs benefit people with schizophrenia?

   A: The medications correct the excessive dopamine activity at the brain's synapses. Excessive dopamine is at the heart of many schizophrenia symptoms.

5. What physical and behavioral differences do we see in Augustine after he has been on medication for four weeks?

   A: Physical: His hair is short and he is clean-shaven. He is neatly dressed. Behavioral: Although he speaks slowly and somewhat without affect, he converses with the doctor.

6. How did Augustine's thought processes change after his being on the medication?

   A: He says he no longer has grandiose ideas. He thinks about obtaining realistic work.

7. Since this video clip is quite old, Augustine was probably taking one of the phenothiazines. Relate what the text says about the effect of these drugs to the alterations in Augustine's symptoms.

   A: The phenothiazines reduce the positive symptoms, such as the delusions, more than the negative symptoms, such as flat affect and poverty of speech. This is consistent with Augustine's postmedication improvement. Although he spoke better, his affect was flat and the doctor prompted him by asking him questions repeatedly. Augustine said that his grandiose thoughts were gone.

Comer Video Segments

(See the Video Guide in Appendix E for detailed descriptions.)

Segment 2 Medical Procedures Used in Mental Hospitals in the First Half of the Twentieth Century
Segment 3 Modern-Day Mental Hospital Ward
Segments 38 and 39 Antipsychotic Drugs
Segment 40 Deinstitutionalization and Homelessness
Segment 41 Therapy Discussion Group: Patients with Severe Mental Disorders
Segment 42 Prefrontal Lobotomy Procedure, 1942
Segment 43 Patients Before and After Prefrontal Lobotomy, 1944
Segment 44 Lobotomized Persons at a State Hospital Today
Segment 53 Drug Therapy Research
Segment 113 Recovery from Schizophrenia

Overhead Transparencies

Transparency 39, Figure 15–1, p. 458, The Effectiveness of Antipsychotic Drugs

DSM-IV Masters

E–38, DSM-IV Diagnostic Criteria for Schizophrenia
E–39, DSM-IV Diagnostic Criteria for Paranoid Type, Disorganized Type, and Catatonic Type Schizophrenia
E–40, DSM-IV Diagnostic Criteria for Undifferentiated Type and Residual Type
E–41, DSM-IV Diagnostic Criteria for Schizoaffective Disorder
E–42, DSM-IV Diagnostic Criteria for Delusional Disorder

CLASS DEMONSTRATIONS AND ACTIVITIES

Neuroleptic Drugs

Discuss some of the controversies that surround neuroleptic drugs. An ongoing controversy involves the control and costs of the blood tests necessary to monitor patients who take Clozaril.

"Here's $25,000 to be awarded to . . . "

Have groups of students compete for an award to be given to the best token economy.

"Let's Write a Self-Help Bestseller."

Discuss the fact that there are few (if any) self-help books for persons with schizophrenia (there are several for families). Divide students into groups, then ask each group to write an outline for such a manual. The results will be interesting.

CHAPTER

16 Disorders of Memory and Other Cognitive Functions

TOPIC OVERVIEW

Dissociative Disorders

Dissociative Amnesia
Dissociative Fugue
Dissociative Identity Disorder (Multiple Personality Disorder)
Explanations of Dissociative Disorders
Treatments for Dissociative Disorders

Organic Memory Disorders

The Biology of Memory
Amnestic Disorders
Dementias
What Treatments Are Available for Organic Memory Disorders?

Crossroads: Enormous Interest but Limited Knowledge

LEARNING OBJECTIVES

1. Describe the general characteristics of the dissociative disorders: dissociative amnesia, dissociative fugue, and dissociative identity disorder (multiple personality disorder).
2. Describe and discuss the types of amnesia: localized amnesia, selective amnesia, generalized amnesia, and continuous amnesia. Distinguish between retrograde amnesia and anterograde amnesia.

3. Discuss the explanations of dissociative disorder to include psychodynamic explanations, behavioral explanations, state-dependent learning, and self-hypnosis.
4. Distinguish between short-term memory and long-term memory. Summarize the anatomy and biochemistry of memory.
5. Describe the dementias, including Alzheimer's disease, Pick's disease, Creutzfeldt-Jakob disease, subcortical dementias, and Parkinson's disease.
6. Discuss treatments for amnestic disorders and dementias.

KEY TERMS

acetylcholine
alternative personality
Alzheimer's disease
amnestic disorders
amnestic episode
anterograde amnesia
beta-amyloid protein
brain surgery
co-conscious subpersonality
confabulate
continuous amnesia
Creutzfeldt-Jakob disease
declarative memory
dementias
diencephalon
dissociative amnesia
dissociative disorders
dissociative fugue
dissociative identity disorder
encode
engram
estrogen
evoked potential
fusion
gene mutation
generalized amnesia
glutamate
head injuries
Huntington's disease
hypnotic amnesia
hypnotic therapy, or hypnotherapy
iatrogenic
identity
Korsakoff's syndrome
localized amnesia
long-term memory
long-term potentiation (LTP)
memory
multiple personality disorder
mutually amnesic
mutually cognizant
neurofibrillary tangles
one-way amnesic
Parkinson's disease
Pick's disease
prefrontal lobes
primary personality
procedural memory
proteins
repression
retrieval
retrograde amnesia
selective amnesia
self-hypnosis
senile plaques
short-term memory, or working memory
sodium amobarbital
sodium pentobarbital
state-dependent learning
stroke
subpersonality
switching
tacrine
temporal lobes
vascular dementia, or multi-infarct dementia
vitamin B (thiamine)

MEDIA RESOURCES

CD-ROM Video Questions

The following is a list of video questions as they appear on the Abnormal Psychology CD-ROM that accompanies each textbook. As a homework assignment, have your students watch the video clip and then answer these questions. Students can answer the questions directly into a text box appearing next to the video clip. When they have finished answering these questions, they can print out their assignment and hand it in for grading.

Also use these CD-ROM segments as assignments to expose your students to material prior to your lectures.

"Tony" Multiple Personality Disorder

1. The narrator says that Tony suffers from multiple personality disorder. What is this disorder called today?

   A: dissociative identity disorder

2. To how many personalities does Tony have?

   A: 53

3. What are some of the things we see happening before Tony "switches" personalities?

   A: He rubs his forehead and around his eyes; he blinks a lot; he coughs; he appears restless; at one point he appeared to be crying.

4. What type of relationship do Tony's personalities seem to have?

   A: They appear to be mutually cognizant of each other, although Tony can't control them.

5. How do Tony's subpersonalities differ?

   A: He says they are all different, even having different voices. One seems to hold all of Tony's memories, one is a child, and one he calls the "Imposter."

6. What does Tony's therapist appear to be trying to get Tony to do? What might be her reason for doing this?

   A: She is trying to bring out the little boy subpersonality. Because dissociative identity disorder is often associated with severe childhood abuse, she may be trying to get him to remember what happened in his childhood.

7. Some people say that dissociative identity disorder is *iatrogenic*. What does that mean? Do you think that Tony's dissociative identity disorder is in any way iatrogenic?

   A: Iatrogenic means a disorder that is itself caused by treatment. It is hard to say for sure, but the therapist is trying to get Tony to let the "little boy" out. Some might say that she was encouraging the creation of a little boy personality.

8. The main characteristic of dissociative disorders is disconnection from memory. What example does Tony give of this?

   A: He mentions being told by one of his "selves" that he was at a wedding. He had no recollection of it.

9. How does Tony keep track of what goes on in his life?

   A: The subpersonalities, whom he refers to as "we," have to tell him or he is unaware of much of what goes on in his life.

"Walter" Alzheimer's Disease

1. What DSM-IV criteria for Alzheimer's does Walter manifest?

   A: Memory impairment; disturbance in executive functioning; impairment in social functioning. We can also assume that he is impaired in occupational functioning.

2. Refer to the discussion of Harry in your text. What characteristics does Walter share with Harry?

   A: difficulty completing tasks; forgetting appointments; dependent on his wife; appears to be in good health

3. What is different about the brains of people with Alzheimer's?

   A: Alzheimer's patients have structural changes in their brains, including the presence of neurofibrillary tangles and senile plaques. These features interfere with the communication between neurons and also cause these neurons to die.

4. How would you characterize Walter's state of mind?

   A: He is forgetful and, at times, agitated. He resists his wife's efforts to make him stop shaving. He appears to pay no attention to her directions and comments.

5. What does Walter's wife appear to be experiencing as she tries to help him get dressed?

   A: frustration and anger; a sense of powerlessness to get Walter's cooperation or attention; stress; low; overwhelmed

6. What medication might Walter be taking? For what purpose is it prescribed?

   A: Tacarine or donepezil. Both prevent the breakdown of acetylcholine, the neurotransmitter that is at low levels in people with Alzheimer's disease. The drugs may improve Walter's short-term memory and reasoning ability, as well as his use of language and coping abilities.

7. If Walter is taking medication, why is his functioning still poor?

   A: The medications are of limited benefit in general, and sometimes they do not help everyone. They are of more use in the early stages of Alzheimer's. Because the drugs would not have been prescribed until after Walter was diagnosed, his disease may have been too advanced for him to benefit from the medications, which might have helped at one time. However, assuming that Walter is on the medications, he might be worse off if he were not taking the drugs.

8. If you were a physician treating Walter, what recommendations would you make for his wife?

   A: She should join a support group, get someone to help out at home so she can have time away from Walter, become fully educated about the nature and course of the disease, and obtain psychotherapy when her stress begins to build.

Comer Video Segments

(See the Video Guide in Appendix E for detailed descriptions.)

Segment 45 Early Care of Multiple Personality Disorder
Segment 54 Left and Right Brain Hemispheres
Segment 215 Woman with Alzheimer's Disease
Segment 216 Man with Severe Amnestic Disorder
Segment 217 Man with Multiple Personality Disorder

Overhead Transparencies

Transparency 40, Figure 16–3, p. 499, Dementia and Age
Transparency 41, Figure 16–4, p. 501, The Aging Brain

Transparency Masters

TM–21, Table 16–4, p. 493, Comparison of Memory Disorders

DSM-IV Masters

E–43, DSM-IV Diagnostic Criteria for Dementia Due to Other General Medical Conditions
E–44, DSM-IV Diagnostic Criteria for Dissociative Amnesia and Dissociative Fugue
E–45, DSM-IV Diagnostic Criteria for Dissociative Identity Disorder and Depersonalization Disorder

CLASS DEMONSTRATIONS AND ACTIVITIES

The Genetics of Alzheimer's Disease

Lead a discussion of whether students would want to know if they were at high risk for developing Alzheimer's disease, now that a new test is available. Even though there has been a test for Huntington's disease, a disease with a genetic basis, many individuals at risk prefer not to know. Discuss the pros and cons of knowing or not knowing.

Development of Dissociative Disorders

Lead a discussion of why some people who are sexually abused as children develop dissociative identity disorder while most don't. Research indicates that individuals who develop dissociative disorders are much more susceptible to self-hypnosis and hypnotic suggestion than the average person. Additionally, why is this disorder more common among females than males? Are there regions of the country where this disorder is more prevalent?

Alzheimer's Disease

Ask students to volunteer personal information of how their family members take care of an Alzheimer's patient. Is the patient in a nursing home? Is the patient who is being cared for at home in the early stages of his or her illness? Would the caregiver prefer to have the patient residing at home rather than placed in a nursing home?

Open Discussion or Group Work: The Genetics of Alzheimer's Disease

Present recent advances in genetic testing, which enable doctors and their patients to determine whether a person is at risk for developing particular disorders or illnesses. Either lead a discussion or divide students into groups to discuss advantages and disadvantages of knowing such information. To focus the discussion, you can let students know that there is a new test that can determine whether a person is at high risk for developing Alzheimer's disease.

Presume You Are an Expert . . . (The Development of Dissociative Disorders)

Tell the students that you received a phone call from your senator last night. He or she recognizes that you are doing a fine job instructing students on the issue of childhood abuse. Your senator wants you and several students to come to Washington, D.C., to testify before a Senate subcommittee about the effects of the abuse on children. Ask students to prepare a 5-minute presentation outlining a position on why some people who are sexually abused as children develop dissociative identity disorder while most don't. One position might be: "It is actually normal for dissociative disorder to develop following severe abuse." A second position is: "Only in unusual cases or examples does dissociative disorder develop as a result of childhood sexual abuse." Have groups present their discussions and positions.

Open Discussion of Alzheimer's and Caregivers

Ask students to volunteer personal information of their family's experience of taking care of a person with Alzheimer's. Is the person in a nursing home or at home? Was the person at home during the early stages of the illness? Would the caregiver or family prefer to have them at home?

"Here's $25,000 to be awarded to . . . "

Given the common awareness and sometimes erroneous information about memory disorders, many elderly persons often worry about their memory. Some elderly worry that their memory is worsening, perhaps due to a degenerative disorder. Announce that the local chapter of the American Association of Retired Persons (AARP) will be giving a $25,000 award to help alleviate these worries by assisting the elderly in performing simple, at-home evaluations to determine whether their memory is indeed deteriorating (and, therefore, that a professional referral should be considered). Ask groups to create criteria or guidelines for distinguishing normal forgetfulness and a memory problem due to brain pathology. Point out that forgetfulness can also be due to undiagnosed depression, alcohol misuse, or drug interactions.

The Anonymous Five-Minute Essay

Ask students to write what they believe or know about getting old. Compare what is commonly "known," which is rife with misinformation and myths (e.g., "You forget things," "You lose interest in sex," "You're in pain all the time"), to the actual facts about later life.

Group Work: Dissociative Identity Disorder

Tell the class that you have been called as expert witness at a trial of a person who is claiming, as his defense, that he has multiple personality disorder. You will be questioned as to the validity of the diagnostic category (which is still being debated among psychologists.) Divide students into groups and assign them either the position that multiple personality disorder is or is not a valid disorder. Have groups present their arguments.

CHAPTER

17 Personality Disorders

TOPIC OVERVIEW

LEARNING OBJECTIVES

1. Define and discuss explanations and treatments for the "odd" personality disorders, including paranoid, schizoid, and schizotypal.
2. Define and discuss explanations and treatments for the "dramatic" personality disorders, including antisocial, borderline, histrionic, and narcissistic.

3. Define and discuss explanations and treatments for the "anxious" personality disorders, including avoidant, dependent, and obsessive-compulsive.
4. Discuss difficulties involved in the categorizing of personality disorders.
5. Summarize the state of the field with respect to personality disorders.

KEY TERMS

anal regressive
antisocial personality disorder
"anxious" personality disorders
avoidant personality disorder
bodily illusion
borderline personality disorder
comorbidity
dependent personality disorder
dichotomous thinking
digressive speech
"dramatic" personality disorders
histrionic personality disorder
hysterical personality disorder
ideas of reference
narcissistic personality disorder
obsessive-compulsive personality disorder
"odd" personality disorders
paranoid personality disorder
passive-aggressive personality disorder
personality
personality disorder
personality traits
psychopathy
schizoid personality disorder
schizophrenia-spectrum disorders
schizotypal personality disorder
social phobias
sociopathy

MEDIA RESOURCES

CD-ROM Video Questions

The following is a list of video questions as they appear on the Abnormal Psychology CD-ROM that accompanies each textbook. As a homework assignment, have your students watch the video clip and then answer these questions. Students can answer the questions directly into a text box appearing next to the video clip. When they have finished answering these questions, they can print out their assignment and hand it in for grading.

Also use these CD-ROM segments as assignments to expose your students to material prior to your lectures.

"Bill" Obsessive-Compulsive Disorder

1. What are the indications that Bill is preoccupied with order, perfection, or control?

   A: He takes many more napkins than he needs, unable to pass them up. In the past, he could not pass up a rubber band without picking it up. Now he cannot pass up a penny without picking it up. He cannot eat french fries without first putting them in meticulous order.

2. In addition to preoccupation with order, perfection, and control, what are the other characteristics of someone with obsessive-compulsive personality disorder?

   A: They lose all flexibility, openness, and efficiency. Their insistence on doing everything "right" impairs their productivity. They set unreasonably high standards for themselves and others. They can never be satisfied with their performance, but they refuse to delegate responsibility or to work with a team, convinced that others are too careless or incompetent to do the job. They tend to be rigid and stubborn. They live by a strict personal code and use it as a yardstick for measuring others. They may have trouble expressing affection, and their relationships are often stiff and superficial. In addition, they are generally stingy. Some cannot throw away objects that are worn out or useless.

3. Referring to your answer to question #2, do we have any evidence that Bill has any of these features of obsessive-compulsive personality disorder?

   A: We have no direct evidence that he expresses any of those features. His preoccupation and desire for control is limited to certain objects—napkins, pennies, rubber bands, and french fries, and we have no indication that he was otherwise unproductive.

4. What did he do to help himself cope with his obsessions?

   A: He acted on his urges so he could get on with what he had to do. He said he would be preoccupied with picking up a penny and if he did not pick it up, the rest of the day would be ruined. If he picked up the penny that "called" out to him, he would not be anxious.

5. Refer to the video questions for Bill in Chapter 6. Was there any question in your mind that Bill could be diagnosed with obsessive-compulsive disorder?

   A: No. He clearly met the DSM-IV criteria for obsessive-compulsive disorder.

6. What defining characteristics distinguish obsessive-compulsive disorder from obsessive-compulsive personality disorder?

   A: People with obsessive-compulsive personality disorder do not manifest obsessions and compulsive behaviors. In obsessive-compulsive disorder (OCD), the individual has excessive obsessions and compulsions so that he or she acts in a way that causes the person significant distress. People with OCD do not necessarily have problems relating to others, as do people with obsessive-compulsive personality disorder. OCD is an anxiety disorder, and the obsessions and compulsions are sometimes a way to cope with anxiety. OCD does not involve being rigid and stubborn, or being stingy or unable to throw out useless objects. There is also nothing in the criteria for OCD that indicates people with OCD cannot get along well with others or be good colleagues, friends, and family members. The focus of obsessive-compulsive disorder is the maladaptive thoughts and behaviors that cause distress. The focus of obsessive-compulsive personality disorder is a maladaptive way of getting things done (or not done) and difficulties in getting along with others. People with obsessive-compulsive disorder know that they have a problem and that it is causing distress. Bill readily admits this. However, individuals with obsessive-compulsive personality disorder generally do not believe that anything is wrong with them.

7. Have researchers found any specific link between obsessive-compulsive personality disorder and obsessive-compulsive anxiety disorder?

   A: Some clinicians believe they are related, but researchers have found no specific link. If a person has obsessive-compulsive anxiety disorder, he or she is more likely to have another personality disorder (avoidant, histrionic, schizotypal, or dependent) than obsessive-compulsive personality disorder.

8. Note that in the video questions for Bill in Chapter 6, we suggested that behavioral treatment might help Bill, as it is an effective treatment for obsessive-compulsive anxiety disorder. Is behavioral treatment the therapy of choice for people with obsessive-compulsive personality disorder?

   A: No. Individuals with the personality disorder often appear to respond better to psychodynamic or cognitive therapy.

9. Why are psychodynamic and cognitive therapies the preferred treatment for obsessive-compulsive personality disorder?

   A: Psychodynamic therapists try to help patients recognize and accept their feelings and underlying insecurities. Cognitive therapists focus on helping them change their perfectionism, indecisiveness, procrastination, and chronic worrying.

Comer Video Segments

(See the Video Guide in Appendix E for detailed descriptions.)

Segment 103 Compulsive Hoarding and Compulsive Symmetry, Order, and Balance
Segment 104 Perfectionism: Obsessive Compulsive Disorder *versus* Obsessive Compulsive Personality Disorder
Segment 202 Aggression, Violence, and the Brain
Segment 204 Assessing Psychopathy
Segment 219 Psychopathy

Overhead Transparencies

Transparency 42, Figure 17–1, p. 511, Prominent and Central Features of DSM-IV's Ten Personality Disorders

Transparency 43, Figure 17–2, p. 513, Whom Do You Trust?

Transparency 44, Figure 17–3, p. 521, Are Some Cultures More Antisocial Than Others?

Transparency Masters

TM–22, Table 17–2, p. 524, Comparison of Personality Disorders

DSM-IV Masters

E–46, DSM-IV General Diagnostic Criteria for a Personality Disorder

E–47, DSM-IV Diagnostic Criteria for Paranoid Personality Disorder and Schizoid Personality Disorder

E–48, DSM-IV Diagnostic Criteria for Schizotypal Personality Disorder

E–49, DSM-IV Diagnostic Criteria for Antisocial Personality Disorder and Borderline Personality Disorder

E–50, DSM-IV Diagnostic Criteria for Histrionic Personality Disorder and Narcissistic Personality Disorder

E–51, DSM-IV Diagnostic Criteria for Avoidant Personality Disorder and Dependent Personality Disorder

E–52, DSM-IV Diagnostic Criteria for Obsessive-Compulsive Personality Disorder

CLASS DEMONSTRATIONS AND ACTIVITIES

Profiles of Personality Disorders

Ask students to form small groups and then assign each group a personality disorder. Give each group a brief description, such as a possible patient profile, for its personality disorder. On an overhead transparency, summarize the diagnostic criteria each group comes up with for its disorder. You can compare the types of behaviors with the DSM-IV masters E–46 through E–52 (in Appendix D), which gives the criteria for different personality disorders. Facilitate a discussion of each disorder.

Personality Disorders and Success

Lead a discussion with the intent of identifying when a specific personality disorder might be an advantage to a person or vocation. Could narcissistic personality be an advantage for a beauty pageant contestant? Could an antisocial personality be helpful to a prizefighter or professional hockey player? Develop a list on an overhead transparency; is there a pattern that is forming?

Reinforcement

Ask the students in small groups to analyze the most typical reinforcement in their lives. What are some examples of reinforcers in their roles as college students? As family members? What patterns are the most common in a small group? In a class? On an overhead transparency list the types of reinforcers students have generated. Continue the discussion in terms of how personality disorders are reinforced.

Therapy-Resistant Personality Disorders

Personality disorders are resistant to treatment efforts. Individuals with personality disorders rarely volunteer for treatment. Many times they seek therapy because of external pressure, from the courts, or from demands by friends and family. Ask students if we should invest the effort to "cure" individuals who believe that they do not have any problems. When might forced treatment be appropriate, if ever?

Narcissism in the United States

Ask students if narcissism is becoming more common in the United States. If so, why? What role does narcissism play in the lives of politicians? Rock and movie stars? Business executives? Is there both a narcissistic style and a narcissistic personality disorder? What would the similarities and differences be? Develop a list of student responses on an overhead transparency.

Similarities and Differences in Narcissist and Histrionic Personality Disorders

Ask students to form small groups and list ways in which they think Nancy the Narcissist and her twin sister, Heloise the Histrionic, would differ from and resemble each other, especially in their interactions with other people. You can make an overhead transparency from the DSM-IV Master E–50 (in Appendix D) and show it for reference to the class. Explore Nancy's and Heloise's behaviors and the students' perceptions and reactions to the transparency.

The Student Personality Disorder

Lead a discussion on the question: Do students see themselves in each of the personality disorders? If so, why does this happen? What criteria should be used to separate the "normal" students from individuals with diagnosable personality disorders?

Role-Playing Personality Disorders

Ask students to form small groups, then ask each group to role-play one of the following personality disorders: (1) narcissistic, (2) obsessive-compulsive, (3) antisocial, or (4) histrionic. Use the criteria from the DSM-IV Masters listed for this chapter as the basis of these exercises. Have each group present its examples to the class.

Personality Disorders and Levels of Maladaptive Behaviors

Start a discussion with the question, Are personality disorders mental disorders? Personality disorders are maladaptive ways of dealing with reality that interfere with functioning. Although they are coded on Axis II of the DSM-IV, are they really mental disorders? Does calling these behaviors mental disorders excuse the individual and allow him or her not to take responsibility for his or her behavior?

New Age/Psychic or Personality Disorder

Lead a class discussion on schizotypal symptoms that may include magical thinking, such as mind reading and clairvoyance; odd perceptions, such as hallucinations about hearing the voice of a dead friend; and other unusual thoughts. How are New Age/psychic persons similar to schizotypal persons? How do they differ? Do the students think that most psychic experiences are due to schizotypal personality disorder? If not, how could they detect the differences between someone with schizotypal personality disorder and a person with psychic abilities?

CHAPTER

18 Disorders of Childhood and Old Age

TOPIC OVERVIEW

Disorders of Childhood and Adolescence
Childhood Anxiety Disorders
Childhood Depression
Disruptive Behavior Disorders
Attention-Deficit/Hyperactivity Disorder
Elimination Disorders

Long-Term Disorders That Begin in Childhood
Autism
Mental Retardation

Disorders of Later Life
Mood, Anxiety, and Substance-Related Disorders
Delirium and Dementia
Issues Affecting the Mental Health of the Elderly

Crossroads: Clinicians Discover the Young and the Elderly

LEARNING OBJECTIVES

1. Describe the prevalence of mental disorders among children and adolescents.
2. Describe persistent childhood anxiety disorders, childhood depression, and conduct disorder.
3. Describe the prevalence, symptoms, causes, and treatments of attention-deficit/hyperactivity disorder (ADHD).

4. Name and describe the elimination disorders. Discuss possible treatments.
5. Describe the symptoms of autistic disorder. Discuss the various etiologies and treatments that have been proposed.
6. Describe the prevalence of the various types of mental retardation, and discuss the environmental, genetic, and biological factors that contribute to mental retardation. Describe and evaluate treatments and therapies for individuals with mental retardation, including normalization programs and behavioral techniques.
7. Describe and explain depression and anxiety among the elderly and discuss appropriate treatment.
8. Distinguish between dementia and delirium.
9. Discuss substance-use disorders among the elderly.
10. Describe Alzheimer's disease, including putative causes and possible treatments.

KEY TERMS

amniocentesis
anoxia
attention-deficit/hyperactivity disorder (ADHD)
augmentative communication system
autistic disorder, or autism
cerebellum
conduct disorder
cretinism
dating skills program
deinstitutionalization
delirium
dementia
discrimination due to ethnicity
Down syndrome
echolalia
encephalitis
encopresis
enuresis
fetal alcohol syndrome
fragile X syndrome
geropsychology
group home
health maintenance
intelligence quotient (IQ)
lead poisoning
long-term care
mainstreaming
meningitis
mental retardation
methylphenidate (Ritalin)
mild retardation
moderate retardation
nominal aphasia
normalization
oppositional defiant disorder
perseveration of sameness
pervasive developmental disorder
phenylalanine
phenylketonuria (PKU)
play therapy
profound retardation
pronominal reversal
recessive genes
rubella
school phobia, or school refusal
self-injurious behavior
self-stimulatory behavior
separation anxiety disorder
severe retardation
shaped
sheltered workshop
sign language
simultaneous communication
special education
state school
syphilis
Tay-Sachs disease
theory of mind
token economy program
trisomy 21

MEDIA RESOURCES

CD-ROM Video Questions

The following is a list of video questions as they appear on the Abnormal Psychology CD-ROM that accompanies each textbook. As a homework assignment, have your students watch the video clip and then answer these questions. Students can answer the questions directly into a text box appearing next to the video clip. When they have finished answering these questions, they can print out their assignment and hand it in for grading.

Also use these CD-ROM segments as assignments to expose your students to material prior to your lectures.

"Michael" Attention-Deficit/Hyperactivity Disorder

1. Michael's mother says that he has attention-deficit/hyperactivity disorder (ADHD). What behaviors did you see that fit the diagnostic criteria?

   A: 1. inattention: failure to follow through on instructions and failure to finish work; difficulty in organizing tasks (started and stopped cleaning his room); avoidance of, dislike of, and reluctance to engage in tasks that require sustained mental effort (cleaning his room); 2. hyperactivity-impulsivity: frequent running about, interrupting of, and intruding on others (especially his brother's chores)

2. What behaviors did we not see that his mother suggested he had trouble with?

   A: getting along with fellow students and teachers; unable to follow instructions at school

3. In addition to the behaviors that fit the DSM-IV criteria for ADHD, what other behaviors did you see Michael engage in?

   A: disobedience to and arguing with his father; challenging his father's instructions; messing up his room more, instead of cleaning it up

4. The DSM-IV criteria require either six behaviors related to inattention or six related to hyperactivity-impulsivity. Based only on the behaviors you did see, are you prepared to make a diagnosis of ADHD for Michael? If not, what other diagnosis might you rule out?

   A: The symptoms we saw in the video are not sufficient to meet the diagnostic criteria. We should rule out a diagnosis of oppositional defiant disorder.

5. Which of Michael's behaviors fit the DSM-IV criteria for oppositional defiant disorder?

   A: 1. arguing with his father; 2. refusal to comply with his father's request or rules; 3. deliberately annoying his brother; 4. His mother's report about Michael kicking his teacher suggests anger, resentment, spitefulness, and vindictiveness.

6. Research indicates that children with ADHD may also have other mental health problems. In addition to ADHD and oppositional defiant disorder, what other disorders should be ruled out?

   A: anxiety disorders and depression

7. Michael's mother places a lot of blame on Michael's teachers for his problems at school, while expressing resentment for what she feels are teachers' placing the blame on her. According to the text, who needs to be involved in treatment of children with ADHD? What aspect of the DSM-IV diagnostic criteria addresses this?

   A: The criteria specify that ADHD affects functioning in at least two settings. These settings would most likely be home and school. As noted in the text, parents and teachers both need to address the behaviors of children with ADHD. Teachers and parents need to work together, not blame each other.

"Joseph" Autism

1. At the beginning of the video, a girl criticizes students in Joseph's school for not paying attention to Joseph, not including him in activities, and trying to "find" Joseph. Based upon what you observed of Joseph's behavior, can you blame them? Why or why not?

   A: Joseph seemed to be oblivious to and uninterested in what was going on around him. When a man asked what Joseph thought about the woman's criticism of his schoolmates, he indicated that he did not hear the conversation. It would be difficult for teenagers to try to engage Joseph when he appears to be so out of touch with his surroundings.

2. What unique talents does Joseph display?

   A: Joseph can make amazing mathematical calculations and identify the day of the week on which any date falls.

3. How does Joseph explain his talents?

   A: He does not explain them. He says that they are just in his head.

4. When asked to describe what a film was "about" that Joseph "starred" in, what is Joseph's response?

   A: He says that someone was filming him and that he was in a room looking outside. He is not able to say what the film is about.

5. Based upon his limited description of the film made about him, how could we characterize Joseph's cognitive development?

   A: It is very childlike in its concreteness. Joseph cannot say what something means. He can only state the facts that he recalls from the situation.

6. At the very end of the movie, Joseph demonstrates a form of speaking characteristic of many people with autism. Describe it and state the term for it.

   A: Joseph repeated the narrator's summation of Joseph's comment about the film. The narrator said, "That was it." Joseph then said, "That was it." This is known as echolalia, the exact echoing of phrases spoken by others.

7. In what way did Joseph's behavior fit the description of autism in the text?

   A: Joseph was very rigid. His facial expressions and tone of voice did not change.

8. Joseph is a savant. What is a savant, and where does the word come from?

   A: *Savant* is French for "knowing." A savant is someone with a major mental disorder or intellectual handicap that has some spectacular ability or some area of exceptional ability.

"George and Charles" Savant Syndrome

1. What are George and Charles able to do?

   A: They can determine the day of the month for any date, far into the past and the future.

2. Referring to the boy on the left as George, and the boy on the right as Charles, what behaviors did George manifest that were absent in Charles?

   A: Charles seemed to more often look at the notes of the man asking the questions. Then he would put a finger to the front of his head, as if thinking, and appear to be "writing" on the palm of his hand.

3. What speech characteristic associated with autism did George and Charles manifest?

   A: They both repeated the man's statements verbatim. This is known as echolalia.

4. Why couldn't George and Charles figure out the product of 4 × 7 but they could add 14 + 11?

   A: There is no explanation for this lapse, just as there is no explanation for their extraordinary powers.

5. They could remember the date on which someone taught them math (referred to in the video as "McBride") but they could not recall being taught anything. What does this indicate?

   A: This indicates that they recall only certain aspects of experiences, such as the day and date when something happened. They seem to be fixated on this.

6. What does their inability to solve the simple word problem indicate? How does this relate to Joseph's (see the video on Autism) inability to say what a film was "about"?

   A: Charles and George's inability to solve the word problem correctly indicates the concrete level of their thinking. Their answer was 20 cents, but they did not know that this was incorrect, nor did they know how to arrive at the correct answer.

7. George and Charles are referred to as "savants." What is a savant, and where does the word come from?

   A: *Savant* is French for "knowing." A savant is someone with a major mental disorder or intellectual handicap that has some spectacular ability or some area of exceptional ability.

8. Read Box 18–5 (page 562) in your text. People are fascinated by the savant syndrome. Do you feel that psychologists or other members of the public are breaching any ethical or moral principles when they film savants demonstrating their talents and show these films to the public? Do you think people like Joseph, George, and Charles like to be "tested" and filmed? Do you think these individuals are being exploited by the media and public?

   A: Answers will vary. Students may indicate that they believe these people are being exploited, or they may feel that the subjects don't seem to notice or care.

Comer Video Segments

(See the Video Guide in Appendix E for detailed descriptions.)

Segment 28 Therapy Reaction Tapes A and D
Segment 29 Family Dynamics Reaction Tape
Segment 46 Clinical Picture of Autism
Segment 47 Dr. Ivar Lovaas Treats Young Autistic Child with Behavioral Intervention
Segment 48 Adult with Autism
Segment 102 Obsessive-Compulsive Disorder in Childhood and Adolescence
Segment 105 Compulsive Vocalizations (Noise Making) by a Child with Obsessive-Compulsive Disorder
Segment 107 Young Man with Tourette's Syndrome
Segment 115 Children with Attention-Deficit/Hyperactivity Disorder (ADHD)
Segment 116 Adult with Attention-Deficit Disorder (ADD)

Segment 117 Desire for Isolation by Person with Autism: Parents and Family Interactions
Segment 118 Peer-Mediated Interventions for Persons with Autism
Segment 119 Music and Psychological Functioning: A Case Study in Autism
Segment 120 Impact of Autism on the Family
Segment 121 The Savant Syndrome (Short Version on CD-ROM)
Segment 122 Adapting to One's Symptoms
Segment 215 Woman with Alzheimer's Disease
Segment 218 Temple Grandin, an Extremely High-Functioning and High-Achieving Person with Autism, and Research on Autism

Overhead Transparencies

Transparency 45, Figure 18–1, p. 551, Early Misbehavior
Transparency 46, Figure 18–2, p. 553, Teenage Crime
Transparency 47, Figure 18–3, p. 555, The Rise of Ritalin
Transparency 48, Figure 18–4, p. 568, Mental Retardation and Socioeconomic Class
Transparency 49, Figure 18–6, p. 576, Ethnicity and Old Age

Transparency Masters

TM–23, Table 18–4, p. 558, Comparison of Childhood Disorders

DSM-IV Masters

E–53, DSM-IV Diagnostic Criteria for Mental Retardation
E–54, DSM-IV Diagnostic Criteria for Reading Disorder, Mathematics Disorder, and Disorder of Written Expression
E–55, DSM-IV Diagnostic Criteria for Developmental Coordination Disorder and Expressive Language Disorder
E–56, DSM-IV Diagnostic Criteria for Autistic Disorder
E–57, DSM-IV Diagnostic Criteria for Attention-Deficit/Hyperactivity Disorder
E–58, DSM-IV Diagnostic Criteria for Attention-Deficit/Hyperactivity Disorder
E–59, DSM-IV Diagnostic Criteria for Conduct Disorder
E–60, DSM-IV Diagnostic Criteria for Conduct Disorder
E–61, DSM-IV Diagnostic Criteria for Oppositional Defiant Disorder
E–62, DSM-IV Diagnostic Criteria for Encopresis and Enuresis
E–63, DSM-IV Diagnostic Criteria for Separation Anxiety Disorder
E–64, DSM-IV Diagnostic Criteria for Dementia of the Alzheimer's Type

CLASS DEMONSTRATIONS AND ACTIVITIES

Children's Problems

Lead a discussion about ways to help children deal with such family adjustments as divorce, financial changes, and death. Ask for student input into the types of problems these children can be expected to encounter.

Presume You Are a Teacher . . .

Johnny is 7 years old and in the first grade. He has trouble sitting still, often loses things, is very loud, and acts very impulsively. He is disruptive to your classroom. You are fairly certain he has ADHD. You are meeting with his parents tomorrow night during Parent-Teacher Night. As typically happens at these events, you and the child's parents will have 10 minutes together. You want to convince them to seek an evaluation. What do you say? Do you recommend a formal evaluation by a mental health professional? Why or why not?

Presume You Are a Mental Health Professional . . .

Johnny is 7 years old and in the first grade. He has trouble sitting still, often loses things, is very loud, and acts very impulsively. Your evaluation has determined that he meets criteria for ADHD. His parents are coming to your office tomorrow to discuss the results. How do you tell them? What if they feel that they've done something wrong? Do you recommend psychotherapy? Do you recommend medication?

Ritalin

The use of stimulant medications such as Ritalin has led to one of the more effective treatments for attention-deficit/hyperactivity disorder. The drugs reduce the activity-level problems, thereby making the child more manageable at home and in the classroom. Ask your students to put themselves in the roles of parents, teachers, and children and to discuss the implications, both pro and con, of using stimulant medications to control children's behavior.

Presume You Are an Expert . . .

Tell the students that you received a phone call from your senator last night at home. He or she recognized that you are doing a fine job instructing students on the issue of childhood abuse. Your senator wants you and several students to come to Washington, D.C., to testify before a Senate subcommittee on a new law intended to prevent the abuse of children. Ask students to prepare a 5-minute presentation outlining a recommendation for a law that might reduce child abuse. Remind them that their testimony will influence law. Also remind them that their testimony is "expert" and that they may be challenged about the validity of what they are saying.

Presume You Are a Therapist . . .

Lead a discussion on the ethical issues of counseling with children and adolescents. As minors, their parents have a legal right to information about their treatment. How would students—acting as therapist—deal with confidentiality issues? What do they think a parent should have the right to know? How would they explain the various aspects of confidentiality to an elementary school child? To an adolescent?

Group Work: Special Problems of the Elderly

Divide students into groups. Ask each group to create a list of problems or difficulties (vulnerabilities) that the elderly in particular face. These would include declining health, decreasing support system (e.g., widowhood, loss of friends), unintentional medication overuse, and abuse. Alternatively, give each group one of the vulnerabilities and ask it to come up with a creative solution to it.

Mainstreaming

Lead a discussion on the topic of mainstreaming mentally retarded students. What are the pros and cons of this issue? Does mainstreaming risk setting up the retarded child for social rejection? Many students will have been exposed to this practice in the K–12 schooling.

Open Discussion: Learning Disabilities

Lead a discussion on how students feel about labeling learning disabilities (LDs) as mental illness. Learning disabled students show few, if any, signs of emotional disturbance, and some authorities question classifying learning disabilities as psychological disorders. Inform the class that several students in your class will fit into this classification. Discuss the advantages and disadvantages of calling LDs mental illness.

Group Work: Alzheimer's and Suicide

Inform the class that you and they have been hired by an attorney working on the following case: a doctor helped a woman with Alzheimer's disease commit suicide. The woman was in the early stages of the disease and had not lost any physical or mental abilities, but was quite despondent over the diagnosis and wanted to preserve her family from having to deal with her suffering. The two sides of the debate are that (1) this was acceptable and allowable, versus (2) it was not acceptable and should not be allowed. Divide students into groups, then assign each group one of these two positions. Have the groups prepare and present their argument.

CHAPTER

19 Law, Society, and the Mental Health Profession

TOPIC OVERVIEW

How Do Clinicians Influence the Criminal Justice System?
Criminal Commitment and Insanity During Commission of a Crime
Criminal Commitment and Incompetence to Stand Trial

How Do the Legislative and Judicial Systems Influence Mental Health Care?
Civil Commitment
Protecting Patients' Rights

In What Other Ways Do the Clinical and Legal Fields Interact?
Malpractice Suits
Jury Selection

What Ethical Principles Guide Mental Health Professionals?

Mental Health, Business, and Economics
Bringing Mental Health Services to the Workplace
The Economics of Mental Health

The Person Within the Profession

Crossroads: Operating Within a Larger System

LEARNING OBJECTIVES

1. Define and discuss criminal commitment and insanity during the commission of a crime.
2. Discuss criticisms of the insanity defense.

3. Define and discuss criminal commitment and incompetence to stand trial.
4. Compare and contrast the M'Naghten test, the irresistible impulse test, and the Durham test.
5. Define civil commitment and include the topics of why one ought to consider commitment, current procedures, emergency commitments, who is dangerous, and criticisms of civil commitment.
6. Define and discuss the concept of protecting patients' rights. Include the topic of the right to treatment, the right to refuse treatment, and other patients' rights.
7. Discuss the concepts of business and mental health and economics and mental health.

KEY TERMS

American Law Institute (ALI) test
civil commitment
code of ethics
confidentiality
criminal commitment
dangerousness
Durham test
duty to protect
electroconvulsive therapy
employee assistance program
guilty but mentally ill
guilty with diminished capacity
irresistible impulse test
jury selection
malpractice lawsuit
managed care program
mental incompetent
mentally disordered sex offenders
minimum standard of proof
M'Naghten rule
not guilty by reason of insanity
parens patriae
peer review system
police power
professional boundaries
protection and advocacy system
psychosurgery
right to refuse treatment
right to treatment
stress-reduction and problem-solving seminars
two-physician certificate (2 PC)

MEDIA RESOURCES

CD-ROM Video Questions

The following is a list of video questions as they appear on the Abnormal Psychology CD-ROM that accompanies each textbook. As a homework assignment, have your students watch the video clip and then answer these questions. Students can answer the questions directly into a text box appearing next to the video clip. When they have finished answering these questions, they can print out their assignment and hand it in for grading.

Also use these CD-ROM segments as assignments to expose your students to material prior to your lectures.

"Mark"

1. What types of tests were used to assess the nature of Mark's aggression?

   A: preliminary neurological assessment, followed by a CAT scan

2. Why were neurological tests indicated?

   A: Mark had manifested a gradual change in personality and temperament. He lost control of his temper more and more as time went on, until the day he attacked his girlfriend's daughter.

3. What was Mark's reaction to his violent assault on the girl?

A: He did not know why he did it. He had never reacted that way before, and he was accustomed to dealing with young children, as he had a daughter of his own.

4. What did the first series of tests indicate?

   A: Mark had a tumor.

5. Why did this tumor cause Mark to be aggressive and violent?

   A: The parts of the brain affected by the tumor are those involved with aggression.

6. How did Mark's behavior change after the tumor was surgically removed?

   A: He could control his temper even better than before. He had no further outbreaks of violence.

7. Why would Mark likely be found not criminally responsible for the attack?

   A: He had a disorder that made it impossible to control his behavior.

8. Is Mark likely to act violently in the future?

   A: We can never say for sure, but because the violence was attributed to the tumor and the tumor was removed, future violence is not likely. His wife said that he controls his temper better now than before.

The Mind of the Psychopath

1. What is the name of Dr. Hare's assessment instrument, and what is it designed to detect?

   A: The Hare Psychopathy Checklist-Revised (PCL-R) is designed to detect psychopathy.

2. What are some specific characteristics that describe psychopaths?

   A: lacking in empathy and emotional affect; egocentric; grandiose; predatory; callous; impulsive, manipulative, and glib

3. What behaviors does the PCL-R measure?

   A: glibness and superficial charm, conning and manipulative behavior, lack of remorse and guilt, and impulsiveness

4. If you administered the test to a client who was charged with assault and the client received a score of 40, what would that score suggest?

   A: The client was likely to commit future acts of violence.

5. Why would this client be held accountable for his crime?

   A: He knew what he was doing. His assaultive behavior was likely part of his personality, because psychopathy includes cognitive, behavioral, and affective features.

6. If the judge wanted to know if the client would be likely to reoffend, how would you respond?

   A: The PCL-R has been deemed to be valid and reliable in predicting future violence. Among incarcerated persons, those who are deemed psychopaths according to the test are three times more likely to reoffend and four times more likely to violently reoffend. Twenty percent of inmates serving time for violent crime score high on the PCL-R.

"Pat" The Mind of the Psychopath

1. For what crimes is Pat serving time in prison?

   A: manslaughter and robbery

2. Pat wants to be paroled from prison. To do so he has to convince the judge that he is not likely to commit further crimes. What fact is in his favor? What fact will hurt his chances?

   A: It is indicated that prison officials believe that Pat is trying to learn a new way of being. However, because he is involved in Dr. Hare's study, he most likely has been diagnosed with psychopathy. Psychopaths are more likely to reoffend and to violently reoffend.

3. Why don't the prison treatment programs used on the normal offender help psychopaths?

   A: The standard programs are designed to help prisoners deal with their anxiety and improve their self-esteem. This is not the psychopath's problem. The psychopath's behavior is deviant from that of the rest of society. A psychopath has to learn a whole new way of being.

4. Did it seem that Pat had benefited from prison programs?

   A: Yes, for the narrator indicated that prison officials seemed to believe that Pat had changed.

5. What do researchers need to find out in order to design an effective treatment for psychopathy?

   A: They need to understand what causes this constellation of behaviors.

Comer Video Segments

(See the Video Guide in Appendix E for detailed descriptions.)

Segment 1 Deinstitutionalization and Jailing the Mentally Ill

Segment 2 Medical Procedures Used in Mental Hospitals in the First Half of the Twentieth Century
Segment 3 Modern-Day Mental Hospital Ward
Segment 19 Early Electroconvulsive Therapies
Segment 28 Therapy Reaction Tapes E and F
Segment 31 Sociocultural Overview of Opioid Dependence
Segment 32 Methadone Treatment Program, 1973
Segment 39 Antipsychotic Drugs
Segment 40 Deinstitutionalization and Homelessness
Segment 42 Prefrontal Lobotomy Procedure, 1942
Segment 43 Patients Before and After Prefrontal Lobotomy, 1944
Segment 44 Lobotomized Persons at a State Hospital Today
Segments 49 and 50 Patients' Rights
Segment 202 Aggression, Violence, and the Brain
Segments 204 and 219 Psychopathy

Overhead Transparencies

Transparency 50, Figure 19–2, p. 606, Mental Health Spending

CLASS DEMONSTRATIONS AND ACTIVITIES

Group Work: "Presume you are a therapist . . ."

Divide students into groups, then present them with the following issue: you are a therapist seeing a 16-year-old female patient. She discloses to you that she is sexually active with multiple partners, and that she occasionally (once a month) gets drunk and then drives. You are seriously concerned about her safety. Do you have an obligation to inform the parents, even over the objections of the patient (i.e., are you obliged to break confidentiality)? Assign these two positions: one is that confidentiality should not be broken, the other is that it should be. Alternatively, have groups argue from the perspective of the adolescent versus the perspective of the parents.

Group Work: The Defendant's Mental State

Divide students into small groups. The issue is whether juries should take information about the defendant's mental state into account in their deliberations about guilt (i.e., whether a defendant's mental state should affect a verdict). Present a specific example from national headlines in which an insanity plea was successful (e.g., Lorena Bobbitt or Theodore Kazinski). One side should be assigned the task of working for the prosecuting attorney (i.e., arguing that mental state does not influence culpability). The other side, working for the defense attorney, should argue that mental state is relevant and should result in a verdict of not guilty by reason of insanity. Ask each group to present its argument to the class. Point out at the end of the discussion that such an arrangement is almost always present in such cases: the two sides will hire their own advisors, who will argue their particular position (resulting in somewhat embarrassing contradictions being presented by two different "mental health experts").

Open Discussion: Homelessness and Mental Health

Lead a discussion on the issue of homeless people. How much has the revolving-door syndrome of mental hospitals contributed to this problem? Should selected patients be kept in a hospital setting for longer periods of time? What about the problem of individuals who do not seek or want treatment for their disorders? Should they be forced into treatment?

Open Discussion: Therapist Abuse

Lead a discussion on the consequences that should be imposed on therapists who seduce their clients. Should they lose their licenses? Should they be prosecuted for sexual abuse or rape? When would it be acceptable for a therapist to develop a relationship with a former client?

Open Discussion: Who Is Responsible?

Present a hypothetical example of a severely mentally ill person committing murder. Ask the class to discuss the culpability of the person's parents in the behavior. Ask some to take the role of advising the plaintiff's attorney (i.e., take the perspective that the parents are responsible), and ask others to adopt the role of advisor to the defense attorney (i.e., take the perspective that the parents are not responsible).

"Presume you are a therapist . . . ": Duty to Warn

Present the following case to the class: you are a therapist, and your client tells you that he intends to kill a woman he was having obsessional thoughts about, a woman he met once at a party. What do you do?

In August 1969, Prosenjit Poddar was in treatment and told his therapist that he intended to kill Tatiana Tarasoff, a woman he was having obsessional thoughts about, a woman he met once at a party. The therapist notified the police, who arrested Poddar and held him briefly. (Neither Tarasoff nor her family was informed of the threat.) Two months later, Poddar killed Tarasoff. The young woman's parents sued the therapist and his employer, the University of California, charging that they should have been warned of the man's intention. The California Supreme Court ruled in favor of the Tarasoffs, saying that "when a therapist determines . . . that a patient presents a serious danger of violence to another, he incurs an obligation to use reasonable care to protect the intended victim."

Open Discussion: The Insanity Defense

The insanity plea is grossly misunderstood in our society. On March 30, 1981, John Hinckley aimed and fired six hollow-tipped, exploding bullets from a .22-caliber revolver at President Ronald Reagan. One of the bullets ricocheted off the presidential limousine and entered Reagan's chest. Another hit a police officer, another a secret service agent, and another James Brady, the president's press secretary, who was paralyzed as a result. The act was caught on film. In June 1982, Hinckley stood trial and was found not guilty by reason of insanity. He was committed to Saint Elizabeth's Hospital in Washington, D.C., to stay there until he is viewed by the hospital as no longer dangerous as a result of his mental illness.

Discuss the differences between descriptive responsibility (Did the person do the action?) and ascriptive responsibility (Is the person responsible for behaving in this fashion?). The following arguments can be presented: Thomas S. Szasz argues that "[b]y codifying acts of violence as expressions of mental illness, we neatly rid ourselves of the task of dealing with criminal offenses as more or less rational, goal-directed acts, no different in principle from other forms of conduct" (1963, p. 141). In other words, the insanity defense is a way for society to avoid taking responsibility. It has also been argued that the insanity defense actually does the exact opposite. Alan A. Stone argues that "[t]he insanity defense is in every sense the exception that proves the rule. It allows the courts to treat every other defendant as someone who chose between good and evil" (Stone, 1975). By not pleading insanity, everyone who stands before a court is saying, "I was responsible for what I am found guilty of doing."

APPENDIX

A Teaching References and Readings

Allen, R. R., & Rueter, T. (1990). *Teaching assistant strategies: An introduction to college teaching.* Dubuque, IA: Kendall/Hunt.

Benjamin, L. T., & Lowman, K. D. (Eds.) (1981). *Activities handbook for the teaching of psychology.* Washington, DC: American Psychological Association.

Benjamin, L. T., Daniel, R. S., & Brewer, C. L. (Eds.) (1985). *Handbook for teaching introductory psychology.* Hillsdale, NJ: Erlbaum.

Bradley-Johnson, S., & Lesiak, J. L. (1989). *Problems in written expression: Assessment and remediation.* New York: Guilford.

Bronstein, P., & Uina, K. (1988). *Teaching a psychology of people: Resources for gender and sociocultural awareness.* Washington, DC: American Psychological Association.

Charles, C. M. (1992). *Building classroom discipline* (4th ed). White Plains, NY: Longman.

Diogenes, R., & Vestal, L. B. (1994). *Prentice Hall critical thinking resource manual for psychology.* Upper Saddle River, NJ: Prentice Hall.

Gardner, R. M. (1980). *Exercises for general psychology.* Minneapolis: Burgess.

Gleitman, H. (1984). Introducing psychology. *American Psychologist, 39,* 421–427.

Golub, S., & Freedman, R. J. (Eds.) (1987). *Psychology of women: Resources for a core curriculum.* New York: Garland.

Herb, D. O. (1974). What psychology is about. *American Psychologist, 29,* 71–79.

Hock, R. (1992). *Forty studies that changed psychology.* Upper Saddle River, NJ: Prentice Hall.

Johnson, G. R. (1995). *First steps to excellence in college teaching.* Madison, WI: Magna Publishing.

Johnson, M., & Wertheimer, M. (Eds.) (1979). *The psychology teacher's resource book: First course.* Washington, DC: American Psychological Association.

Keller, F., & Sherman, J. (1974). *The Keller plan handbook.* Menlo Park, CA: W. A. Benjamin.

McKeachie, W. J. (1990). *Teaching tips: A guidebook for the beginning college teacher* (9th ed). Lexington, MA: D.C. Heath.

McKenzie, S., & Cangemi, J. P. (1978). What new students in introduction to psychology really want to learn: A survey. *Journal of Instructional Psychology, 5,* 5–7.

McLeod, R. B. (1971). The teaching of psychology. *American Psychologist, 26,* 245–249.

Magnan, R. (1990). *147 practical tips for teaching professors.* Madison, WI: Magna Publishing.

Makosky, U. P., Whittemore, L. G., & Rogers, A. J. (Eds.) (1987). *Activities handbook for the teaching of psychology. Vol. 2.* Washington, DC: American Psychological Association.

Makosky, U. P., Whittemore, L. G., & Skutley, M. L. (Eds.) (1990). *Activities handbook for the teaching of psy-*

chology. Vol. 3. Washington, DC: American Psychological Association.

Neff, A., & Weimer, M. (Eds.) (1989). *Classroom communications: Collected readings for effective discussion and questioning.* Madison, WI: Magna Publishing.

Parrott, L. (1994). *How to write psychology papers.* New York: Harper/Collins.

Pettijohn, T. (1994). *Sources: Notable selections in psychology*. Guilford, CT: Dushkin Publishing.

Pregent, R. (1994). *Charting your course: How to prepare to teach more effectively.* Madison, WI: Magna Publishing.

Radford, J., & Rose, D. (Eds.) (1980). *The teaching of psychology.* New York: John Wiley & Sons.

Ryan, J. B. (1974). *Keller's personalized system of instruction: An appraisal.* Washington, DC: American Psychological Association.

Schoenfeld, A. C., & Magnan, R. (1994). *Mentor in a manual: Climbing the academic ladder to tenure.* Madison, WI: Magna Publishing.

Shapiro, E. S. (1989). *Academic skills problems: Direct assessment and intervention.* New York: Guilford.

Silverstein, B. (1982). Teaching a large lecture course in psychology: Turning defeat into victory. *Teaching of Psychology, 9,* 150–155.

Smith, R. A. (1995). *Challenging your perceptions: Thinking critically about psychology.* Pacific Grove, CA: Brooks/Cole.

Weimer, M., & Neff, R. A. (Eds.) (1990). *Teaching college: Collected reading for the new instructor.* Madison, WI: Magna Publishing.

Weimer, M., Parrett, J., & Kerns, M. (1988). *How am I teaching: Forms and activities for acquiring instructional input.* Madison, WI: Magna Publishing.

Whitford, F. W. (1996). *Teaching psychology: A guide for the new instructor* (2nd ed). Upper Saddle River, NJ: Prentice Hall.

Whitford, F. W. (1998). *Quick guide to the internet for psychology, 1998.* Needham Heights, MA: Allyn & Bacon.

Whitford, F. W. (1999). *Quick guide to the internet for psychology, 1999.* Needham Heights, MA: Allyn & Bacon.

APPENDIX

B Internet Sites

Listed here are a variety of sites about mental illness description, causes, and treatment, psychopharmacology, neuroscience, and other topics related directly or indirectly to abnormal psychology. Students can be encouraged or instructed to visit these sites for either class activities or assignments. Several sites have links to electronic journals and other resources that students may use to research for a writing assignment.

These pages can be photocopied and distributed to students at the beginning of the course. This list comprises primarily general sites that are excellent starting points for an Internet search on a specific topic. A brief list of recommended specific sites with information about particular disorders or topics is also provided.

Many of these links are very dense with information and will require substantial "loading time" unless the user has a high-speed Internet connection. At the time of publication of this IRM, all these sites were "alive."

These sites can also be found at **http://www.worthpublishers.com/comerabnormalpsychology4e**

Non-Specific Sites Useful for Starting Internet Searches

http://www.apa.org (American Psychological Association)

The APA's home page contains a wealth of information about the APA, the largest scientific and professional organization representing psychology in the United States, and includes numerous links to information about mental illness and its treatment. A page on the site gives the basics of library research for psychology studies (www.apa.org/science/lib.html).

http://www.psycport.com/

PsycPORT was developed by the American Psychological Association (APA), and is intended to provide quality psychological and mental health information and resources available on the Web.

http://www.psychologicalscience.org (American Psychological Society)

The APS's home page. This site contains a wealth of information on this organization, including schedules for conventions, teaching, research, and other psychological society information.

http://www.nmha.org (The National Mental Health Association)

Through its national office and more than 300 affiliates nationwide, NMHA is dedicated to improving the mental health of all individuals and achieving victory over mental illnesses.

http://www.nih.gov (National Institutes of Health)

The major government funding agency for the study of health issues, including mental health, addictions, and aging. NIH comprises several institutes, including the National Institute of Mental Health, the National Institute of Alcoholism and Alcohol Abuse, and the National Institute on Drug Abuse, which deal with mental health issues in particular.

http://www.nimh.nih.gov (National Institute of Mental Health—NIMH)

The home page of NIMH, a component of NIH. NIMH is the federal agency that conducts and supports (funds) research on mental illness and mental health.

http://www.psychwww.com (Psych Web Resources)
This site lists web resources for clinical psychology, behavioral medicine, and mental health.

http://www.nami.org (National Alliance for the Mentally Ill—NAMI)
The home page of NAMI has links to other sites and searchable indexes of mental disorders.

http://www.mentalhealth.com (Internet Mental Health)
Internet Mental Health is an extensive and fairly comprehensive site full of mental health information. It includes a glossary of terms used in pharmacology, descriptions of all the disorders, and a long list of links to other English-language Internet sites that provide "more than 10 pages of free, scientifically sound mental health information." This site provides extensive information about all of the DSM disorders, and is a very useful starting page for Internet searches.

http://www.psychologicalscience.net (Psychological Science on the Net)
This is a general purpose "bookmark" with over 8,500 links to sites related to psychology. It includes WWW Psychology Search, which helps the surfer find documents on psychology-related web sites.

http://www.med.nyu.edu/Psych/public.html (Psychiatry Information for the General Public)
Includes on-line screenings for various disorders and links to abnormal psychology and treatment-related sites.

http://krantzj.hanover.edu/(Psychology Department of Hanover College)
The web page of the Psychology Department of Hanover College has a variety of links to numerous tutorials on psychology (such as basic neural processes), links to online journals, psychological societies and psychological software, as well as links to other sites.

http://psychcentral.com (Psych Central)
Psych Central is Dr. John Grohol's Mental Health Page, a "personalized one-stop index for psychology, support, and mental health issues, resources, and people on the Internet, since 1995." The resources page has an extensive listing of sites related to abnormal psychology.

http://www.realtime.net/~mmjw
A listing of specific mental health resources, in particular, of self-help sites and links.

http://ctiwebct.york.ac.uk/journals/journals.html
Links to Psychological Journals is an index of 1,600+ online psychology and social science journals. It links you to journal home pages and journal information on the web.

http://www-ai.ijs.si/eliza-cgi-bin/eliza_script
"Eliza" is the interactive software program that attempts to use basic artificial intelligence concepts and strategies to imitate certain aspects of a therapeutic conversation. Some people think it performs rudimentary client-centered therapy quite well.

The Brain and Neuroscience

http://www.med.harvard.edu/AANLIB/home.html
Information, images, and QuickTime movies all related to the brain. Included is a discussion on the pathology of Alzheimer's disease. A complete reference to the brain.

http://www.nlm.nih.gov/research/visible/visible_human.html
The Visible Human Project is creating a complete, anatomically detailed, three-dimensional representation of both the male and female human bodies.

http://www.bic.mni.mcgill.ca/demos/
From the McConnell Brain Imaging Center. The site features brain-imaging demos that require a graphics browser. These are interesting examples of brain imaging techniques.

http://faculty.washington.edu/chudler/ehceduc.html
Extremely detailed site that consists of links for neuroscience education. This site is large enough to spend several days exploring.

History of Abnormal Psychology

http://www.museum-london.org.uk/MOLsite/exhibits/bedlam/f_bed.htm
This site tells the fascinating 750-year-old story of Bethlem Royal Hospital, popularly known as "Bedlam." Bethlem is the world's oldest institution caring for people with mental disorders. It has been a part of London since 1247 and many people, rich and poor, have played a part in its history.

http://www.netaxs.com/people/aca3/LPM.HTM
"The world's first virtual museum of psychology . . . The museum's main goal is to present a variety of fun and educational exhibits which present a broad

overview of psychology and its many facets. The exhibits are designed to be friendly enough for anyone to enjoy, but also present a wealth of interesting information. These exhibits will constantly be revised and added to as the museum is further refined." (From page's "Information Desk")

Obsessive-Compulsive Disorder

http://www.fairlite.com/ocd (O.C.D. Web Server)

A comprehensive site that details both research and treatment of obsessive-compulsive disorder.

Mood Disorders and Suicide

http://www.moodswing.org/bdfaq.html

This text-only site contains answers to frequently asked questions about bipolar disorder.

http://bipolar.mentalhelp.net/

A site that includes the symptoms, treatments, and online support groups for bipolar disorder.

http://www.geocities.com/HotSprings/8094

A site on depression that includes the symptoms, options for treatments, and links to related sites.

http://sandbox.xerox.com/pair/cw/testing.html

This site includes the Clinical Depression Screening Test, a quick test of depressive symptoms, as well as some advice for individuals who score in the depressed range.

http://www.siec.ca (Suicide Information and Education Center)

A good source for the topic of suicide and suicide prevention.

Psychosocial Factors in Physical Disorders

http://www.mindspring.com/~louisalasher/

This site contains information on factitious disorder by proxy and Munchausen syndrome by proxy.

http://www.mc.vanderbilt.edu/peds/pidl/adolesc/convreac.html

A referenced text discussion of conversion and somatization disorders.

http://www.cloud9.net:80/~thorpy/

This extensive site contains a complete listing of the sleep disorders, including links to research and a discussion of treatments.

http://www.ncf.carleton.ca:80/freenet/rootdir/menus/social.services/cfseir/CFSEIR.HP.html (Chronic Fatigue Syndrome)

A comprehensive page that discusses the many factors associated with chronic fatigue syndrome.

Eating Disorders

http://www.eating-disorders.com (The Center for Eating Disorders)

This site contains discussion of symptoms, support groups, and links to other sites to explore the eating disorders.

http://www.something-fishy.org

A major site on all eating disorders including descriptions, diagnosis, and treatments.

Substance-Related Disorders

http://www.recovery.org/aa/

A large site containing the history of Alcoholics Anonymous (AA), meeting sites and regional meetings, on-line meetings, and other resources.

http://www.12step-recovery.org/

AL-ANON (and ALATEEN for younger members) is a worldwide organization that offers a self-help recovery program for families and friends of alcoholics, whether or not the alcoholic seeks help or even recognizes the existence of a drinking problem.

http://www.ccsa.ca/ (Canadian Centre on Substance Abuse)

The Canadian Centre on Substance Abuse is a non-profit organization working to minimize the harm associated with the use of alcohol, tobacco, and other drugs.

http://www.health.org/aboutn.htm

The National Clearinghouse for Alcohol and Drug Information (NCADI) is the information service of the Center for Substance Abuse Prevention of the U.S. Department of Health & Human Services. NCADI is the world's largest resource for current information and materials concerning substance-abuse prevention.

Sexual Disorders and Gender Identity Disorders

http://www.qrd.org/QRD/orgs/NAMBLA/journal.and.research.reports

References for the study of pedophilia.

http://www.sca-recovery.org (Sexual Compulsives Anonymous)

SCA is a fellowship of men and women who share their experience, strength, and hope with each other, that they may solve their common problem and help others to recover from sexual compulsion.

Schizophrenia

http://members.aol.com/leonardjk/support.htm

This site contains a listing of support organizations in the United States for people with schizophrenia and their families.

http://www.schizophrenia.com/

The Schizophrenia Home Page contains links to chat rooms and to sites for families of affected individuals and individuals with schizophrenia. It also contains suggestions for dealing with this disorder.

Disorders of Memory and Other Cognitive Functions

http://www.issd.org/isdguide.htm

The guidelines present a broad outline of what has thus far seemed to be effective treatment for Dissociative Identity Disorder (DID). The guidelines are not intended to replace the therapist's clinical judgment, but they do aim to summarize what most commonly has been found to benefit DID patients. Where a clear divergence of opinion exists in the field, the guidelines attempt to present both sides of the issue.

http://www.voiceofwomen.com/centerarticle.html

The Spectrum of Dissociative Disorders: An Overview of Diagnosis and Treatment. A referenced and detailed discussion of dissociative disorders. Additionally, an extensive discussion of treatments for this disorder.

http://www.biostat.wustl.edu/alzheimer

The Alzheimer page is an educational service created by and sponsored by the Washington University Alzheimer's Disease Research Center.

http://alzweb.org

The aim of the Alzheimer web is to provide a resource for researchers in the field of Alzheimer's disease and for the people who have an interest in research developments.

http://www.alz.org (The Alzheimer's Association)

The Alzheimer's Association is the national voluntary health agency dedicated to researching the prevention, cure, and treatment of Alzheimer's disease and related disorders, and providing support and assistance to afflicted patients and their families.

Disorders of Childhood and Old Age

http://www.ummed.edu/pub/o/ozbayrak/aspclin.html

Asperger's disorder is a milder variant of autistic disorder. Both Asperger's disorder and autistic disorder are in fact subgroups of a larger diagnostic category. This larger category is called either Autistic Spectrum Disorders or Pervasive Developmental Disorders.

http://www.stanford.edu/group/dss/Info.by.disability/Attention.Deficit.Disorder/

This site contains links to attention deficit disorder (ADD) and attention-deficit/hyperactivity disorder (ADHD) sites.

http://members.tripod.com/~tourette13/

This site discusses how Tourette's syndrome (TS) is a neurological disorder characterized by tics or involuntary, rapid, sudden movements or vocalizations that occur repeatedly in the same way.

http://www.vh.org/Providers/Conferences/CPS/42.html

A division of the Virtual Hospital that discusses Tourette's syndrome, its causes and treatments.

http://www.thearc.org (Association for Retarded Citizens—ARC)

Law, Society, and the Mental Health Profession

http://bama.ua.edu/~jhooper

Links to the field of forensic psychiatry.

http://bama.ua.edu/~jhooper/law-psy.html

This Law for Psychiatrists page discusses how most psychiatrists have to deal with the law since there are many legal issues related to mental illness, such as civil commitment, informed consent, and competency.

http://bama.ua.edu/~jhooper/psy-law.html

This site defines mental illness specifically for attorneys.

http://bama.ua.edu/~jhooper/insanity.html

This site is a brief summary of the insanity defense.

http://jh4.net/lm/dir.html

A large listing of the major cases in forensic psychiatry.

http://jh4.net/sp/ct.html

All the major Supreme Court decisions dealing with mental health.

http://www.apa.org/journals/law.html

A journal on psychology, public policy, and law.

http://www.psychlaws.org/

This is the site of the Treatment Advocacy Center, a nonprofit organization dedicated to eliminating legal and clinical barriers for Americans with severe brain disorders who are not receiving appropriate medical care. The focus is on schizophrenia and manic-depressive illness (bipolar disorder).

APPENDIX

C Transparency Masters

Transparency Number	Table	Textbook Page	Title
TM-1	Table 1-1	21	Profiles of Mental Health Professionals
TM-2	Table 2-1	33	Relative Strengths and Weaknesses of Research Methods
TM-3 a & b	Table 3-2	54	Defense Mechanisms to the Rescue
TM-4	Table 3-4	79	Comparing the Models
TM-5	Table 4-1	94	Sample Items from the Beck Depression Inventory
TM-6	Table 5-2	122	Anxiety Disorders Profile
TM-7	Table 6-3	159	Anxiety Disorders Profile
TM-8	Table 7-2	199	Mood Disorders Profile
TM-9	Table 7-3	209	Internal and External Attributions
TM-10	Table 8-1	229	Mood Disorders and Treatment
TM-11	Table 9-1	252	Most Common Causes of Death in the United States
TM-12	Table 9-2	262	Common Predictors of Suicide
TM-13	Table 10-4	298	Disorders That Have Physical Symptoms
TM-14 a & b	Table 10-6	306	Most Stressful Life Events
TM-15 a & b	Table 11-3	331	Anorexia Nervosa vs. Bulimia Nervosa
TM-16 a & b	Table 11-4	341	Sample Items from the Eating Disorder Inventory II
TM-17	Table 12-2	353	Relationships Between Sex, Weight, Oral Alcohol Consumption, and Blood Alcohol Level
TM-18	Table 12-3	359	Risks and Consequences of Drug Misuse
TM-19	Table 14-2	435	Type I vs. Type II Schizophrenia
TM-20	Table 14-3	437	An Array of Psychotic Disorders
TM-21	Table 16-4	493	Comparison of Memory Disorders
TM-22	Table 17-2	524	Comparison of Personality Disorders
TM-23	Table 18-4	558	Comparison of Childhood Disorders

Table 1-1

Profiles of Mental Health Professionals

	DEGREE	BEGAN TO PRACTICE	CURRENT NUMBER	MEDIAN AGE	PERCENT MALE
Psychiatrists	M.D., D.O.	1840s	33,486	52	75
Psychologists	Ph.D., Psy.D., Ed.D.	Late 1940s	69,817	48	52
Social workers	M.S.W., D.S.W.	Early 1950s	188,792	47	23
Marriage and family therapists	Various	1940s	46,227	52	45

Source: Barber, 1999; Zarin et al., 1988; Peterson et al., 1996; Knowlton, 1995

Table 2-1

Relative Strengths and Weaknesses of Research Methods

	PROVIDES INDIVIDUAL INFORMATION (IDIOGRAPHIC)	PROVIDES GENERAL INFORMATION (NOMOTHETIC)	PROVIDES CAUSAL INFORMATION	STATISTICAL ANALYSIS IS POSSIBLE	REPLICABLE
Case study	Yes	No	No	No	No
Correlational method	No	Yes	No	Yes	Yes
Experimental method	No	Yes	Yes	Yes	Yes

TM-2
Ronald J. Comer: Abnormal Psychology, 4/e

Table 3-2 Defense Mechanisms to the Rescue

DEFENSE	OPERATION	EXAMPLE
Repression	Person avoids anxiety by simply not allowing painful or dangerous thoughts to become conscious.	An executive's desire to run amok and attack his boss and colleagues at a board meeting is denied access to his awareness.
Denial	Person simply refuses to acknowledge the existence of an external source of anxiety.	You are not prepared for tomorrow's final exam, but you tell yourself that it's not actually an important exam and that there's no good reason not to go to a movie tonight.
Fantasy	Person imagines events as a means of satisfying unacceptable, anxiety-producing desires that would otherwise go unfulfilled.	An aggressive driver cuts in front of you and pulls into the last remaining parking space. You later fantasize about getting out of your car and beating the person to a pulp in front of admiring onlookers.
Projection	Person attributes own unacceptable impulses, motives, or desires to other individuals.	The executive who repressed his destructive desires may project his anger onto his boss and claim that it is actually the boss who is hostile.
Rationalization	Person creates a socially acceptable reason for an action that actually reflects unacceptable motives.	A student explains away poor grades by citing the importance of the "total experience" of going to college and claiming that too much emphasis on grades would actually interfere with a well-rounded education.
Reaction formation	Person adopts behavior that is the exact opposite of impulses he or she is afraid to acknowledge.	A man experiences homosexual feelings and responds by taking a strong antihomosexual stance.

Table 3-2

Defense Mechanisms to the Rescue (Continued)

DEFENSE	OPERATION	EXAMPLE
Displacement	Person displaces hostility away from a dangerous object and onto a safer substitute.	After your parking spot was taken, you released your pent-up anger by starting a fight with your roommate.
Intellectualization (isolation)	Person represses emotional reactions in favor of overly logical response to a problem.	A woman who has been beaten and raped gives a detached, methodical description of the effects that such attacks may have on victims.
Undoing	Person tries to make up for unacceptable desires or acts, frequently through ritualistic behavior.	A woman who has aggressive feelings toward her husband dusts and straightens their wedding photograph every time such thoughts occur to her.
Regression	Person retreats from an upsetting conflict to an early developmental stage at which no one is expected to behave maturely or responsibly.	A boy who cannot cope with the anger he feels toward his rejecting mother regresses to infantile behavior, soiling his clothes and no longer taking care of his basic needs.
Overcompensation	Person tries to cover up a personal weakness by focusing on another, more desirable trait.	A very shy young woman overcompensates for her weak social skills by spending many hours in the gym trying to perfect her physical condition.
Sublimation	Person expresses sexual and aggressive energy in ways that are acceptable to society.	Athletes, artists, surgeons, and other highly dedicated and skilled people may be reaching their high levels of accomplishment by directing otherwise potentially harmful energies into their work.

Table 3-4

Comparing the Models

	BIOLOGICAL	PSYCHODYNAMIC	BEHAVIORAL	COGNITIVE	HUMANISTIC	EXISTENTIAL	SOCIO-CULTURAL
Cause of dysfunction	Biological malfunction	Underlying conflicts	Maladaptive learning	Maladaptive thinking	Self-deceit	Avoidance of responsibility	Family or social stress
Research support	Strong	Modest	Strong	Strong	Weak	Weak	Moderate
Consumer designation	Patient	Patient	Client	Client	Patient or client	Patient or client	Client
Therapist role	Doctor	Interpreter	Teacher	Persuader	Observer	Collaborator	Social facilitator
Key therapist technique	Biological intervention	Free association and interpretation	Conditioning	Reasoning	Reflection	Varied	Social inter-vention
Therapy goal	Biological repair	Broad psychological change	Functional behaviors	Adaptive thinking	Self-actualization	Authentic life	Effective family or social system

TM-4
Ronald J. Comer: Abnormal Psychology, 4/e

Table 4-1

Sample Items from the Beck Depression Inventory

ITEMS	INVENTORY	
Suicidal ideas	0	I don't have any thoughts of killing myself.
	1	I have thoughts of killing myself but I would not carry them out.
	2	I would like to kill myself.
	3	I would kill myself if I had the chance.
Work inhibition	0	I can work about as well as before.
	1	It takes extra effort to get started at doing something.
	2	I have to push myself very hard to do anything.
	3	I can't do any work at all.
Loss of libido	0	I have not noticed any recent change in my interest in sex.
	1	I am less interested in sex than I used to be.
	2	I am much less interested in sex now.
	3	I have lost interest in sex completely.

Table 5-2

Anxiety Disorders Profile

	ONE-YEAR PREVALENCE (%)	FEMALE:MALE RATIO	TYPICAL AGE AT ONSET	PREVALENCE AMONG CLOSE RELATIVES	PERCENTAGE RECEIVING TREATMENT
Generalized anxiety disorder	4.0%	2:1	0–20 years	Elevated	27%
Specific phobias	9.0	2:1	Variable	Elevated	12%
Social phobias	8.0	3:2	10–20 years	Elevated	21%

Source: APA, 2000, 1994; Kessler et al., 1999, 1994; Regier et al., 1993; Blazer et al., 1991; Davidson et al., 1991; Eaton et al., 1991.

Table 6-3

Anxiety Disorders Profile

	ONE-YEAR PREVALENCE (%)	FEMALE:MALE RATIO	TYPICAL AGE AT ONSET	PREVALENCE AMONG CLOSE RELATIVES	PERCENTAGE RECEIVING TREATMENT
Panic disorder	2.3%	5:2	15–35 years	Elevated	54.4%
Obsessive-compulsive disorder	2.0	1:1	4–25 years	Elevated	41.3
Acute and posttraumatic stress disorders	3.9	2:1	Variable	Unknown	Unknown

Source: APA, 2000, 1994; Kessler et al., 1994; Regier et al., 1933; Davidson et al., 1991; Eaton et al., 1991; Boyd et al., 1990.

TM-7
Ronald J. Comer: Abnormal Psychology, 4/e

Table 7-2

Mood Disorders Profile

	ONE-YEAR PREVALENCE (%)	FEMALE: MALE RATIO	TYPICAL AGE AT ONSET (YEARS)	PREVALENCE AMONG FIRST-DEGREE RELATIVES	PERCENTAGE RECEIVING TREATMENT
Major depressive disorder	5–10%	2:1	24–29	Elevated	49%
Dysthymic disorder	2.5–5.4	Between 3:2 and 2:1	10–25	Elevated	37.8
Bipolar I disorder	0.7	1:1	15–44	Elevated	58.9
Bipolar II disorder	0.5	1:1	15–44	Elevated	58.9
Cyclothymic disorder	0.4	1:1	15–25	Elevated	Unknown

Source: APA, 2000, 1994; Kessler et al., 1994; Regier et al., 1993; Weissman et al., 1991.

Table 7-3

Internal and External Attributions

Event: "I failed my psych test today"

	INTERNAL		EXTERNAL	
	STABLE	UNSTABLE	STABLE	UNSTABLE
Global	"I have a problem with test anxiety."	"Getting into an argument with my roommate threw my whole day off."	"Written tests are an unfair way to assess knowledge."	"No one does well on tests that are given the day after vacation."
Specific	"I just have no grasp of psychology."	"I got upset and froze when I couldn't answer the first two questions."	"Everyone knows that this professor enjoys giving unfair tests."	"This professor didn't put much thought into the test because of the pressure of her book deadline."

TM-9
Ronald J. Comer: Abnormal Psychology, 4/e

Table 8-1

Mood Disorders and Treatment

DISORDER	MOST EFFECTIVE TREATMENT	AVERAGE LENGTH OF INITIAL TREATMENT (WEEKS)	PERCENT IMPROVED BY TREATMENT
Major depressive disorder	Cognitive or interpersonal psychotherapy	20	60%
	Antidepressant drugs	20	60
	ECT	2	60
Dysthymic disorder	Cognitive or interpersonal psychotherapy	20	60
	Antidepressant drugs	20	60
Bipolar I disorder	Antibipolar drugs	Indefinite	60
Bipolar II disorder	Antibipolar drugs	Indefinite	60
Cyclothymic disorder	Psychotherapy or antibipolar drugs	20 to indefinite	Unknown

TM-10
Ronald J. Comer: Abnormal Psychology, 4/e

Table 9-1

Most Common Causes of Death in the United States

RANK	CAUSE	DEATHS PER YEAR	PERCENTAGE OF TOTAL DEATHS
1	Heart disease	733,834	31.6%
2	Cancer	544,278	23.4
3	Stroke	160,431	6.9
4	Lung diseases	106,146	4.6
5	Accidents	93,874	4.0
6	Pneumonia and influenza	82,579	3.6
7	Diabetes	61,559	2.7
8	AIDS	32,655	1.4
9	**Suicide**	**30,862**	**1.3**
10	Liver disease	25,135	1.1

Source: Ash, 1999; U.S. National Center for Health Statistics.

Table 9-2

Common Predictors of Suicide

1. Depressive disorder and certain other mental disorders
2. Alcoholism and other forms of substance abuse
3. Suicide ideation, talk, preparation; certain religious ideas
4. Prior suicide attempts
5. Lethal methods
6. Isolation, living alone, loss of support
7. Hopelessness, cognitive rigidity
8. Being an older white male
9. Modeling, suicide in the family, genetics
10. Economic or work problems; certain occupations
11. Marital problems, family pathology
12. Stress and stressful events
13. Anger, aggression, irritability
14. Physical illness
15. Repetition and combination of factors 1 to 14

Source: Adapted from Maris, 1992.

Table 10-4

Disorders That Have Physical Symptoms

DISORDER	VOLUNTARY CONTROL OF SYMPTOMS?	SYMPTOMS LINKED TO PSYCHOSOCIAL FACTOR?	AN APPARENT GOAL?
Malingering	Yes	Maybe	Yes
Factitious disorder	Yes	Yes	No*
Somatoform disorder	No	Yes	Maybe
Psychophysiological disorder	No	Yes	Maybe
Physical illness	No	Maybe	No

*Except for medical attention.

Source: Adapted from Hyler & Spitzer, 1978.

Table 10-6

Most Stressful Life Events

ADULTS: "SOCIAL ADJUSTMENT RATING SCALE"*

1. Death of spouse
2. Divorce
3. Marital separation
4. Jail term
5. Death of close family member
6. Personal injury or illness
7. Marriage
8. Fired at work
9. Marital reconciliation
10. Retirement
11. Change in health of family member
12. Pregnancy
13. Sex difficulties
14. Gain of new family member
15. Business readjustment
16. Change in financial state
17. Death of close friend
18. Change to different line of work
19. Change in number of arguments with spouse
20. Mortgage over $10,000
21. Foreclosure of mortgage or loan
22. Change in responsibilities at work

*Full scale has 43 items.

Source: Holmes & Rahe, 1967; Crandall et al., 1992.

Table 10-6

Most Stressful Life Events (Continued)

STUDENTS: "UNDERGRADUATE STRESS QUESTIONNAIRE"†

1. Death (family member or friend)
2. Had a lot of tests
3. It's finals week
4. Applying to graduate school
5. Victim of a crime
6. Assignments in all classes due the same day
7. Breaking up with boy-/girlfriend
8. Found out boy-/girlfriend cheated on you
9. Lots of deadlines to meet
10. Property stolen
11. You have a hard upcoming week
12. Went into a test unprepared
13. Lost something (especially wallet)
14. Death of a pet
15. Did worse than expected on test
16. Had an interview
17. Had projects, research papers due
18. Did badly on a test
19. Parents getting divorce
20. Dependent on other people
21. Having roommate conflicts
22. Car/bike broke down, flat tire, etc.

†Full scale has 83 items.

Source: Holmes & Rahe, 1967; Crandall et al., 1992.

Table 11-3

Anorexia Nervosa vs. Bulimia Nervosa

RESTRICTING-TYPE ANOREXIA NERVOSA	BULIMIA NERVOSA
Refusal to maintain a minimum body weight for healthy functioning	Underweight, normal weight, near-normal weight, or overweight
Hunger and disorder denied; often proud of weight management and more satisfied with body	Intense hunger experienced; binge–purge experienced as abnormal; greater body dissatisfaction
Less antisocial behavior	Greater tendency to antisocial behavior and alcohol abuse
Amenorrhea of at least 3 months' duration common	Irregular menstrual periods common; amenorrhea uncommon unless body weight is low
Mistrust of others, particularly professionals	More trusting of people who wish to help
Tend to be obsessional	Tend to be dramatic
Greater self-control, but emotionally over-controlled, with problems experiencing and expressing feelings	More impulsivity and emotional instability

TM-15a
Ronald J. Comer: Abnormal Psychology, 4/e

Table 11-3

Anorexia Nervosa vs. Bulimia Nervosa (Continued)

RESTRICTING-TYPE ANOREXIA NERVOSA	BULIMIA NERVOSA
More likely to be sexually immature and inexperienced	More sexually experienced and sexually active
Females more likely to reject traditional feminine role	Females more likely to embrace traditional feminine role
Age of onset often around 14–18	Age of onset around 15–21
Greater tendency for maximum pre-disorder weight to be near normal for age	Greater tendency for maximum pre-disorder weight to be slightly greater than normal
Lesser familial predisposition to obesity	Greater familial predisposition to obesity
Greater tendency toward pre-disorder compliance with parents	Greater tendency toward pre-disorder conflict with parents
Tendency to deny family conflict	Tendency to perceive intense family conflict

Source: APA, 2000, 1994; Levine, 1987; Andersen, 1985; Garner et al., 1985; Neuman & Halvorson, 1983.

Table 11-4

Sample Items from the Eating Disorder Inventory II

For each item, decide if the item is true about you ALWAYS (A), USUALLY (U), OFTEN (O), SOMETIMES (S), RARELY (R), or NEVER (N). Circle the letter that corresponds to your rating.

A	U	O	S	R	N	I think that my stomach is too big.
A	U	O	S	R	N	I eat when I am upset.
A	U	O	S	R	N	I stuff myself with food.
A	U	O	S	R	N	I think about dieting.
A	U	O	S	R	N	I think that my thighs are too large.
A	U	O	S	R	N	I feel ineffective as a person.
A	U	O	S	R	N	I feel extremely guilty after overeating.
A	U	O	S	R	N	I am terrified of gaining weight.
A	U	O	S	R	N	I get confused about what emotion I am feeling.
A	U	O	S	R	N	I feel inadequate.

Table 11-4

Sample Items from the Eating Disorder Inventory II (Continued)

For each item, decide if the item is true about you ALWAYS (A), USUALLY (U), OFTEN (O), SOMETIMES (S), RARELY (R), or NEVER (N). Circle the letter that corresponds to your rating.

A	U	O	S	R	N	I have gone on eating binges where I felt that I could not stop.
A	U	O	S	R	N	As a child, I tried very hard to avoid disappointing my parents and teachers.
A	U	O	S	R	N	I have trouble expressing my emotions to others.
A	U	O	S	R	N	I get confused as to whether or not I am hungry.
A	U	O	S	R	N	I have a low opinion of myself.
A	U	O	S	R	N	I think my hips are too big.
A	U	O	S	R	N	If I gain a pound, I worry that I will keep gaining.
A	U	O	S	R	N	I have the thought of trying to vomit in order to lose weight.
A	U	O	S	R	N	I think my buttocks are too large.
A	U	O	S	R	N	I eat or drink in secrecy.
A	U	O	S	R	N	I would like to be in total control of my bodily urges.

Source: Garner, Olmsted, & Polivy, 1991, 1984.

Table 12-2

Relationships Between Sex, Weight, Oral Alcohol Consumption, and Blood Alcohol Level

		Blood Alcohol Level (percent)					
Absolute Alcohol (Ounces)	Beverage Intake*	Female (100 lb.)	Male (100 lb.)	Female (150 lb.)	Male (150 lb.)	Female (200 lb.)	Male (200 lb.)
1/2	1 oz. spirits† 1 glass wine 1 can beer	0.045	0.037	0.03	0.025	0.022	0.019
1	2 oz. spirits 2 glasses wine 2 cans beer	0.090	0.075	0.06	0.050	0.045	0.037
2	4 oz. spirits 4 glasses wine 4 cans beer	0.180	0.150	0.12	0.100	0.090	0.070
3	6 oz. spirits 6 glasses wine 6 cans beer	0.270	0.220	0.18	0.150	0.130	0.110
4	8 oz. spirits 8 glasses wine 8 cans beer	0.360	0.300	0.24	0.200	0.180	0.150
5	10 oz. spirits 10 glasses wine 10 cans beer	0.450	0.370	0.30	0.250	0.220	0.180

*In 1 hour.
†100-proof spirits

Source: Ray & Ksir, 1993, p. 194.

Table 12-3

Risks and Consequences of Drug Misuse

	INTOXICATION POTENTIAL	DEPENDENCY POTENTIAL	RISK OF ORGAN DAMAGE OR DEATH	RISK OF SEVERE SOCIAL OR ECONOMIC CONSEQUENCES	RISK OF SEVERE OR LONG-LASTING MENTAL AND BEHAVIORAL CHANGE
Opioids	High	High	Low	High	Low to moderate
Sedative-hypnotics					
Barbiturates	Moderate	Moderate to high	Moderate to high	Moderate to high	Low
Benzodiazepines	Moderate	Low	Low	Low	Low
Stimulants (cocaine, amphetamines)	High	High	Moderate	Low to moderate	Moderate to high
Alcohol	High	Moderate	High	High	High
Cannabis	High	Low to moderate	Low	Low to moderate	Low
Mixed drug classes	High	High	High	High	High

Source: APA, 2000, 1994; Gold, 1986, p. 28.

Table 14-2

Type I vs. Type II Schizophrenia

	TYPE I	TYPE II
Symptoms	Positive symptoms: Delusions Hallucinations Inappropriate affect Positive formal thought disorders	Negative symptoms: Avolition Social withdrawal Blunted and flat affect Alogia
Premorbid adjustment	Relatively good	Relatively poor
Responsiveness to traditional antipsychotic drugs	Good	Poor
Outcome of disorder	Fair	Poor
Biological features	Abnormal neurotransmitter activity	Abnormal brain structures

Source: Adapted from Crow, 1985, 1982, 1980.

Table 14-3

An Array of Psychotic Disorders

DISORDER	KEY FEATURES	DURATION	LIFETIME PREVALENCE
Schizophrenia	Various psychotic symptoms such as delusions, hallucinations, disorganized speech, flat or inappropriate affect, and catatonia.	6 months or more	1.0%
Brief psychotic disorder	Various psychotic symptoms such as delusions, hallucinations, disorganized speech, flat or inappropriate affect, and catatonia.	Less than 1 month	Unknown
Schizophreniform disorder	Various psychotic symptoms such as delusions, hallucinations, disorganized speech, flat or inappropriate affect, and catatonia.	1 to 5 months	0.2%
Schizoaffective disorder	Marked symptoms of both schizophrenia and a mood disorder.	6 months or more	Unknown
Delusional disorder	Persistent delusions that are not bizarre and not due to schizophrenia. Persecutory, jealous, grandiose, and somatic delusions are common.	1 month or more	0.1%
Shared psychotic disorder	Person adopts delusions that are held by another individual, such as a parent or sibling. Also known as *folie à deux*.	No minimum length	Unknown
Psychotic disorder due to a general medical condition	Hallucinations or delusions caused by a medical illness or brain damage.	No minimum length	Unknown
Substance-induced psychotic disorder	Hallucinations or delusions caused directly by a substance, such as an abused drug.	No minimum length	Unknown

Table 16-4

Comparison of Memory Disorders

	ANTEROGRADE (CONTINUOUS) AMNESIA	RETROGRADE (LOCALIZED, SELECTIVE, AND GENERALIZED) AMNESIA	DECLARATIVE MEMORY LOSS	PROCEDURAL MEMORY LOSS	ORGANIC CAUSES
Dissociative amnesia	Sometimes	Yes	Yes	Sometimes	No
Dissociative fugue	Sometimes	Yes	Yes	Sometimes	No
Multiple personality disorder	Yes	Yes	Yes	Yes	No
Amnestic disorders	Yes	Sometimes	Yes	Sometimes	Yes
Dementias	Yes	Yes	Yes	Yes	Yes

Table 17-2

Comparison of Personality Disorders

	DSM-IV CLUSTER	SIMILAR DISORDERS ON AXIS I	RESPONSIVENESS TO TREATMENT
Paranoid	Odd	Schizophrenia; delusional disorder	Modest
Schizoid	Odd	Schizophrenia; delusional disorder	Modest
Schizotypal	Odd	Schizophrenia; delusional disorder	Modest
Antisocial	Dramatic	Conduct disorder	Poor
Borderline	Dramatic	Mood disorders	Moderate
Histrionic	Dramatic	Somatoform disorders; mood disorders	Modest
Narcissistic	Dramatic	Cyclothymic disorder (mild bipolar disorder)	Poor
Avoidant	Anxious	Social phobia	Moderate
Dependent	Anxious	Separation anxiety disorder; dysthymic disorder (mild depressive disorder)	Moderate
Obsessive-compulsive	Anxious	Obsessive-compulsive anxiety disorder	Moderate

Ronald J. Comer: Abnormal Psychology, 4/e

Table 18-4

Comparison of Childhood Disorders

DISORDER	USUAL AGE OF IDENTIFICATION	PREVALENCE AMONG ALL CHILDREN	GENDER WITH GREATER PREVALENCE	ELEVATED FAMILY HISTORY	RECOVERY BY ADULTHOOD
Separation anxiety disorder	Before 12 years	4%	Females	Yes	Often
Conduct disorder	7–15 years	1–10%	Males	Yes	Often
ADHD	Before 12 years	5%	Males	Yes	Often
Enuresis	5–8 years	5%	Males	Yes	Usually
Encopresis	After 4 years	1%	Males	Unclear	Usually
Learning disorders	6–9 years	5%	Males	Yes	Often
Autism	0–3 years	0.05%	Males	Yes	Sometimes
Mental retardation	Before 10 years	1%	Males	Unclear	Sometimes

TM-23
Ronald J. Comer: Abnormal Psychology, 4/e

APPENDIX

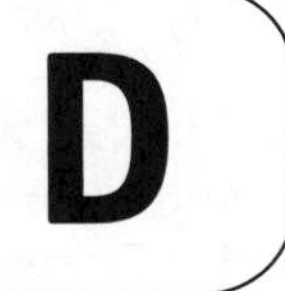

D DSM-IV Masters

Contents	Description

What's New in DMS-IV?

The *DSM-IV Text Revision* (APA, 2000) has changed the diagnostic criteria for a number of disorders in DMS-IV.

Disorder	DSM-IV (APA, 1994)	DSM-IV Text Revision (APA, 2000)
Tourette's Disorder	Symptoms must cause marked distress or significant impairment in order to warrant diagnosis.	Diagnosis is warranted even if symptoms do not cause marked distress or significant impairment.
Chronic Motor or Vocal Tic Disorder	Symptoms must cause marked distress or significant impairment in order to warrant diagnosis.	Diagnosis is warranted even if symptoms do not cause marked distress or significant impairment.
Transient Tic Disorder	Symptoms must cause marked distress or significant impairment in order to warrant diagnosis.	Diagnosis is warranted even if symptoms do not cause marked distress or significant impairment.
Dementia Due to Other General Medical Conditions	Lists as Distinct Axis I disorders: *Dementia due to HIV disease* *Dementia due to head trauma* *Dementia due to Parkinson's disease* *Dementia due to Huntington's disease* *Dementia due to Pick's disease* *Dementia due to Creutzfeldt-Jakob disease*	These are no longer listed as distinct Axis I disorders. Instead, they are grouped together as *Dementia due to other general medical conditions,* with the particular medical condition coded on Axis III.
Personality Change Due to a General Medical Condition	Diagnosis is not warranted if the personality change occurs as part of dementia.	A diagnosis is warranted even in cases of dementia when the personality change is prominent.
Exhibitionism	Sexually arousing fantasies, sexual urges, or behaviors must cause significant distress or impairment in order to warrant diagnosis.	Diagnosis is warranted if person acts on sexual urges, even if such actions do not cause marked distress, impairment, or interpersonal difficulty. If person manifests only sexual urges or fantasies (not actions), these must cause marked distress or interpersonal difficulty to warrant diagnosis.
Frotteurism	Sexually arousing fantasies, sexual urges, or behaviors must cause significant distress or impairment in order to warrant diagnosis.	Diagnosis is warranted if person acts on sexual urges, even if such actions do not cause marked distress, impairment, or interpersonal difficulty. If person manifests only sexual urges or fantasies (not actions), these must cause marked distress or interpersonal difficulty to warrant diagnosis.

Source: APA, 2000

What's New in DMS-IV? (Continued)

The *DSM-IV Text Revision* (APA, 2000) has changed the diagnostic criteria for a number of disorders in DMS-IV.

Disorder	DSM-IV (APA, 1994)	DSM-IV Text Revision (APA, 2000)
Pedophilia	Sexually arousing fantasies, sexual urges, or behaviors must cause significant distress or impairment in order to warrant diagnosis.	Diagnosis is warranted if person acts on sexual urges, even if such actions do not cause marked distress, impairment, or interpersonal difficulty. If person manifests only sexual urges or fantasies (not actions), these must cause marked distress or interpersonal difficulty to warrant diagnosis.
Sexual Sadism	Sexually arousing fantasies, sexual urges, or behaviors must cause significant distress or impairment in order to warrant diagnosis.	Diagnosis is warranted if person acts on sexual urges with a non-consenting person, even if such actions do not cause the patient marked distress, impairment, or interpersonal difficulty. If the individual manifests only sexual urges or fantasies (not actions), these must cause marked distress or interpersonal difficulty to warrant diagnosis.
Voyeurism	Sexually arousing fantasies, sexual urges, or behaviors must cause significant distress or impairment in order to warrant diagnosis.	Diagnosis is warranted if person acts on sexual urges, even if such actions do not cause marked distress, impairment, or interpersonal difficulty. If person manifests only sexual urges or fantasies (not actions), these must cause marked distress or interpersonal difficulty to warrant diagnosis.

Source: APA, 2000

Axis I Disorders in DSM-IV

Disorders Usually First Diagnosed in Infancy, Childhood, and Adolescence
Disorders in this group tend to emerge and sometimes dissipate before adult life. They include pervasive developmental disorders (such as autism); learning disorders; attention-deficit hyperactivity disorder; conduct disorders; and separation anxiety disorder.

Delirium, Dementia, Amnestic, and Other Cognitive Disorders
These disorders are dominated by impairment in cognitive functioning. They include Alzheimer's disease and Huntington's disease.

Mental Disorders Due to a General Medical Condition
These are mental disorders that are caused primarily by a general medical disorder. They include mood disorder due to a general medical condition.

Substance-Related Disorders
These disorders are brought about by the use of substances that affect the central nervous system, such as alcohol use disorders, opioid use disorders, amphetamine use disorders, cocaine use disorders, and hallucinogen use disorders.

Schizophrenia and Other Psychotic Disorders
In this group of disorders, functioning deteriorates until the patient reaches a state of psychosis, or loss of contact with reality.

Mood Disorders
Disorders in this group are marked by severe disturbances of mood that cause people to feel extremely and inappropriately sad or elated for extended periods of time. They include major depressive disorder and bipolar disorder.

Anxiety Disorders
Anxiety is the predominant disturbance in this group of disorders. They include generalized anxiety disorders, phobic disorders, panic disorder, obsessive-compulsive disorder, acute stress disorder, and posttraumatic stress disorder.

Somatoform Disorders
These disorders, marked by physical symptoms that apparently are caused primarily by psychological rather than physiological factors, include pain disorders, conversion disorders, somatization disorder, and hypochondriasis.

Factitious Disorders
People with these disorders intentionally produce or feign psychological or physical symptoms.

Source: APA, 2000, 1994

Axis I Disorders in DSM-IV (Continued)

Dissociative Disorders
These disorders are characterized by a change in the usually integrated functions of memory and identity. They include dissociative amnesia; dissociative fugue; and dissociative identity disorder (multiple personality disorder).

Eating Disorders
People with these disorders display abnormal patterns of eating that significantly impair their functioning. The disorders include anorexia nervosa and bulimia nervosa.

Sexual Disorders and Gender Identity Disorders
These disorders in sexual functioning, behavior, or preferences include paraphilias, sexual dysfunctions, and gender identity disorder.

Sleep Disorders
People with these disorders display chronic sleep problems. The disorders include primary insomnia, primary hypersomnia, sleep terror disorder, and sleepwalking disorder.

Impulse-Control Disorders
People with these disorders are chronically unable to resist impulses, drives, or temptations to perform certain acts that are harmful to them or to others. The disorders include pathological gambling; kleptomania; pyromania; and intermittent explosive disorders.

Adjustment Disorder
The primary feature of these disorders is a maladaptive reaction to a clear stressor such as divorce or business difficulties that occur within three months after the onset of the stressor.

Other Conditions That May Be a Focus of Clinical Attention
This category consists of certain conditions or problems that are worth noting because they cause significant impairment, such as relational problems, problems related to abuse or neglect, medication-induced movement disorders, and psychophysiological disorders.

Source: APA, 2000, 1994

Global Assessment of Functioning (GAF) Scale

Consider psychological, social, and occupational functioning on a hypothetical continuum of mental health–illness. Do not include impairment in functioning due to physical (or environmental) limitations.

Code [Note: Use intermediate codes when appropriate (e.g., 45, 68, 72).]

91–100 Superior functioning in a wide range of activities. Life's problems never seem to get out of hand, is sought out by others because of his or her many positive qualities. No symptoms.

81–90 Absent or minimal symptoms (e.g., mild anxiety before an exam), good functioning in all areas, interested and involved in a wide range of activities, socially effective, generally satisfied with life, no more than everyday problems or concerns (e.g., an occasional argument with family members).

71–80 If symptoms are present, they are transient and expectable reactions to psychosocial stressors (e.g., difficulty concentrating after family argument); no more than slight impairment in social, occupational, or school functioning (e.g., temporarily falling behind in schoolwork).

61–70 Some mild symptoms (e.g., depressed mood and mild insomnia) or some difficulty in social, occupational, or school functioning (e.g., occasional truancy, or theft within the household), but generally functioning pretty well, has some meaningful interpersonal relationships.

51–60 Moderate symptoms (e.g., flat affect and circumstantial speech, occasional panic attacks) or moderate difficulty in social, occupational, or school functioning (e.g., new friends, conflicts with peers or co-workers).

41–50 Serious symptoms (e.g., suicidal ideation, severe obsessional rituals, frequent shoplifting) or any serious impairment in social, occupational, or school functioning (e.g., no friends, unable to keep a job).

Source: APA, 2000, 1994

Global Assessment of Functioning (GAF) Scale (Continued)

31–40 Some impairment in reality testing or communication (e.g., speech is at times illogical, obscure, or irrelevant) or major impairment in several areas, such as work or school, family relations, judgment, thinking, or mood (e.g., depressed man avoids friends, neglects family, and is unable to work; child frequently beats up younger children, is defiant at home, and is failing at school).

21–30 Behavior is considerably influenced by delusions or hallucinations or serious impairment in communication or judgment (e.g., sometimes incoherent, acts grossly inappropriately, suicidal preoccupation) or inability to function in almost all areas (e.g., stays in bed all day; no job, home, or friends).

11–20 Some danger of hurting self or others (e.g., suicide attempts without clear expectation of death; frequently violent; manic excitement) or occasionally fails to maintain minimal personal hygiene (e.g., smears feces) or gross impairment in communication (e.g., largely incoherent or mute).

1–10 Persistent danger of severely hurting self or others (e.g., recurrent violence) or persistent inability to maintain minimal personal hygiene or serious suicidal act with clear expectation of death.

0 Inadequate information.

Source: APA, 2000, 1994

Criteria for Agoraphobia

Note: Agoraphobia is not a codable disorder. Code the specific disorder in which the Agoraphobia occurs (e.g., 300.21 Panic Attack with Agoraphobia or 300.22 Agoraphobia Without History of Panic Disorder).

A. Anxiety about being in places or situations from which escape might be difficult (or embarrassing) or in which help may not be available in the event of having an unexpected or situationally predisposed Panic Attack or panic-like symptoms. Agoraphobic fears typically involve characteristic clusters of situations that include being outside the home alone; being in a crowd or standing in a line; being on a bridge; and traveling in a bus, train, or automobile.

   Note: Consider the diagnosis of Specific Phobia if the avoidance is limited to one or only a few specific situations, or Social Phobia if the avoidance is limited to social situations.

B. The situations are avoided (e.g., travel is restricted) or else are endured with marked distress or with anxiety about having a Panic Attack or panic-like symptoms, or require the presence of a companion.

C. The anxiety of phobic avoidance is not better accounted for by another mental disorder, such as Social Phobia (e.g., avoidance limited to social situations because of fear of embarrassment), Specific Phobia (e.g., avoidance limited to a single situation like elevators), Obsessive-Compulsive Disorder (e.g., avoidance of dirt in someone with an obsession about contamination), Posttraumatic Stress Disorder (e.g., avoidance of stimuli associated with a severe stressor), or Separation Anxiety Disorder (e.g., avoidance of leaving home or relatives).

Source: APA, 2000, 1994

Diagnostic Criteria for Specific Phobia

A. Marked and persistent fear that is excessive or unreasonable, cued by the presence or anticipation of a specific object or situation (e.g., flying, heights, animals, receiving an injection, seeing blood).

B. Exposure to the phobic stimulus almost invariably provokes an immediate anxiety response, which may take the form of a situationally bound or situationally predisposed Panic Attack. Note: In children, the anxiety may be expressed by crying, tantrums, freezing, or clinging.

C. The person recognizes that the fear is excessive or unreasonable. Note: In children, this feature may be absent.

D. The phobic situation(s) is (are) avoided or else is endured with intense anxiety or distress.

E. The avoidance, anxious anticipation, or distress in the feared situation(s) interferes significantly with the person's normal routine, occupational (academic) functioning, or social activities or relationships, or there is a marked distress about having the phobia.

F. In individuals under 18 years, the duration is at least 6 months.

G. The anxiety, Panic Attacks, or phobic avoidance associated with the specific object or situation are not better accounted for by another mental disorder, such as Obsessive-Compulsive Disorder (e.g., fear of dirt in someone with an obsession about contamination), Posttraumatic Stress Disorder (e.g., avoidance of stimuli associated with a severe stressor), Separation Anxiety Disorder (e.g., avoidance of school), Social Phobia (e.g., avoidance of social situations because of fear of embarrassment), Panic Disorder With Agoraphobia, or Agoraphobia Without History of Panic Disorder.

Specify type:

Animal Type

Natural Environment Type (e.g., heights, storms, water)

Blood-Injection-Injury Type

Situational Type (e.g., airplanes, elevators, enclosed places)

Other Type (e.g., phobic avoidance of situations that may lead to choking, vomiting, or contracting an illness; in children, avoidance of loud sounds or costumed characters)

Source: APA, 2000, 1994

Diagnostic Criteria for Social Phobia

A. A marked and persistent fear of one or more social or performance situations in which the person is exposed to unfamiliar people or to possible scrutiny by others. The individual fears that he or she will act in a way (or show anxiety symptoms) that will be humiliating or embarrassing. Note: In children, there must be evidence of the capacity for age-appropriate social relationships with familiar people and the anxiety must occur in peer settings, not just in interactions with adults.

B. Exposure to the feared social situation almost invariably provokes anxiety which may take the form of a situationally bound or situationally predisposed Panic Attack. Note: In children, the anxiety may be expressed by crying, tantrums, freezing, or shrinking from social situations with unfamiliar people.

C. The person recognizes that the fear is excessive or unreasonable. Note: In children, this feature may be absent.

D. The feared social or performance situations are avoided or else are endured with intense anxiety or distress.

E. The avoidance, anxious anticipation, or distress in the feared social or performance situation(s) interferes significantly with the person's normal routine, occupational (academic) functioning, or social activities or relationships, or there is a marked distress about having the phobia.

F. In individuals under 18 years, the duration is at least 6 months.

G. The fear of avoidance is not due to the direct physiological effects of a substance (e.g., a drug of abuse, a medication) or a general medical condition and is not better accounted for by another mental disorder (e.g., Panic Disorder With or Without Agoraphobia, Separation Anxiety Disorder, Body Dysmorphic Disorder, a Pervasive Developmental Disorder, or Schizoid Personality Disorder).

H. If a general medical condition or another mental disorder is present, the fear in Criterion A is unrelated to it, e.g., the fear is not of Stuttering, trembling in Parkinson's disease, or exhibiting abnormal eating behavior in Anorexia or Bulimia Nervosa.

Source: APA, 2000, 1994

Diagnostic Criteria for Generalized Anxiety Disorder

A. Excessive anxiety and worry (apprehensive expectation), occurring more days than not for at least 6 months, about a number of events or activities (such as work or school performance).

B. The person finds it difficult to control the worry.

C. The anxiety and worry are associated with three (or more) of the following six symptoms (with at least some symptoms present for more days than not for the past 6 months). Note: Only one item is required in children.
   (1) restlessness or feeling keyed up or on edge
   (2) being easily fatigued
   (3) difficulty concentrating or mind going blank
   (4) irritability
   (5) muscle tension
   (6) sleep disturbance (difficulty falling or staying asleep, or restless unsatisfying sleep)

D. The focus of the anxiety and worry is not confined to features of an Axis 1 disorder, e.g., the anxiety or worry is not about having a Panic Attack (as in Panic Disorder), being embarrassed in public (as in Social Phobia), being contaminated (as in Obsessive-Compulsive Disorder), being away from home or close relatives (as in Separation Anxiety Disorder), gaining weight (as in Anorexia Nervosa), having multiple physical complaints (as in Hypochondriasis), and the anxiety and worry do not occur exclusively during Posttraumatic Stress Disorder.

E. The anxiety, worry, or physical symptoms cause clinically significant distress or impairment in social, occupational, or other important areas of functioning.

F. The disturbance is not due to the direct physiological effects of a substance (e.g., a drug of abuse, a medication) or a general medical condition (e.g., hyperthyroidism) and does not exclusively occur during a Mood Disorder, a Psychotic Disorder, or a Pervasive Developmental Disorder.

Source: APA, 2000, 1994

Criteria for Panic Attack

Note: A Panic Attack is not a codable disorder. Code the specific diagnosis in which the Panic Attack occurs (e.g., 300.21 Panic Attack with Agoraphobia).

A discrete period of intense fear or discomfort, in which four (or more) of the following symptoms developed abruptly and reached a peak within 10 minutes:

(1) palpitations, pounding heart, or accelerated heart rate
(2) sweating
(3) trembling or shaking
(4) sensations of shortness of breath or smothering
(5) feeling of choking
(6) chest pain or discomfort
(7) nausea or abdominal distress
(8) feeling dizzy, unsteady, lightheaded, or faint
(9) derealization (feelings of unreality) or depersonalization (being detached from oneself)
(10) fear of losing control or going crazy
(11) fear of dying
(12) paresthesias (numbness or tingling sensations)
(13) chills or hot flushes

Source: APA, 2000, 1994

Diagnostic Criteria for Obsessive-Compulsive Disorder

A. Either obsessions or compulsions:

Obsessions as defined by (1), (2), (3), and (4):

(1) recurrent and persistent thoughts, impulses, or images that are experienced, at some time during the disturbance, as intrusive and inappropriate and that cause marked anxiety or distress
(2) the thoughts, impulses, or images are not simply excessive worries about real-life problems
(3) the person attempts to ignore or suppress such thoughts, impulses, or images, or to neutralize them with some other thought or action
(4) the person recognizes that the obsessional thoughts, impulses, or images are a product of his or her own mind (not imposed from without as in thought insertion)

Compulsions are defined by (1) and (2):

(1) repetitive behaviors (e.g., hand washing, ordering, checking) or mental acts (e.g., praying, counting, repeating words silently) that the person feels driven to perform in response to an obsession, or according to rules that must be applied rigidly
(2) the behaviors or mental acts are aimed at preventing or reducing distress or preventing some dreaded event or situation; however, these behaviors or mental acts either are not connected in a realistic way with what they are designed to neutralize or prevent or are clearly excessive

B. At some point during the course of the disorder, the person has recognized that the obsessions or compulsions are excessive or unreasonable. Note: This does not apply to children.

C. The obsessions or compulsions cause marked distress, are time consuming (take more than 1 hour a day), or significantly interfere with the person's normal routine, occupational (or academic) functioning, or usual social activities or relationships.

D. If another Axis I disorder is present, the content of the obsessions or compulsions is not restricted to it (e.g., preoccupation with food in the presence of an Eating Disorder; hair pulling in the presence of Trichotillomania; concern with appearance in the presence of Body Dysmorphic Disorder; preoccupation with having a serious illness in the presence of Hypochondriasis; preoccupation with sexual urges or fantasies in the presence of a Paraphilia; or guilty ruminations in the presence of a Major Depressive Disorder).

E. The disturbance is not due to the direct physiological effects of a substance (e.g., a drug of abuse, a medication) or a general medical condition.

Source: APA, 2000, 1994

Diagnostic Criteria for Posttraumatic Stress Disorder

A. The person has been exposed to a traumatic event in which both of the following were present:
   (1) The person experienced, witnessed, or was confronted with an event or events that involved actual or threatened death or serious injury, or a threat to the physical integrity of self or others
   (2) The person's response involved intense fear, helplessness, or horror. Note: In children, this may be expressed instead by disorganized or agitated behavior.

B. The traumatic event is persistently reexperienced in one or more of the following ways:
   (1) recurrent and intrusive distressing recollections of the event, including images, thoughts, or perceptions. Note: In young children, repetitive play may occur in which themes or aspects of the trauma are expressed.
   (2) recurrent distressing dreams of the event. Note: In children, there may be frightening dreams without recognizable content.
   (3) acting or feeling as if the traumatic event were recurring (includes a sense of reliving the experience, illusions, hallucinations, and dissociative flashback episodes, including those that occur on awakening or when intoxicated). In young children, trauma-specific reenactment may occur.
   (4) intense psychological distress at exposure to internal or external cues that symbolize or resemble an aspect of the traumatic event
   (5) physiological reactivity on exposure to internal or external cues that symbolize or resemble an aspect of the traumatic event

C. Persistent avoidance of stimuli associated with the trauma and numbing of general responsiveness (not present before the trauma), as indicated by three (or more) of the following:
   (1) efforts to avoid thoughts, feelings, or conversations associated with the trauma
   (2) efforts to avoid activities, places, or people that arouse recollections of the trauma
   (3) inability to recall an important aspect of the trauma
   (4) markedly diminished interest or participation in significant activities
   (5) feeling of detachment or estrangement from others
   (6) restricted range of affect (e.g., unable to have loving feelings)
   (7) sense of a foreshortened future (e.g., does not expect to have a career, marriage, children or a normal life span)

D. Persistent symptoms of increased arousal (not present before the trauma), as indicated by two (or more) of the following:
   (1) difficulty falling or staying asleep
   (2) irritability or outbursts of anger
   (3) difficulty concentrating
   (4) hypervigilance
   (5) exaggerated startle response

Source: APA, 2000, 1994

Diagnostic Criteria for Posttraumatic Stress Disorder (Continued)

E. Duration of the disturbance (symptoms in criteria B, C, D) is more than 1 month.

F. The disturbance causes clinically significant distress or impairment in social, occupational, or other important areas of functioning.

Specify if:

Acute: if duration of symptoms is less than 3 months

Chronic: if duration of symptoms is 3 months or more

Specify if:

With Delayed Onset: if onset of symptoms is at least 6 months after the stressor

Source: APA, 2000, 1994

Criteria for Major Depressive Episode

A. Five (or more) of the following symptoms have been present during the same 2-week period and represent a change from the previous functioning; at least one of the symptoms is either (1) depressed mood or (2) loss of interest or pleasure.

Note: Do not include symptoms that are clearly due to a general medical condition, or mood-incongruent delusions or hallucinations.

(1) depressed mood most of the day, nearly every day, as indicated by either subjective report (e.g., feels sad or empty) or observation made by others (e.g., appears tearful).

(2) markedly diminished interest or pleasure in all, or almost all, activities most of the day, nearly every day (as indicated by either subjective account or observations made by others)

(3) significant weight loss when not dieting or weight gain (e.g., a change of more than 5% of body weight in a month), a decrease or increase in appetite nearly every day. Note: In children, consider failure to make expected weight gains.

(4) insomnia or hypersomnia nearly every day

(5) psychomotor agitation or retardation nearly every day (observable by others)

(6) fatigue or loss of energy nearly every day

(7) feelings of worthlessness or excessive or inappropriate guilt (which may be delusional) nearly every day

(8) diminished ability to think or concentrate, or indecisiveness, nearly every day (either by subjective account or observed by others)

(9) recurrent thoughts of death (not just fear of dying), recurrent suicidal ideation without a specific plan, or a suicide attempt or a specific plan for committing suicide

B. The symptoms do not meet criteria for a Mixed Episode.

C. The symptoms cause clinically significant distress or impairment in social, occupational, or other important areas of functioning.

D. The symptoms are not due to the direct physiological effects of a substance (e.g., a drug of abuse, a medication) or a general medical condition (e.g., hypothyroidism).

E. The symptoms are not better accounted for by Bereavement, i.e., after the loss of a loved one, the symptoms persist for longer than 2 months or are characterized by marked functional impairment, morbid preoccupation with worthlessness, suicidal ideation, psychotic symptoms, or psychomotor retardation.

Source: APA, 2000, 1994

Criteria for Manic Episode

A. A distinct period of abnormally and persistently elevated, expansive, or irritable mood lasting at least 1 week (or any duration if hospitalization is necessary).

B. During the period of mood disturbance, three (or more) of the following symptoms have persisted (four if the mood is only irritable) and have been present to a significant degree:
   (1) inflated self-esteem or grandiosity
   (2) decreased need for sleep (e.g., feels rested after only 3 hours of sleep)
   (3) more talkative than usual or pressure to keep talking
   (4) flight of ideas or subjective experience that thoughts are racing
   (5) distractibility (i.e., attention too easily drawn to unimportant or irrelevant external stimuli)
   (6) increase in goal-directed activity (either socially, at work or school, or sexually) or psychomotor agitation
   (7) excessive involvement in pleasurable activities that have a high potential for painful consequences (e.g., engaging in unrestrained buying sprees, sexual indiscretions, or foolish business investments)

C. The symptoms do not meet the criteria for a Mixed Episode.

D. The mood disturbance is sufficiently severe to cause marked impairment in occupational functioning or in usual social activities or relationships with others, or to necessitate hospitalization to prevent harm to self or others, or there are psychotic features.

E. The symptoms are not due to the direct physiological effects of a substance (e.g., a drug of abuse, a medication, or other treatment) or a general medical condition (e.g., hyperthyroidism).

Source: APA, 2000, 1994

Criteria for Mixed Episode

A. The criteria are met both for a Manic Episode and for a Major Depressive Episode (except for duration) nearly every day during at least a 1-week period.

B. The mood disturbance is sufficiently severe to cause marked impairment in occupational functioning or in usual social activities or relationships with others, or to necessitate hospitalization to prevent harm to self or others, or there are psychotic features.

C. The symptoms are not due to the direct physiological effects of a substance (e.g., a drug of abuse, a medication, or other treatment) or a general medical condition (e.g., hyperthyroidism).

Diagnostic Criteria for Major Depressive Disorder, Single Episode

A. Presence of a single Major Depressive Episode

B. The Major Depressive Episode is not better accounted for by Schizoaffective Disorder and is not superimposed on Schizophrenia, Schizophreniform Disorder, Delusional Disorder, or Psychotic Disorder Not Otherwise Specified.

C. There has never been a Manic Episode, a Mixed Episode, or a Hypomanic Episode. Note: This exclusion does not apply if all the manic-like, mixed-like, or hypomanic-like episodes are substance or treatment induced or are due to the direct physiological effects of a general medical condition.

Source: APA, 2000, 1994

Diagnostic Criteria for Dysthymic Disorder

A. Depressed mood for most of the day, for more days than not, as indicated either by subjective account or observation by others, for at least 2 years. Note: In children and adolescents, mood can be irritable and duration must be at least 1 year.

B. Presence, while depressed, of two (or more) of the following:
   (1) poor appetite or overeating
   (2) insomnia or hypersomnia
   (3) low energy or fatigue
   (4) low self-esteem
   (5) poor concentration or difficulty making decisions
   (6) feelings of hopelessness

C. During the 2-year period (1 year for children or adolescents) of the disturbance, the person has never been without the symptoms in Criteria A and B for more than 2 months at a time.

D. No Major Depressive Episode has been present during the first 2 years of the disturbance (1 year for children and adolescents); i.e., the disturbance is not better accounted for by chronic Major Depressive Disorder, or Major Depressive Disorder, In Partial Remission.

   Note: There may have been a previous Major Depressive Episode provided there was a full remission (no significant signs or symptoms for 2 months) before development of the Dysthymic Disorder. In addition, after the initial 2 years (1 year in children or adolescents) of Dysthymic Disorder, there may be superimposed episodes of Major Depressive Disorder, in which case both diagnoses may be given when the criteria are met for a Major Depressive Episode.

E. There has never been a Manic Episode, a Mixed Episode, or a Hypomanic Episode, and criteria have never been met for Cyclothymic Disorder.

F. The disturbance does not occur exclusively during the course of a chronic Psychotic Disorder, such as Schizophrenia or Delusional Disorder.

G. The symptoms are not due to the direct physiological effects of a substance (e.g., a drug of abuse, a medication) or a general medical condition (e.g., hypothyroidism).

H. The symptoms cause clinically significant distress or impairment in social, occupational, or other important areas of functioning.

Specify if:

Early Onset: if onset is before age 21 years

Late Onset: if onset is age 21 or older

Source: APA, 2000, 1994

Diagnostic Criteria for Bipolar I Disorder, Single Manic Episode

A. Presence of only one Manic Episode and no past major Depressive Episodes.

Note: Recurrence is defined as either a change in polarity from depression or an interval of at least 2 months without manic symptoms.

B. The Manic Episode is not better accounted for by Schizoaffective Disorder and is not superimposed on Schizophrenia, Schizophreniform Disorder, Delusional Disorder, or Psychotic Disorder Not Otherwise Specified.

Diagnostic Criteria for Bipolar II Disorder

A. Presence (or history) of one or more Major Depressive Episodes.

B. Presence (or history) of at least one Hypomanic Episode.

C. There has never been a Manic Episode or a Mixed Episode.

D. The mood symptoms in criteria A and B are not better accounted for by Schizophrenia, Schizophreniform Disorder, Delusional Disorder, or Psychotic Disorder Not Otherwise Specified.

E. The symptoms cause clinically significant distress or impairment in social, occupational, or other important areas of functioning.

Source: APA, 2000, 1994

Diagnostic Criteria for Cyclothymic Disorder

A. For at least 2 years, the presence of numerous periods with hypomanic symptoms and numerous periods with depressive symptoms that do not meet criteria for a Major Depressive Episode. Note: In children and adolescents, the duration must be at least 1 year.

B. During the above 2-year period (1 year in children and adolescents), the person has not been without the symptoms in Criterion A for more than 2 months at a time.

C. No Major Depressive Episode, Manic Episode, or Mixed Episode has been present during the first 2 years of the disturbance.

D. The symptoms in Criterion A are not better accounted for by Schizoaffective Disorder and are not superimposed on Schizophrenia, Schizophreniform Disorder, or Psychotic Disorder Not Otherwise Specified.

E. The symptoms are not due to the direct physiological effects of a substance (e.g., a drug of abuse, a medication) or a general medical condition (e.g., hyperthyroidism).

F. The symptoms cause clinically significant distress or impairment in social, occupational, or other important areas of functioning.

Source: APA, 2000, 1994

Diagnostic Criteria for Somatization Disorder

A. A history of many physical complaints beginning before age 30 years that occur over a period of several years and result in treatment being sought or significant impairment in social, occupational, or other important areas of functioning.

B. Each of the following criteria must have been met, with individual symptoms occurring at any time during the course of the disturbance.
   (1) Four pain symptoms: a history of pain related to at least four different sites or functions (e.g., head, abdomen, back, joints, extremities, chest, rectum, during menstruation, during sexual intercourse, or during urination)
   (2) Two gastrointestinal symptoms: a history of at least two gastrointestional symptoms other than pain (e.g., nausea, bloating, vomiting other than during pregnancy, diarrhea, or intolerance of several different foods)
   (3) One sexual symptom: a history of at least one sexual or reproductive symptom other than pain (e.g., sexual indifference, erectile or ejaculatory dysfunction, irregular menses, excessive menstrual bleeding, vomiting throughout pregnancy)
   (4) One pseudoneurological symptom: a history of at least one symptom or deficit suggesting a neurological condition not limited to pain (conversion symptoms such as impaired coordination or balance, paralysis or localized weakness, difficulty swallowing or lump in throat, aphonia, urinary retention, hallucinations, loss of touch or pain, double vision, blindness, deafness, seizures; dissociative symptoms such as amnesia; or loss of consciousness other than fainting)

C. Either (1) or (2):
   (1) After appropriate investigation, each of the symptoms in Criterion B cannot be fully explained by a known general medical condition or the direct effects of a substance (e.g., a drug of abuse, a medication)
   (2) When there is a related general medical condition, the physical complaints or resulting social or occupational impairment are in excess of what would be expected from the history, physical examination, or laboratory findings

D. The symptoms are not intentionally produced or feigned (as in Factitious Disorder or Malingering).

Source: APA, 2000, 1994

Diagnostic Criteria for Conversion Disorder

A. One or more symptoms or deficits affecting voluntary motor or sensory function that suggest a neurological or other general medical condition.

B. Psychological factors are judged to be associated with the symptom or deficit because the initiation or exacerbation of the symptom or deficit is preceded by conflicts or other stressors.

C. The symptom or deficit is not intentionally produced or feigned (as in Factitious Disorder or Malingering).

D. The symptom or deficit cannot, after appropriate investigation, be fully explained by a general medical condition, or by the direct effects of a substance, or as a culturally sanctioned behavior or experience.

E. The symptom or deficit causes clinically significant distress or impairment in social, occupational, or other important areas of functioning or warrants medical evaluation.

F. The symptom or deficit is not limited to pain or sexual dysfunction, does not occur exclusively during the course of the Somatization Disorder, and is not better accounted for by another mental disorder.

Source: APA, 2000, 1994

Diagnostic Criteria for Pain Disorder

A. Pain in one or more anatomical sites is the predominant focus of the clinical presentation and is of sufficient severity to warrant clinical attention.

B. The pain causes clinically significant distress or impairment in social, occupational, or other important areas of functioning.

C. Psychological factors are judged to have an important role in the onset, severity, exacerbation, or maintenance of the pain.

D. The symptom or deficit is not intentionally produced or feigned (as in Factitious Disorder or Malingering).

E. The pain is not better accounted for by a Mood, Anxiety, or Psychotic Disorder and does not meet criteria for Dyspareunia.

Diagnostic Criteria for Hypochondriasis

A. Preoccupation with fears of having, or the idea that one has, a serious disease based on the person's misinterpretation of bodily symptoms.

B. The preoccupation persists despite appropriate medical evaluation and reassurance.

C. The belief in Criterion A is not of delusional intensity (as in Delusional Disorder, Somatic Type) and is not restricted to a circumscribed concern about appearance (as in Body Dysmorphic Disorder).

D. The preoccupation causes clinically significant distress or impairment in social, occupational, or other important areas of functioning.

E. The duration of the disturbance is at least 6 months.

F. The preoccupation is not better accounted for by Generalized Anxiety Disorder, Obsessive-Compulsive Disorder, Panic Disorder, a Major Depressive Episode, Separation Anxiety, or another Somatoform Disorder.

Source: APA, 2000, 1994

Diagnostic Criteria for Body Dysmorphic Disorder

A. Preoccupation with an imagined defect in appearance. If a slight physical anomaly is present, the person's concern is markedly excessive.

B. The preoccupation causes clinically significant distress or impairment in social, occupational, or other important areas of functioning.

C. The preoccupation is not better accounted for by another mental disorder (e.g., dissatisfaction with body shape and size in Anorexia Nervosa).

Diagnostic Criteria for Factitious Disorder

A. Intentional production or feigning of physical or psychological signs or symptoms.

B. The motivation for the behavior is to assume a sick role.

C. External incentives for the behavior (such as economic gain, avoiding legal responsibility, or improving physical well-being, as in Malingering) are absent.

Source: APA, 2000, 1994

Diagnostic Criteria for Anorexia Nervosa

A. Refusal to maintain body weight at or above a minimally normal weight for age and height (e.g., weight loss leading to maintenance of body weight less than 85% of that expected; or failure to make expected weight gain during period of growth, leading to body weight less than 85% of that expected).

B. Intense fear of gaining weight or becoming fat, even though underweight.

C. Disturbance in the way in which one's body weight or shape is experienced, undue influence of body weight or shape on self-evaluation, or denial of the seriousness of the current low body weight.

D. In postmenarcheal females, amenorrhea, i.e., the absence of at least three consecutive menstrual cycles. (A woman is considered to have amenorrhea if her periods occur only following hormone administration, e.g., estrogen.)

Specify type:

Restricting Type: during the current episode of Anorexia Nervosa, the person has not regularly engaged in binge-eating or purging behavior (i.e., self-induced vomiting or the misuse of laxatives, diuretics, or enemas)

Binge-Eating/Purging Type: during the current episode of Anorexia Nervosa, the person has regularly engaged in binge-eating or purging behavior (i.e., self-induced vomiting or the misuse of laxatives, diuretics, or enemas)

Source: APA, 2000, 1994

Diagnostic Criteria for Bulimia Nervosa

A. Recurrent episodes of binge-eating. An episode of binge eating is characterized by both of the following:
   (1) Eating, in a discrete period of time (e.g., within any 2-hour period), an amount of food that is definitely larger than most people would eat during that similar period of time under similar circumstances
   (2) A sense of lack of control over eating during the episode (e.g., a feeling that one cannot stop eating or control what or how much one is eating)

B. Recurrent inappropriate compensatory behavior in order to prevent weight gain, such as self-induced vomiting; misuse of laxatives, diuretics, enemas, or other medications; fasting; or excessive exercise.

C. The binge eating and inappropriate compensatory behavior both occur, on average, at least twice a week for 3 months.

D. Self-evaluation is unduly influenced by body shape and weight.

E. The disturbance does not occur exclusively during episodes of Anorexia Nervosa.

Specify type:

Purging Type: during the current episode of Bulimia Nervosa, the person has regularly engaged in self-induced vomiting or the misuse of laxatives, diuretics, or enemas.

Nonpurging Type: during the current episode of Bulimia Nervosa, the person has used other inappropriate compensatory behaviors, such as fasting or excessive exercise, but has not regularly engaged in self-induced vomiting or the misuse of laxatives, diuretics, or enemas.

Source: APA, 2000, 1994

Criteria for Substance Dependence

A maladaptive pattern of substance use, leading to clinically significant impairment or distress, as manifested by three (or more) of the following, occurring at any time in the same 12-month period:

(1) tolerance as defined by either of the following:
   (a) a need for markedly increased amounts of the substance to achieve intoxication or desired effect
   (b) markedly diminished effect with continued use of the same amount of the substance
(2) withdrawal, as manifested by either of the following:
   (a) the characteristic withdrawal syndrome for the substance (refer to Criteria A and B of the criteria sets for Withdrawal from the specific substances)
   (b) the same (or a closely related) substance is taken to relieve or avoid withdrawal symptoms
(3) the substance is often taken in larger amounts or over a longer period than was intended
(4) there is a persistent desire or unsuccessful effort to cut down or control substance use
(5) a great deal of time is spent in activities necessary to obtain the substance (e.g., visiting multiple doctors or driving long distances), use the substance (e.g., chainsmoking), or recover from its effects
(6) important social, occupational, or recreational activities are given up or reduced because of substance use
(7) the substance use is continued despite knowledge of having a persistent or recurrent physical or psychological problem that is likely to be exacerbated by the substance (e.g., current cocaine use despite recognition of cocaine-induced depression, or continued drinking despite recognition that an ulcer was made worse by alcohol consumption)

Source: APA, 2000, 1994

Criteria for Substance Abuse

A. A maladaptive pattern of substance use leading to clinically significant impairment or distress, as manifested by one (or more) of the following, occurring within a 12-month period:
   (1) recurring substance use resulting in failure to fulfill major role obligations at work, school, or home (e.g., repeated absences or poor work performance related to substance use; substance-related absences, suspensions, or expulsions from school; neglect of children or household
   (2) recurrent substance use in situations in which it is physically hazardous (e.g., driving an automobile or operating a machine when impaired by substance use)
   (3) recurrent substance-related legal problems (e.g., arrests for substance-related disorderly conduct)
   (4) continued substance use despite having persistent or recurrent social or interpersonal problems caused or exacerbated by the effects of the substance (e.g., arguments with spouse about consequences of intoxication, physical fights)

B. The symptoms have never met the criteria for Substance Dependence for this class of substance.

Source: APA, 2000, 1994

Diagnostic Criteria for Hypoactive Sexual Desire Disorder

A. Persistently or recurrently deficient (or absent) sexual fantasies and desire for sexual activity. The judgment of deficiency or absence is made by the clinician, taking into account the factors that affect sexual functioning, such as age and the context of the person's life.

B. The disturbance causes marked distress or interpersonal difficulty.

C. The sexual dysfunction is not better accounted for by another Axis I disorder (except another Sexual Dysfunction) and is not due exclusively to the direct physiological effects of a substance (e.g., a drug of abuse, a medication) or a general medical condition.

Diagnostic Criteria for Sexual Aversion Disorder

A. Persistent or recurrent extreme aversion to, and avoidance of, all (or almost all) genital sexual contact with a sexual partner.

B. The disturbance causes marked distress or interpersonal difficulty.

C. The sexual dysfunction is not better accounted for by another Axis I disorder (except another Sexual Dysfunction).

Source: APA, 2000, 1994

Diagnostic Criteria for Female Sexual Arousal Disorder

A. Persistent or recurrent inability to attain, or to maintain until completion of the sexual activity, an adequate lubrication-swelling response to sexual excitement.

B. The disturbance causes marked distress or interpersonal difficulty.

C. The sexual dysfunction is not better accounted for by another Axis I disorder (except another Sexual Dysfunction) and is not due exclusively to the direct physiological effects of a substance (e.g., a drug of abuse, a medication) or a general medical condition.

Diagnostic Criteria for Male Erectile Disorder

A. Persistent or recurrent inability to attain, or to maintain until completion of the sexual activity, an adequate erection.

B. The disturbance causes marked distress or interpersonal difficulty.

C. The erectile dysfunction is not better accounted for by another Axis I disorder (other than a Sexual Dysfunction) and is not due exclusively to the direct physiological effects of a substance (e.g., a drug of abuse, a medication) or a general medical condition.

Source: APA, 2000, 1994

Diagnostic Criteria for Female Orgasmic Disorder

A. The persistent or recurrent delay in, or absence of, orgasm following a normal sexual excitement phase. Women exhibit wide variability in the type or intensity of stimulation that triggers orgasm. The diagnosis of Female Orgasmic Disorder should be based on the clinician's judgment that the woman's orgasmic capacity is less than would be reasonable for her age, sexual experience, and the adequacy of stimulation she receives.

B. The disturbance causes marked distress or interpersonal difficulty.

C. The orgasmic dysfunction is not better accounted for by another Axis I disorder (except another Sexual Dysfunction) and is not due exclusively to the direct physiological effects of a substance (e.g., a drug of abuse, a medication) or a general medical condition.

Diagnostic Criteria for Male Orgasmic Disorder

A. Persistent or recurrent delay in, or absence of, orgasm following a normal sexual excitement phase during sexual activity that the clinician, taking into account the person's age, judges to be adequate in focus, intensity, and duration.

B. The disturbance causes marked distress or interpersonal difficulty.

C. The orgasmic dysfunction is not better accounted for by another Axis I disorder (except another Sexual Dysfunction) and is not due exclusively to the direct physiological effects of a substance (e.g., a drug of abuse, a medication) or a general medical condition.

Source: APA, 2000, 1994

Diagnostic Criteria for Premature Ejaculation

A. Persistent or recurrent ejaculation with minimal sexual stimulation before, on, or shortly after penetration and before the person wishes it. The clinician must take into account factors that affect duration of the excitement phase, such as age, novelty of sexual partner or situation, and recent frequency of sexual activity.

B. The disturbance causes marked distress or interpersonal difficulty.

C. The premature ejaculation is not due exclusively to the direct effects of a substance (e.g., withdrawal from opioids).

Diagnostic Criteria for Dyspareunia

A. Recurrent or persistent genital pain associated with sexual intercourse in either a male or a female.

B. The disturbance causes marked distress or interpersonal difficulty.

C. The disturbance is not caused exclusively by Vaginismus or lack of lubrication, is not better accounted for by another Axis I disorder (except another Sexual Dysfunction), and is not due exclusively to the direct physiological effects of a substance (e.g., a drug of abuse, a medication) or a general medical condition.

Diagnostic Criteria for Vaginismus

A. Recurrent or persistent involuntary spasm of the musculature of the outer third of the vagina that interferes with sexual intercourse.

B. The disturbance causes marked distress or interpersonal difficulty.

C. The disturbance is not better accounted for by another Axis I disorder (e.g., Somatization Disorder) and is not due exclusively to the direct physiological effects of a general medical condition.

Source: APA, 2000, 1994

Diagnostic Criteria for Exhibitionism

A. Over a period of at least 6 months, recurrent, intense sexually arousing fantasies, sexual urges, or behaviors involving the exposure of one's genitals to an unsuspecting stranger.

B. The person has acted on these sexual urges, or the sexual urges or fantasies cause marked distress or interpersonal difficulty.

Diagnostic Criteria for Fetishism

A. Over a period of at least 6 months, recurrent, intense sexually arousing fantasies, sexual urges, or behaviors involving the use of nonliving objects (e.g., female undergarments).

B. The person has acted on these sexual urges, or the sexual urges or fantasies cause marked distress or interpersonal difficulty.

C. The fetish objects are not limited to articles of female clothing used in cross-dressing (as in Transvestic Fetishism) or devices designed for the purpose of tactile genital stimulation (e.g., a vibrator).

Diagnostic Criteria for Frotteurism

A. Over a period of at least 6 months, recurrent, intense sexually arousing fantasies, sexual urges, or behaviors involving touching and rubbing against a nonconsenting person.

B. The person has acted on these sexual urges, or the sexual urges or fantasies cause marked distress or interpersonal difficulty.

Diagnostic Criteria for Pedophilia

A. Over a period of at least 6 months, recurrent, intense sexually arousing fantasies, sexual urges, or behaviors involving sexual activity with a prepubescent child or children (generally age 13 years or younger).

B. The person has acted on these sexual urges, or the sexual urges or fantasies cause marked distress or interpersonal difficulty.

C. The person is at least 16 years and at least 5 years older than the child or children in Criterion A.

Note: Do not include an individual in late adolescence involved in an ongoing sexual relationship with a 12- or 13-year-old.

Source: APA, 2000, 1994

Diagnostic Criteria for Sexual Masochism

A. Over a period of at least 6 months, recurrent, intense sexually arousing fantasies, sexual urges, or behaviors involving the act (real, not simulated) of being humiliated, beaten, bound, or otherwise made to suffer.

B. The person has acted on these sexual urges, or the sexual urges or fantasies cause marked distress or interpersonal difficulty.

Diagnostic Criteria for Sexual Sadism

A. Over a period of at least 6 months, recurrent, intense sexually arousing fantasies, sexual urges, or behaviors involving acts (real, not simulated) in which the psychological or physical suffering (including humiliation) of the victim is sexually exciting to the person.

B. The person has acted on these sexual urges with a non-consenting person, or the sexual urges or fantasies cause marked distress or interpersonal difficulty.

Diagnostic Criteria for Transvestic Fetishism

A. Over a period of at least 6 months, in a heterosexual male, recurrent, intense sexually arousing fantasies, sexual urges, or behaviors involving cross-dressing.

B. The person has acted on these sexual urges, or the sexual urges or fantasies cause marked distress or interpersonal difficulty.

Diagnostic Criteria for Voyeurism

A. Over a period of at least 6 months, recurrent, intense sexually arousing fantasies, sexual urges, or behaviors involving the act of observing an unsuspecting person who is naked, in the process of disrobing, or engaging in sexual activity.

B. The person has acted on these sexual urges, or the sexual urges or fantasies cause marked distress or interpersonal difficulty.

Source: APA, 2000, 1994

Diagnostic Criteria for Gender Identity Disorder

A. A strong and persistent cross-gender identification (not merely a desire for any perceived cultural advantages of being the other sex).

In children, the disturbance is manifested by four (or more) of the following:

(1) repeatedly stated desire to be, or insistence that he or she is, the other sex
(2) in boys, preference for cross-dressing or simulating female attire; in girls, insistence on wearing only stereotypical masculine clothing
(3) strong and persistent preferences for cross-sex roles in make-believe play or persistent fantasies about being the other sex
(4) intense desire to participate in the stereotypical games and pastimes of the other sex
(5) strong preference for playmates of other sex

In adolescents and adults, the disturbance is manifested by symptoms such as a stated desire to be the other sex, frequent passing as the other sex, desire to live and be treated as the other sex, or the conviction that he or she has the typical feelings and reactions of the other sex.

B. Persistent discomfort with his or her sex or sense of inappropriateness in the gender role of that sex.

In children, the disturbance is manifested by any of the following: in boys, assertion that his penis or testes are disgusting or will disappear or assertion that it would be better not to have a penis, or aversion toward rough-and-tumble play and rejection of male stereotypical toys, games, and activities; in girls, rejection of urinating in a sitting position, assertion that she has or will grow a penis, or assertion that she does not want to grow breasts or menstruate, or marked aversion toward normative feminine clothing.

In adolescents and adults, the disturbance is manifested by symptoms such as preoccupation with getting rid of primary and secondary sex characteristics (e.g., request for hormones, surgery, or other procedures to physically alter sexual characteristics that simulate the other sex), or belief that he or she was born the wrong sex.

C. The disturbance is not concurrent with a physical intersex condition.

D. The disturbance causes clinically significant distress or impairment in social, occupational, or other important areas of functioning.

Source: APA, 2000, 1994

Diagnostic Criteria for Schizophrenia

A. Characteristic symptoms: Two (or more) of the following, each present for a significant portion of time during a 1-month period (or less if successfully treated):
   (1) delusions
   (2) hallucinations
   (3) disorganized speech (e.g., frequent derailment or incoherence)
   (4) grossly disorganized or catatonic behavior
   (5) negative symptoms i.e., affective flattening, alogia, or avolition

   Note: Only one Criterion A symptom is required if delusions are bizarre or hallucinations consist of a voice keeping up a running commentary on the person's behavior or thoughts, or two or more voices conversing with each other.

B. Social/occupational dysfunction: For a significant portion of the time since the onset of the disturbance, one or more major areas of functioning such as work, interpersonal relations, or self-care are markedly below the level achieved prior to the onset (or when the onset is in childhood or adolescence, failure to achieve expected level of interpersonal, academic, or occupational achievement).

C. Duration: Continuous signs of the disturbance persist for at least 6 months. This 6-month period must include at least 1 month of symptoms (or less if successfully treated) that meet Criteria A (i.e., active-phase symptoms) and may include periods of prodromal or residual symptoms. During these prodromal or residual periods, the signs of the disturbance may be manifested by only negative symptoms or two or more symptoms listed in Criteria A present in an attenuated form (e.g., odd beliefs, unusual perceptual experiences).

D. Schizoaffective and Mood Disorder exclusion: Schizoaffective Disorder and Mood Disorder With Psychotic Features have been ruled out because either (1) no Major Depressive, Manic, or Mixed Episodes have occurred concurrently with active-phase symptoms; or (2) if mood episodes have occurred during active-phase symptoms, their total duration has been brief relative to the duration of the active and residual periods.

E. Substance/general medical condition exclusion: The disturbance is not due to the direct physiological effects of a substance (e.g., a drug of abuse, a medication) or a general medical condition.

F. Relationship to a Pervasive Developmental Disorder: If there is history of Autistic Disorder or another Pervasive Developmental Disorder, the additional diagnosis of Schizophrenia is made only if prominent delusions or hallucinations are also present for at least a month (or less if successfully treated).

Source: APA, 2000, 1994

Diagnostic Criteria for Paranoid Type

A type of Schizophrenia in which the following criteria are met:

A. Preoccupation with one or more delusions or frequent auditory hallucinations.

B. None of the following is prominent: disorganized speech, disorganized or catatonic behavior, or flat or inappropriate affect.

Diagnostic Criteria for Disorganized Type

A type of Schizophrenia in which the following criteria are met:

A. All of the following are prominent:
   (1) disorganized speech
   (2) disorganized behavior
   (3) flat or inappropriate affect

B. The criteria are not met for Catatonic Type.

Diagnostic Criteria for Catatonic Type

A type of Schizophrenia in which the following criteria are met:

(1) motoric immobility as evidenced by catalepsy (including waxy flexibility) or stupor
(2) excessive motor activity (that is apparently purposeless and not influenced by external stimuli)
(3) extreme negativism (an apparently motiveless resistance to all instructions, or maintenance of a rigid posture against attempts to be moved) or mutism
(4) peculiarities of voluntary movement as evidenced by posturing (voluntary assumption of inappropriate or bizarre postures), stereotyped movements, prominent mannerisms, or prominent grimacing
(5) echolalia or echopraxia

Source: APA, 2000, 1994

Diagnostic Criteria for Undifferentiated Type

A type of Schizophrenia in which symptoms that meet Criterion A are present, but the crit ria are not met for the Paranoid, Disorganized, or Catatonic Type.

Diagnostic Criteria for Residual Type

A type of Schizophrenia in which the following criteria are met:

A. Absence of prominent delusions, hallucinations, disorganized speech, and grossly di organized or catatonic behavior.

B. There is continuing evidence of the disturbance, as indicated by the presence of neg tive symptoms or two or more symptoms listed in Criterion A for Schizophrenia, pr sent in an attenuated form (e.g., odd beliefs, unusual perceptual experiences).

Source: APA, 2000, 1994

Diagnostic Criteria for Schizoaffective Disorder

A. An uninterrupted period of illness during which, at some time, there is either a Major Depressive Episode, a Manic Episode, or a Mixed Episode concurrent with symptoms that meet Criterion A for Schizophrenia.

Note: The Major Depressive Episode must include Criterion A1: depressed mood.

B. During the same period of illness, there have been delusions or hallucinations for at least two weeks in the absence of prominent mood symptoms.

C. Symptoms that meet criteria for a mood episode are present for a substantial portion of the total duration of the active and residual periods of the illness.

D. The disturbance is not due to the direct physiological effects of a substance (e.g., a drug of abuse, a medication) or a general medical condition.

Source: APA, 2000, 1994

Diagnostic Criteria for Delusional Disorder

A. Nonbizarre delusions (i.e., involving situations that occur in real life, such as being followed, poisoned, infected, loved at a distance, or deceived by spouse or lover, or having a disease) of at least 1 month's duration.

B. Criterion A for Schizophrenia has never been met. Note: Tactile and olfactory hallucinations may be present in Delusional Disorder if they are related to the delusional theme.

C. Apart from the impact of the delusion(s) or its ramifications, functioning is not markedly impaired and behavior is not obviously odd or bizarre.

D. If mood episodes have occurred concurrently with delusions, their total duration has been brief relative to the duration of the delusional periods.

E. The disturbance is not due to the direct physiological effects of a substance (e.g., a drug of abuse, a medication) or a general medical condition.

Specify type (the following types are assigned based on the predominant delusional theme):

Erotomanic Type: delusions that another person, usually of higher status, is in love with the individual.

Grandiose Type: delusions of inflated worth, power, knowledge, identity, or special relationship to a deity or famous person.

Jealous Type: delusions that the individual's sexual partner is unfaithful

Persecutory Type: delusions that the person (or someone to whom the person is close) is being malevolently treated in some way.

Somatic Type: delusions that the person has some physical defect or general medical condition

Mixed Type: delusions characteristic of more than one of the above types but no one theme predominates

Unspecified Type

Source: APA, 2000, 1994

Diagnostic Criteria for Dementia Due to Other General Medical Conditions

A. The development of multiple cognitive deficits manifested by both
   (1) memory impairment (impaired ability to learn new information or to recall previously learned information)
   (2) one (or more) of the following cognitive disturbances:
      (a) aphasia (language disturbance)
      (b) apraxia (impaired ability to carry out motor activities despite intact motor function)
      (c) agnosia (failure to recognize or identify objects despite intact sensory function)
      (d) disturbance in executive functioning (i.e., planning, organizing, sequencing, abstracting)

B. The cognitive deficits in Criteria A1 and A2 each cause significant impairment in social or occupational functioning and represent a significant decline from a previous level of functioning.

C. There is evidence from the history, physical examination, or laboratory findings that the disturbance is the direct physiological consequence of one of the general medical conditions listed below.

D. The deficits do not occur exclusively during the course of a delirium.

Code based on presence or absence of a clinically significant behavioral disturbance:

Without Behavioral Disturbance: if the cognitive disturbance is not accompanied by any clinically significant behavioral disturbance.

With Behavioral Disturbance: if the cognitive disturbance is accompanied by a clinically significant behavioral disturbance (e.g., wandering, agitation).

Also code the general medical condition on Axis III (e.g., HIV infection, head injury, Parkinson's disease, Huntington's disease, Pick's disease, Creutzfeldt-Jakob disease)

Source: APA, 2000, 1994

Diagnostic Criteria for Dissociative Amnesia

A. The predominant disturbance is one or more episodes of inability to recall important personal information, usually of a traumatic or stressful nature, that is too extensive to be explained by ordinary forgetfulness.

B. The disturbance does not occur exclusively during the course of Dissociative Identity Disorder, Dissociative Fugue, Posttraumatic Stress Disorder, Acute Stress Disorder, or Somatization Disorder and is not due to the direct physiological effects of a substance (e.g., a drug of abuse, a medication) or a neurological or other general medical condition (e.g., Amnestic Disorder Due to Head Trauma).

C. The symptoms cause clinically significant distress or impairment in social, occupational, or other important areas of functioning.

Diagnostic Criteria for Dissociative Fugue

A. The predominant disturbance is sudden, unexpected travel away from home or one's customary place of work, with inability to recall one's past.

B. Confusion about personal identity or assumption of a new identity (partial or complete).

C. The disturbance does not occur exclusively during the course of Dissociative Identity Disorder and is not due to the direct physiological effects of a substance (e.g., a drug of abuse, a medication) or a general medical condition (e.g., temporal lobe epilepsy).

D. The symptoms cause clinically significant distress or impairment in social, occupational, or other important areas of functioning.

Source: APA, 2000, 1994

Diagnostic Criteria for Dissociative Identity Disorder

A. The presence of two or more distinct identities or personality states (each with its own relatively enduring pattern of perceiving, relating to, and thinking about the environment and self).

B. At least two of these identities or personality states recurrently take control of the person's behavior.

C. Inability to recall important personal information that is too extensive to be explained by ordinary forgetfulness.

D. The disturbance is not due to the direct physiological effects of a substance (e.g., blackouts or chaotic behavior during Alcohol Intoxication) or a general medical condition (e.g., complex partial seizures).

Diagnostic Criteria for Depersonalization Disorder

A. Persistent or recurrent experiences of feeling detached from, and as if one is an outside observer of, one's mental processes or body (e.g., feeling like one is in a dream).

B. During the depersonalization experience, reality testing remains intact.

C. The depersonalization causes clinically significant distress or impairment in social, occupational, or other important areas of functioning.

D. The depersonalization experience does not occur exclusively during the course of another mental disorder, such as Schizophrenia, Panic Disorder, Acute Stress Disorder, or another Dissociative Disorder, and is not due to the direct physiological effects of a substance (e.g., a drug of abuse, a medication) or a general medical condition (e.g., temporal lobe epilepsy).

Source: APA, 2000, 1994

General Diagnostic Criteria for a Personality Disorder

A. An enduring pattern of inner experience and behavior that deviates markedly from th expectations of the individual's culture. This pattern is manifested in two (or more) c the following areas:

 (1) cognition (i.e., ways of perceiving and interpreting self, other people, and events)
 (2) affectivity (i.e., the range, intensity, ability, and appropriateness of emotional re sponse)
 (3) interpersonal functioning
 (4) impulse control

B. The enduring pattern is inflexible and pervasive across a broad range of personal an social situations.

C. The enduring pattern leads to clinically significant distress or impairment in social, oc cupational, or other important areas of functioning.

D. The pattern is stable and of long duration and its onset can be traced back at least t adolescence or early childhood.

E. The enduring pattern is not better accounted for as a manifestation or consequence c another mental disorder.

F. The enduring pattern is not due to the direct physiological effects of a substance (e.g., drug of abuse, a medication) or a general medical condition (e.g., head trauma).

Source: APA, 2000, 1994

Diagnostic Criteria for Paranoid Personality Disorder

A. A pervasive distrust and suspiciousness of others such that their motives are interpreted as malevolent, beginning by early adulthood and present in a variety of contexts, as indicated by four (or more) of the following:
   (1) suspects, without sufficient basis, that others are exploiting, harming, or deceiving him or her
   (2) is preoccupied with unjustified doubts about the loyalty or trustworthiness of friends or associates
   (3) is reluctant to confide in others because of unwarranted fear that the information will be used maliciously against him or her
   (4) reads hidden, demeaning, or threatening meanings into benign remarks or events
   (5) persistently bears grudges, i.e., is unforgiving of insults, injuries, or slights
   (6) perceives attacks on his or her character or reputation that are not apparent to others and is quick to react angrily or to counterattack
   (7) has recurrent suspicions, without justification, regarding fidelity of spouse or sexual partner

B. Does not occur exclusively during the course of Schizophrenia, a Mood Disorder With Psychotic Features, or another Psychotic Disorder and is not due to the direct physiological effects of a general medical condition.

Diagnostic Criteria for Schizoid Personality Disorder

A. A pervasive pattern of detachment from social relationships and a restricted range of expression of emotions in interpersonal settings, beginning in early adulthood and present in a variety of contexts, as indicated by four (or more) of the following:
   (1) neither desires nor enjoys close relationships, including being part of a family
   (2) almost always chooses solitary activities
   (3) has little, if any, interest in having sexual experiences with another person
   (4) takes pleasure in few, if any, activities
   (5) lacks close friends or confidants other than first-degree relatives
   (6) appears indifferent to the praise or criticism of others
   (7) shows emotional coldness, detachment, or flattened affectivity

B. Does not occur exclusively during the course of Schizophrenia, a Mood Disorder With Psychotic Features, another Psychotic Disorder, or a Pervasive Developmental Disorder and is not due to the direct physiological effects of a general medical condition.

Source: APA, 2000, 1994

Diagnostic Criteria for Schizotypal Personality Disorder

A. A pervasive pattern of social and interpersonal deficits marked by acute discomfort with, and reduced capacity for, close relationships as well as by cognitive or perceptual distortions and eccentricities of behavior, beginning by early adulthood and present in a variety of contexts, as indicated by five (or more) of the following:
  (1) ideas of reference (excluding delusions of reference)
  (2) odd beliefs or magical thinking that influences behavior and is inconsistent with subcultural norms (e.g., superstitiousness, belief in clairvoyance, telepathy, or "sixth sense"; in children and adolescents, bizarre fantasies or preoccupations)
  (3) unusual perceptual experiences, including bodily illusions
  (4) odd thinking and speech (e.g., vague, circumstantial, metaphorical, overelaborate, or stereotyped)
  (5) suspiciousness or paranoid ideation
  (6) inappropriate or constricted affect
  (7) behavior or appearances that is odd, eccentric, or peculiar
  (8) lack of close friends or confidants other than first-degree relatives
  (9) excessive social anxiety that does not diminish with familiarity and tends to be associated with paranoid fears rather than negative judgments about self

B. Does not occur exclusively during the course of Schizophrenia, a Mood Disorder With Psychotic Features, another Psychotic Disorder, or a Pervasive Developmental Disorder.

Source: APA, 2000, 1994

Diagnostic Criteria for Antisocial Personality Disorder

A. There is a pervasive pattern of disregard for and violation of the rights of others occurring since age 15 years, as indicated by three (or more) of the following:
   (1) failure to conform to social norms with respect to lawful behaviors as indicated by repeatedly performing acts that are grounds for arrest
   (2) deceitfulness, as indicated by repeated lying, use of aliases, or conning others for personal profit or pleasure
   (3) impulsivity or failure to plan ahead
   (4) irritability and aggressiveness, as indicated by repeated physical fights or assaults
   (5) reckless disregard for safety of self or others
   (6) consistent irresponsibility, as indicated by repeated failure to sustain consistent work behavior or honor financial obligations
   (7) lack of remorse, as indicated by being indifferent to or rationalizing having hurt, mistreated, or stolen from another

B. The individual is at least age 18 years.

C. There is evidence of Conduct Disorder with onset before age 15 years.

D. The occurrence of antisocial behavior is not exclusively during the course of Schizophrenia or a Manic Episode.

Diagnostic Criteria for Borderline Personality Disorder

A pervasive pattern of instability of interpersonal relationships, self-image, and affects, and marked impulsivity beginning by early adulthood and present in a variety of contexts, as indicated by five (or more) of the following:

(1) frantic efforts to avoid real or imagined abandonment. Note: Do not include suicidal or self-mutilating behavior covered in Criterion 5.
(2) a pattern of unstable and intense interpersonal relationships characterized by alternating between extremes of idealization and devaluation
(3) identity disturbance: markedly and persistently unstable self-image or sense of self
(4) impulsivity in at least two areas that are potentially self-damaging (e.g., spending, sex, substance abuse, reckless driving, binge eating). Note: Do not include suicidal or self-mutilating behavior covered in Criterion 5.
(5) recurrent suicidal behavior, gestures, or threats, or self-mutilating behavior
(6) affective instability due to a marked reactivity of mood (e.g., intense episodic dysphoria, irritability, or anxiety usually lasting a few hours and only rarely more than a few days)
(7) chronic feelings of emptiness
(8) inappropriate, intense anger or difficulty controlling anger (e.g., frequent displays of temper, constant anger, recurrent physical fights)
(9) transient, stress-related paranoid ideation or severe dissociative symptoms

Source: APA, 2000, 1994

Diagnostic Criteria for Histrionic Personality Disorder

A pervasive pattern of excessive emotionality and attention seeking, beginning by early adulthood and present in a variety of contexts, as indicated by five (or more) of the following:

(1) is uncomfortable in situations in which he or she is not the center of attention
(2) interaction with others often characterized by inappropriate sexually seductive or provocative behavior
(3) displays rapidly shifting and shallow expression of emotions
(4) consistently uses physical appearance to draw attention to self
(5) has a style of speech that is excessively impressionistic and lacking in detail
(6) shows self-dramatization, theatricality, and exaggerated expression of emotion
(7) is suggestible, i.e., easily influenced by others or circumstances
(8) considers relationships to be more intimate than they actually are

Diagnostic Criteria for Narcissistic Personality Disorder

A pervasive pattern of grandiosity (in fantasy or behavior), need for admiration, and lack of empathy, beginning by early adulthood and present in a variety of contexts, as indicated by five (or more) of the following:

(1) has a grandiose sense of self-importance (e.g., exaggerates achievements and talents, expects to be recognized as superior without commensurate achievements)
(2) is preoccupied with fantasies of unlimited success, power, brilliance, beauty, or ideal love
(3) believes that he or she is "special" and unique and can only be understood by, or should associate with, other special or high-status people (or institutions)
(4) requires excessive admiration
(5) has a sense of entitlement, i.e., unreasonable expectations of especially favorable treatment or automatic compliance with his or her expectations
(6) is interpersonally exploitative, i.e., takes advantage of others to achieve his or her own ends
(7) lacks empathy: is unwilling to recognize or identify with the feelings and needs of others
(8) is often envious of others or believes that others are envious of him or her
(9) shows arrogant, haughty behaviors or attitudes

Source: APA, 2000, 1994

Diagnostic Criteria for Avoidant Personality Disorder

A pervasive pattern of social inhibition, feelings of inadequacy, and hypersensitivity to negative evaluation, beginning by early adulthood and present in a variety of contexts, as indicated by four (or more) of the following:

(1) avoids occupational activities that involve significant interpersonal contact, because of fears of criticism, disapproval, or rejection
(2) is unwilling to get involved with people unless certain of being liked
(3) shows restraint within intimate relationships because of the fear of being shamed or ridiculed
(4) is preoccupied with being criticized or rejected in social situations
(5) is inhibited in new interpersonal situations because of feelings of inadequacy
(6) views self as socially inept, personally unappealing, or inferior to others
(7) is unusually reluctant to take personal risks or to engage in any new activities because they may prove embarrassing

Diagnostic Criteria for Dependent Personality Disorder

A pervasive and excessive need to be taken care of that leads to submissive and clinging behavior and fears of separation, beginning by early adulthood and present in a variety of contexts, as indicated by five (or more) of the following:

(1) has difficulty making everyday decisions without an excessive amount of advice and reassurance from others
(2) needs others to assume responsibility for most major areas of his or her life
(3) has difficulty expressing disagreement with others because of fear of loss of support or approval. Note: Do not include realistic fears of retribution.
(4) has difficulty initiating projects or doing things on his or her own (because of lack of self-confidence in judgment or abilities rather than a lack of motivation or energy)
(5) goes to excessive lengths to obtain nurturance and support from others, to the point of volunteering to do things that are unpleasant
(6) feels uncomfortable or helpless when alone because of exaggerated fears of being unable to care for himself or herself
(7) urgently seeks another relationship as a source of care and support when a close relationship ends
(8) is unrealistically preoccupied with fears of being left to take care of himself or herself

Source: APA, 2000, 1994

Diagnostic Criteria for Obsessive-Compulsive Personality Disorder

A pervasive pattern of preoccupation with orderliness, perfectionism, and mental and interpersonal control, at the expense of flexibility, openness, and efficiency, beginning by early adulthood and present in a variety of contexts, as indicated by four (or more) of the following:

(1) is preoccupied with details, rules, lists, order, organization, or schedules to the extent that the major point of the activity is lost
(2) shows perfectionism that interferes with task completion (e.g., is unable to complete a project because his or her own overly strict standards are not met)
(3) is excessively devoted to work and productivity to the exclusion of leisure activities and friendships (not accounted for by obvious economic necessity)
(4) is overly conscientious, scrupulous, and inflexible about matters of morality, ethics, or values (not accounted for by cultural or religious identification)
(5) is unable to discard worn-out or worthless objects even when they have no sentimental value
(6) is reluctant to delegate tasks or to work with others unless they submit to exactly his or her way of doing things
(7) adopts a miserly spending style toward both self and others; money is viewed as something to be hoarded for future catastrophes
(8) shows rigidity and stubbornness

Source: APA, 2000, 1994

Diagnostic Criteria for Mental Retardation

A. Significantly subaverage intellectual functioning: an IQ of approximately 70 or below on an individually administered IQ test (for infants, a clinical judgment of significantly subaverage intellectual functioning).

B. Concurrent deficits or impairments in present adaptive functioning (i.e., the person's effectiveness in meeting the standards expected for his or her age by his or her cultural group) in at least two of the following areas: communication, self-care, home living, social/interpersonal skills, use of community resources, self-direction, functional academic skills, work, leisure, health, and safety.

C. The onset is before age 18 years.

Code based on degree of severity reflecting level of intellectual impairment:

Mild Mental Retardation:	IQ level 50–55 to approximately 70
Moderate Mental Retardation:	IQ level 35–40 to 50–55
Severe Mental Retardation:	IQ level 20–25 to 35–40
Profound Mental Retardation:	IQ level below 20 or 25

Source: APA, 2000, 1994

Diagnostic Criteria for Reading Disorder

A. Reading achievement, as measured by individually administered standardized tests of reading accuracy or comprehension, is substantially below that expected given the person's chronological age, measured intelligence, and age-appropriate education.

B. The disturbance in Criterion A significantly interferes with academic achievement or activities of daily living that require reading skills.

C. If a sensory deficit is present, the reading difficulties are in excess of those usually associated with it.

Diagnostic Criteria for Mathematics Disorder

A. Mathematical ability, as measured by individually administered standardized tests, is substantially below that expected given the person's chronological age, measured intelligence, and age-appropriate education.

B. The disturbance in Criterion A significantly interferes with academic achievement or activities of daily living that require mathematical ability.

C. If a sensory deficit is present, the difficulties in mathematical ability are in excess of those usually associated with it.

Diagnostic Criteria for Disorder of Written Expression

A. Writing skills, as measured by individually administered standardized tests (or functional assessments of writing skills), are substantially below those expected given the person's chronological age, measured intelligence, and age-appropriate education.

B. The disturbance in Criterion A significantly interferes with academic achievement or activities of daily living that require the composition of written texts (e.g., writing grammatically correct sentences and organized paragraphs).

C. If a sensory deficit is present, the difficulties with writing skills are in excess of those usually associated with it.

Source: APA, 2000, 1994

Diagnostic Criteria for Developmental Coordination Disorder

A. Performance in daily activities that require motor coordination is substantially below that expected given the person's chronological age and measured intelligence. This may be manifested by marked delays in achieving motor milestones (e.g., walking, crawling, sitting), dropping things, "clumsiness," poor performances in sports, or poor handwriting.

B. The disturbance in Criterion A significantly interferes with academic achievement or activities of daily living.

C. The disturbance is not due to a general medical condition (e.g., cerebral palsy, hemiplegia, or muscular dystrophy) and does not meet criteria for a Pervasive Developmental Disorder.

D. If Mental Retardation is present, the motor difficulties are in excess of those usually associated with it.

Diagnostic Criteria for Expressive Language Disorder

A. The scores obtained from standardized individually administered measures of expressive language development are substantially below those obtained from standardized measures of both nonverbal intellectual capacity and receptive language development. The disturbance may be manifest clinically by symptoms that include having a markedly limited vocabulary, making errors in tense, or having difficulty in recalling words or producing sentences with developmentally appropriate length or complexity.

B. The difficulties with expressive language interfere with academic or occupational achievement or with social communication.

C. Criteria are not met for Mixed-Receptive-Expressive Language Disorder or a Pervasive Developmental Disorder.

D. If Mental Retardation, a speech-motor or sensory deficit, or environmental deprivation is present, the language difficulties are in excess of those usually associated with these problems.

Source: APA, 2000, 1994

Diagnostic Criteria for Autistic Disorder

A. A total of six (or more) items from (1), (2), and (3), with at least two from (1), and one each from (2) and (3):
   (1) qualitative impairment in social interaction, as manifested by at least two of the following:
      (a) marked impairment in the use of multiple nonverbal behaviors such as eye-to-eye gaze, facial expression, body postures, and gestures to regulate social interaction
      (b) failure to develop peer relationships appropriate to developmental level
      (c) a lack of spontaneous seeking to share enjoyment, interests, or achievements with other people (e.g., by a lack of showing, bringing, or pointing out objects of interest)
      (d) lack of social or emotional reciprocity
   (2) qualitative impairments in communication, as manifested by at least one of the following:
      (a) delay in, or total lack of, the development of spoken language (not accompanied by an attempt to compensate through alternative modes of communication such as gesture or mime)
      (b) in individuals with adequate speech, marked impairment in the ability to initiate or sustain a conversation with others
      (c) stereotyped or repetitive use of language or idiosyncratic language
      (d) lack of varied, spontaneous make-believe play or social imitative play appropriate to developmental level
   (3) restricted repetitive and stereotyped patterns of behavior, interests, and activities, as manifested by at least one of the following:
      (a) encompassing preoccupation with one or more stereotyped and restricted patterns of interest that is abnormal either in intensity or focus
      (b) apparently inflexible adherence to specific, nonfunctional routines or rituals
      (c) stereotyped and repetitive motor mannerisms (e.g., hand or finger flapping or twisting, or complex whole-body movements)
      (d) persistent preoccupation with parts of objects

B. Delays or abnormal functioning in at least one of the following areas, with onset prior to age 3 years: (1) social interaction, (2) language as used in social communication, or (3) symbolic or imaginative play.

C. The disturbance is not better accounted for by Rett's Disorder or Childhood Disintegrative Disorder.

Source: APA, 2000, 1994

Diagnostic Criteria for Attention-Deficit/ Hyperactivity Disorder

A. Either (1) or (2):

(1) six (or more) of the following symptoms of inattention have persisted for at least 6 months to a degree that is maladaptive and inconsistent with developmental level:

Inattention

(a) often fails to give close attention to details or makes careless mistakes in schoolwork, work, or other activities
(b) often has difficulty sustaining attention in tasks or play
(c) often does not seem to listen when spoken to directly
(d) often does not follow through on instructions and fails to finish schoolwork, chores, or duties in the workplace (not due to oppositional behavior or failure to understand instructions)
(e) often has difficulty organizing tasks and activities
(f) often avoids, dislikes, or is reluctant to engage in tasks that require sustained mental effort (such as schoolwork or homework)
(g) often loses things necessary for tasks or activities (e.g., toys, school assignments, pencils, books, or tools)
(h) is often easily distracted by extraneous stimuli
(i) is often forgetful in daily activities

(2) six (or more) of the following symptoms of hyperactivity-impulsivity have persisted for at least 6 months to a degree that is maladaptive and inconsistent with developmental level:

Hyperactivity

(a) often fidgets with hands or feet or squirms in seat
(b) often leaves seat in classroom or in other situations in which remaining seated is expected
(c) often runs about or climbs excessively in situations in which it is inappropriate (in adolescents or adults, may be limited to subjective feelings of restlessness)
(d) often has difficulty playing or engaging in leisure activities quietly
(e) is often "on the go" or often acts as if "driven by a motor"
(f) often talks excessively

Impulsivity

(g) often blurts out answers before questions have been completed
(h) often has difficulty awaiting turn
(i) often interrupts or intrudes on others (e.g., butts into conversations or games)

B. Some hyperactive-impulsivity or inattentive symptoms that caused impairment were present before age 7 years.

Source: APA, 2000, 1994

Diagnostic Criteria for Attention-Deficit/ Hyperactivity Disorder (Continued)

C. Some impairment from the symptoms is present in two or more settings (e.g., at schoo [or work] and at home).

D. There must be clear evidence of clinically significant impairment in social, academic, o occupational functioning.

E. The symptoms do not occur exclusively during the course of a Pervasive Developmen tal Disorder, Schizophrenia, or other Psychotic Disorder and are not better accounted fo by another mental disorder (e.g., Mood Disorder, Anxiety Disorder, Dissociative Disor der, or a Personality Disorder).

Attention-Deficit/Hyperactivity Disorder, Combined Type: if both Criteria A1 and A are met for the past 6 months

Attention-Deficit/Hyperactivity Disorder, Predominantly Inattentive Type: if Criterio A1 is met but Criterion A2 is not met for the past 6 months

Attention-Deficit/Hyperactivity Disorder, Predominantly Hyperactive-Impulsive Type if Criterion A2 is met but Criterion A1 is not met for the past 6 months

Source: APA, 2000, 1994

Diagnostic Criteria for Conduct Disorder

A. A repetitive and persistent pattern of behavior in which the basic rights of others or major age-appropriate societal norms or rules are violated, as manifested by the presence of three (or more) of the following criteria in the past 12 months, with at least one criterion present in the past 6 months:

Aggression to people and animals
(1) often bullies, threatens, or intimidates others
(2) often initiates physical fights
(3) has used a weapon that can cause serious physical harm to others (e.g., a bat, brick, broken bottle, knife, gun)
(4) has been physically cruel to people
(5) has been physically cruel to animals
(6) has stolen while confronting a victim (e.g., mugging, purse snatching, extortion, armed robbery)
(7) has forced someone into sexual activity

Destruction of property
(8) has deliberately engaged in fire setting with the intention of causing serious damage
(9) has deliberately destroyed others' property (other than by fire setting)

Deceitfulness or theft
(10) has broken into someone else's house, building, or car
(11) often lies to obtain goods or favors or to avoid obligations (i.e., "cons" others)
(12) has stolen items of nontrivial value without confronting a victim (e.g., shoplifting, but without breaking and entering; forgery)

Serious violations of rules
(13) often stays out at night despite parental prohibitions, beginning before age 13 years
(14) has run away from home overnight at least twice while living in parental or parental surrogate home (or once without returning for a lengthy period)
(15) is often truant from school, beginning before age 13 years

B. The disturbance in behavior causes clinically significant impairment in social, academic, or occupational functioning.

C. If the individual is age 18 years or older, criteria are not met for Antisocial Personality Disorder.

Source: APA, 2000, 1994

Diagnostic Criteria for Conduct Disorder (Continued)

Specify type based on age at onset:

Childhood-Onset Type: onset of at least one criterion characteristic of Conduct Disorder prior to age 10 years

Adolescent-Onset Type: absence of any criteria characteristic of Conduct Disorder prior to age 10 years

Specify severity:

Mild: few if any conduct problems in excess of those required to make the diagnosis and conduct problems cause only minor harm to others

Moderate: number of conduct problems and effect on others intermediate between "mild" and "severe"

Severe: many conduct problems in excess of those required to make the diagnosis or conduct problems cause considerable harm to others

Source: APA, 2000, 1994

Diagnostic Criteria for Oppositional Defiant Disorder

A. A pattern of negativistic, hostile, and defiant behavior lasting at least 6 months, during which four (or more) of the following are present:
   (1) often loses temper
   (2) often argues with adults
   (3) often actively defies or refuses to comply with adults' requests or rules
   (4) often deliberately annoys people
   (5) often blames others for his or her mistakes or misbehavior
   (6) is often touchy or easily annoyed by others
   (7) is often angry or resentful
   (8) is often spiteful or vindictive

   Note: Consider a criterion met only if the behavior occurs more frequently than is typically observed in individuals of comparable age and developmental level.

B. The disturbance in behavior causes clinically significant impairment in social, academic, or occupational functioning.

C. The behaviors do not occur exclusively during the course of a Psychotic or Mood Disorder.

D. Criteria are not met for Conduct Disorder, and, if the individual is age 18 years or older, criteria are not met for Antisocial Personality Disorder.

Source: APA, 2000, 1994

Diagnostic Criteria for Encopresis

A. Repeated passage of feces into inappropriate places (e.g., clothing or floor) whether involuntary or intentional.

B. At least one such event per month for at least 3 months.

C. Chronological age is at least 4 years (or equivalent developmental level).

D. The behavior is not due exclusively to the direct physiological effects of a substance (e.g., laxatives) or a general medical condition except through a mechanism involving constipation.

Diagnostic Criteria for Enuresis

A. Repeated voiding of urine into bed or clothes (whether involuntary or intentional).

B. The behavior is clinically significant as manifested by either a frequency of twice a week for at least 3 consecutive months or the presence of clinically significant distress or impairment in social, academic (occupational), or other important areas of functioning.

C. Chronological age is at least 5 years (or equivalent developmental level).

D. The behavior is not due exclusively to the direct physiological effect of a substance (e.g., a diuretic) or a general medical condition (e.g., diabetes, spina bifida, a seizure disorder).

Source: APA, 2000, 1994

Diagnostic Criteria for Separation Anxiety Disorder

A. Developmentally inappropriate and excessive anxiety concerning separation from home or from those to whom the individual is attached, as evidenced by three (or more) of the following:
   (1) recurrent excessive distress when separation from home or major attachment figures occurs or is anticipated
   (2) persistent and excessive worry about losing, or about possible harm befalling, major attachment figures
   (3) persistent and excessive worry that an untoward event will lead to separation from a major attachment figure (e.g., getting lost or being kidnapped)
   (4) persistent reluctance or refusal to go to school or elsewhere because of fear of separation
   (5) persistently and excessively fearful or reluctant to be alone or without major attachment figures at home or without significant adults in other settings
   (6) persistent reluctance or refusal to go to sleep without being near a major attachment figure or to sleep away from home
   (7) repeated nightmares involving the theme of separation
   (8) repeated complaints of physical symptoms (such as headaches, stomachaches, nausea, or vomiting) when separation from major attachment figures occurs or is anticipated

B. The duration of the disturbance is at least 4 weeks.

C. The onset is before age 18 years.

D. The disturbance causes clinically significant distress or impairment in social, academic (occupational), or other important areas of functioning.

E. The disturbance does not occur exclusively during the courses of a Pervasive Developmental Disorder, Schizophrenia, or other Psychotic Disorder and, in adolescents and adults, is not better accounted for by Panic Disorder With Agoraphobia.

Early Onset: if onset occurs before age 6 years

*Source: APA, 2000, 1994

Diagnostic Criteria for Dementia of the Alzheimer's Type

A. The development of multiple cognitive deficits manifested by both
   (1) Memory impairment (impaired ability to learn new information or to recall previously learned information)
   (2) one (or more) of the following cognitive disturbances:
      (a) aphasia (language disturbance)
      (b) apraxia (impaired ability to carry out motor activities despite intact motor function)
      (c) agnosia (failure to recognize or identify objects despite intact sensory function)
      (d) disturbance in executive functioning (i.e., planning, organizing, sequencing, abstracting)

B. The cognitive deficits in Criteria A1 and A2 each cause significant impairment in social or occupational functioning and represent a significant decline from a previous level of functioning.

C. The course is characterized by gradual onset and continuing cognitive decline.

D. The cognitive deficits in Criteria A1 and A2 are not due to any of the following:
   (1) Other central nervous system conditions that cause progressive deficits in memory and cognition (e.g., cerebrovascular disease, Parkinson's disease, Huntington's disease, subdural hematoma, normal-pressure hydrocephalus, brain tumor)
   (2) systemic conditions that are known to cause dementia (e.g., hypothyroidism, vitamin B12 or folic acid deficiency, niacin deficiency, hypercalcemia, neurosyphilis, HIV infection)
   (3) Substance-induced conditions

E. The deficits do not occur exclusively during the course of a delirium.

F. The disturbance is not better accounted for by another Axis I disorder (e.g., Major Depressive Disorder, Schizophrenia).

Code based on presence or absence of a clinically significant behavioral disturbance:

Without Behavioral Disturbance: if the cognitive disturbance is not accompanied by any clinically significant behavioral disturbance.

With Behavioral Disturbance: if the cognitive disturbance is accompanied by a clinically significant behavioral disturbance (e.g., wandering, agitation).

Specify subtype:

With Early Onset: if onset is age 65 years or below

With Late Onset: if onset is after age 65 years

Source: APA, 2000, 1994

DSM-IV Classification

From the American Psychiatric Association: Diagnostic and Statistical Manual of Mental Disorders, Fourth Edition, Washington, DC, American Psychiatric Association, 1994, Revised, 2000. Reprinted by permission.

(All categories are on Axis I except those indicated otherwise.)

Disorders Usually First Diagnosed in Infancy, Childhood, or Adolescence

Mental Retardation

Note: These are coded on Axis II.

Mild mental retardation
Moderate mental retardation
Severe mental retardation
Profound mental retardation
Mental retardation, severity unspecified

Learning Disorders

Reading disorder
Mathematics disorder
Disorder of written expression
Learning disorder NOS*

Motor Skills Disorder

Developmental coordination disorder

Communication Disorders

Expressive language disorder
Mixed receptive-expressive language disorder
Phonological disorder
Stuttering
Communication disorder NOS*

Pervasive Developmental Disorders

Autistic disorder
Rett's disorder
Childhood disintegrative disorder
Asperger's disorder
Pervasive development disorder NOS*

Attention-Deficit and Disruptive Behavior Disorders

Attention-deficit/hyperactivity disorder
- Combined type
- Predominantly inattentive type
- Predominantly hyperactive-impulsive type
- Attention-deficit/hyperactivity disorder NOS*

Conduct disorder
Oppositional defiant disorder
Disruptive behavior disorder NOS*

Feeding and Eating Disorders of Infancy or Early Childhood

Pica
Rumination disorder
Feeding disorder of infancy or early childhood

Tic Disorders

Tourette's disorder
Chronic motor or vocal tic disorder
Transient tic disorder
Tic disorder NOS*

Elimination Disorders

Encopresis
- With constipation and overflow incontinence
- Without constipation and overflow incontinence

Enuresis (not due to a general medical condition)

Other Disorders of Infancy, Childhood, or Adolescence

Separation anxiety disorder
Selective mutism
Reactive attachment disorder of infancy or early childhood
Stereotypic movement disorder
Disorder of infancy, childhood, or adolescence NOS*

*NOS = Not otherwise specified

DSM-IV Classification (Continued)

From the American Psychiatric Association: Diagnostic and Statistical Manual of Mental Disorders, Fourth Edition, Washington, DC, American Psychiatric Association, 1994, Revised, 2000. Reprinted by permission.

(All categories are on Axis I except those indicated otherwise.)

Delirium, Dementia, and Amnestic and Other Cognitive Disorders

Delirium

Delirium due to . . . *(indicate the general medical condition)*
Substance intoxication delirium
Substance withdrawal delirium
Delirium due to multiple etiologies
Delirium NOS*

Dementia

Dementia of the Alzheimer's type, with early onset
Dementia of the Alzheimer's type, with late onset
Vascular dementia

Dementia Due to Other General Medical Conditions

Dementia due to HIV disease
Dementia due to head trauma
Dementia due to Parkinson's disease
Dementia due to Huntington's disease
Dementia due to Pick's disease
Dementia due to Creutzfeldt-Jakob disease
Dementia due to . . . *(indicate the general medical condition not listed above)*
Substance-induced persisting dementia
Dementia due to multiple etiologies
Dementia NOS*

Amnestic Disorders

Amnestic disorders due to . . . *(indicate the general medical condition)*
Substance-induced persisting amnestic disorder
Amnestic disorder NOS*

Other Cognitive Disorders

Cognitive disorder NOS*

Mental Disorders Due to a General Medical Condition Not Elsewhere Classified

Catatonic disorder due to . . . *(indicate the general medical condition)*
Personality change due to . . . *(indicate the general medical condition)*
Mental disorder NOS* due to . . . *(indicate the general medical condition)*

*NOS = Not otherwise specified

DSM-IV Classification (Continued)

From the American Psychiatric Association: Diagnostic and Statistical Manual of Mental Disorders, Fourth Edition, Washington, DC, American Psychiatric Association, 1994, Revised, 2000. Reprinted by permission.

(All categories are on Axis I except those indicated otherwise.)

Substance-Related Disorders

[Specific substance categories: Alcohol; Amphetamine; Caffeine; Cannabis; Cocaine; Hallucinogen; Inhalant; Nicotine; Opioid; Phencyclidine; Sedative, Hypnotic, or Anxiolytic; Polysubstance; Other or unknown]

Substance Use Disorders

Substance dependence
Substance abuse

Substance-Induced Disorders

Substance intoxication
Substance withdrawal
Substance intoxication delirium
Substance withdrawal delirium
Substance-induced persisting dementia
Substance-induced persisting amnestic disorder
Substance-induced psychotic disorder
Substance-induced mood disorder
Substance-induced anxiety disorder
Substance-induced sexual dysfunction
Substance-induced sleep disorder
Substance-related disorder NOS*

Schizophrenia and Other Psychotic Disorders

Schizophrenia
  Paranoid type
  Disorganized type
  Catatonic type
  Undifferentiated type
  Residual type
Schizophreniform disorder
Schizoaffective disorder
Delusional disorder
Brief psychotic disorder
Shared psychotic disorder
Psychotic disorder due to . . . *(indicate the general medical condition)*
Substance-induced psychotic disorder
Psychotic disorder NOS*

Mood Disorders

Depressive Disorders

Major depressive disorder
Dysthymic disorder
Depressive disorder NOS*

Bipolar Disorders

Bipolar I disorder
Bipolar II disorder
Cyclothymic disorder
Bipolar disorder NOS*
Mood disorder due to . . . *(indicate the general medical condition)*
Substance-induced mood disorder
Mood disorder NOS*

*NOS = Not otherwise specified

DSM-IV Classification (Continued)

From the American Psychiatric Association: Diagnostic and Statistical Manual of Mental Disorders, Fourth Edition, Washington, DC, American Psychiatric Association, 1994, Revised, 2000. Reprinted by permission.

(All categories are on Axis I except those indicated otherwise.)

Anxiety Disorders

Panic disorder without agoraphobia
Panic disorder with agoraphobia
Agoraphobia without history of panic disorder
Specific phobia
Social phobia
Obsessive-compulsive disorder
Posttraumatic stress disorder
Acute stress disorder
Generalized anxiety disorder
Anxiety disorder due to . . . *(indicate the general medical condition)*
Substance-induced anxiety disorder
Anxiety disorder NOS*

Somatoform Disorders

Somatization disorder
Undifferentiated somatoform disorder
Conversion disorder
Pain disorder
Associated with psychological factors
Associated with both psychological factors and a general medical condition
Hypochondriasis
Body dysmorphic disorder
Somatoform disorder NOS*

Factitious Disorders

Factitious disorder
With predominantly psychological signs and symptoms
With predominantly physical signs and symptoms
With combined psychological and physical signs and symptoms
Factitious disorder NOS*

Dissociative Disorders

Dissociative amnesia
Dissociative fugue
Dissociative identity disorder
Depersonalization disorder
Dissociative disorder NOS*

*NOS = Not otherwise specified

DSM-IV Classification (Continued)

From the American Psychiatric Association: Diagnostic and Statistical Manual of Mental Disorders, Fourth Edition, Washington, DC, American Psychiatric Association, 1994, Revised, 2000. Reprinted by permission.

(All categories are on Axis I except those indicated otherwise.)

Sexual and Gender Identity Disorders

Sexual Dysfunctions

Sexual Desire Disorders
Hypoactive sexual desire disorder
Sexual aversion disorder

Sexual Arousal Disorders
Female sexual arousal disorder
Male erectile disorder

Orgasmic Disorders
Female orgasmic disorder
Male orgasmic disorder
Premature ejaculation

Sexual Pain Disorders
Dyspareunia (not due to a general medical condition)
Vaginismus (not due to a general medical condition)

Sexual Dysfunction Due to a General Medical Condition
Substance-induced Sexual Dysfunction
Sexual Dysfunction NOS*

Paraphilias
Exhibitionism
Fetishism
Frotteurism
Pedophilia
Sexual Masochism
Sexual Sadism
Transvestic Fetishism
Voyeurism
Paraphilia NOS*

Gender Identity Disorders
Gender identity disorder
- In children
- In adolescents or adults

Gender identity disorder NOS*
Sexual disorder NOS*

Eating Disorders

Anorexia nervosa
Bulimia nervosa
Eating disorder NOS*

Sleep Disorders

Primary Sleep Disorders

Dyssomnias
Primary insomnia
Primary hypersomnia
Narcolepsy
Breathing-related sleep disorder
Circadian rhythm sleep disorder
Dyssomnia NOS*

Parasomnias
Nightmare disorder
Sleep terror disorder
Sleepwalking disorder
Parasomnia NOS*

Sleep Disorders Related to Another Mental Disorder

Other Sleep Disorders
Sleep disorder due to . . . *(indicate the general medical condition)*
Substance-induced sleep disorder

*NOS = Not otherwise specified

DSM-IV Classification (Continued)

From the American Psychiatric Association: Diagnostic and Statistical Manual of Mental Disorders, Fourth Edition, Washington, DC, American Psychiatric Association, 1994, Revised, 2000. Reprinted by permission.

(All categories are on Axis I except those indicated otherwise.)

Impulse-Control Disorders Not Elsewhere Classified

Intermittent explosive disorder
Kleptomania
Pyromania
Pathological gambling
Trichotillomania
Impulse-control disorder NOS*

Adjustment Disorders

Adjustment disorder
- With depressed mood
- With anxiety
- With mixed anxiety and depressed mood
- With disturbance of conduct
- With mixed disturbance of emotions and conduct
- Unspecified

Personality Disorders

Note: These are coded on Axis II.

Paranoid personality disorder
Schizoid personality disorder
Schizotypal personality disorder
Antisocial personality disorder
Borderline personality disorder
Histrionic personality disorder
Narcissistic personality disorder
Avoidant personality disorder
Dependent personality disorder
Obsessive-compulsive personality disorder
Personality disorder NOS*

*NOS = Not otherwise specified

DSM-IV Classification (Continued)

From the American Psychiatric Association: Diagnostic and Statistical Manual of Mental Disorders, Fourth Edition, Washington, DC, American Psychiatric Association, 1994, Revised, 2000. Reprinted by permission.

(All categories are on Axis I except those indicated otherwise.)

Other Conditions That May Be a Focus of Clinical Attention

Psychological Factors Affecting Medical Condition

Mental disorder affecting medical condition
Psychological symptoms affecting medical condition
Personality traits or coping style affecting medical condition
Maladaptive health behaviors affecting medical condition
Stress-related physiological response affecting medical condition
Other or unspecified psychological factors affecting medical condition

Medication-Induced Movement Disorders

Neuroleptic-induced Parkinsonism
Neuroleptic malignant syndrome
Neuroleptic-induced acute dystonia
Neuroleptic-induced acute akathisia
Neuroleptic-induced tardive dyskinesia
Medication-induced postural tremor
Medication-induced movement disorder NOS*

Other Medication-Induced Disorder

Adverse effects of medication NOS*

Relational Problems

Relational problem related to a mental disorder or general medical condition
Parent-child relational problem
Partner relational problem
Sibling relational problem
Relational problem NOS*

Problems Related to Abuse or Neglect

Physical abuse of child
Sexual abuse of child
Neglect of child
Physical abuse of adult
Sexual abuse of adult

Additional Conditions That May Be a Focus of Clinical Attention

Noncompliance with treatment
Malingering
Adult antisocial behavior
Child or adolescent antisocial behavior
Borderline intellectual functioning
Age-related cognitive decline
Bereavement
Academic problem
Occupational problem
Identity problem
Religious or spiritual problem
Acculturation problem
Phase of life problem

*NOS = Not otherwise specified

APPENDIX

E Video Guide

OVERVIEW

This appendix contains summaries of the video segments excerpted from clinical documentaries or programs. The video segments, each 1 to 8 minutes in length, have been selected by Ron Comer because they provide perfect illustrations for points made in lecture without actually overshadowing the lecture.

The segments include powerful and memorable illustrations of different kinds of disorders, different treatments (often conducted by the originator of the treatment), experiments, historical events and procedures, and major clinical social issues such as deinstitutionalization and jailing people with mental disorders.

In addition, the video package includes reaction tapes—brief video pieces in which an actress or actor talks directly to the student viewer, making comments that a client might make to a therapist or that a therapist might make to a client. Students may then offer their reactions to the statements in class discussions.

There are 4 videotapes in the package:

- Video Segments for Abnormal Psychology—Tape I: Contains Segments 1 through 27
- Video Segments for Abnormal Psychology—Tape II: Contains Segments 28 through 50
- Video Segments for Abnormal Psychology—Tape III: Contains Segments 101 through 122
- Video Segments for Abnormal Psychology—Tape IV: Contains Segments 201 through 219

Locating segments on the videotapes is designed to be straightforward. At the beginning of each of the tapes, push the video machine's counter to zero. Then fast forward to the counter number indicated in the Segment Description in this appendix. For your convenience, both a real time counter number and a digital counter number are provided for each segment. Note that Tape IV lists only the length of the segments.

There are two types of listings in this guide. The first, "Video Segments Ordered Sequentially," includes the counter number, *Source, Description,* and a list of *Relevant Lecture Topics* for each segment. The second, "Video Segments Ordered Topically," includes a list of lecture topics, each with a sublist of recommended video segments.

Lastly, this appendix has a section entitled "Recommendations for Purchase or Rental." This section details where to purchase or rent many of the videos from which the video segments are derived. This section is organized topically.

VIDEO SEGMENTS ORDERED SEQUENTIALLY

Video Segments for Abnormal Psychology—Tape I

Credits (Tape I, Real Time Counter 0:00.20, Digital Counter 0032)

Introduction Professor Comer Introduces the Video Program
(Tape I, Real Time Counter 0:01.37, Digital Counter 0153)

Segment 1 Deinstitutionalization and Jailing the Mentally Ill
(Tape I, Real Time Counter 0:05.10, Digital Counter 0463)
Source: NBC Nightly News, 4/13/93 (NBC News Archives)
Description: This television news report reveals that people with serious mental disorders are increasingly being jailed for minor criminal offenses, such as trespassing. The piece links this trend to the failures of deinstitutionalization and discusses why the trend continues.
Relevant Lecture Topics: 1. Law, Society, and the Mental Health Profession; 2. Deinstitutionalization and Community Mental Health; 3. Treatments for Schizophrenia; 4. General Treatment; Current Trends in Abnormal Psychology; 5. History of Abnormal Psychology; 6. Sociocultural Model

Segment 2 (*Version available on CD-ROM) **Medical Procedures Used in Mental Hospitals in the First Half of the Twentieth Century**
(Tape I, Real Time Counter 0:08.34, Digital Counter 0733)
Sources: "Treatment in Mental Disorders," 1949 (James D. Page); "Prefrontal Lobotomy in the Treatment of Mental Disorders," 1942 (Walter Freeman and James Watts). Courtesy: History of Medicine Division, National Library of Medicine.
Description: The medical treatments used in mental hospitals during the first half of this century were crude, largely ineffective, and often unintentionally cruel. Some of the leading approaches are shown in this segment, including the wet pack, insulin therapy, metrazol therapy, and the lobotomy.
Relevant Lecture Topics: 1. History of Abnormal Psychology; 2. Institutionalization; 3. Biological Treatments; 4. Treatments for Schizophrenia; 5. Treatments for Mood Disorders; 6. General Treatment; 7. Biological Model; 8. Law, Society, and the Mental Health Profession

Segment 3 Modern Day Mental Hospital Ward
(Tape I, Real Time Counter 0:13.38, Digital Counter 1100)
Source: Madness: To Define True Madness, 1991 (BBC-Lionheart Television International)
Description: This video of a ward in a modern mental hospital reveals that hospital conditions today are more humane and activities more plentiful and interesting than those of the past. Yet, at the same time, it also shows that the atmosphere of today's mental hospital wards remains very distinct and the problems of many patients continue to be quite severe.
Relevant Lecture Topics: 1. Institutionalization; 2. Treatments for Schizophrenia; 3. General Treatment, Clinical Picture of Schizophrenia; 4. Current Trends in Abnormal Psychology; 5. History of Abnormal Psychology

Segment 4 PET Scan Procedure and Results: Comparison of schizophrenic and nonschizophrenic twins
(Tape I, Real Time Counter 0:15.32, Digital Counter 1234)
Source: Madness: In Two Minds, 1991 (BBC-Lionheart Television International)
Description: This segment shows a subject receiving a PET scan. It demonstrates both the machinery itself and the kinds of tasks performed during testing. The segment also shows and explains PET scan findings and compares the scans of schizophrenic and nonschizophrenic identical twins.
Relevant Lecture Topics: 1. Clinical Assessment; 2. Schizophrenia; 3. Biological View of Schizophrenia; 4. Research Designs and Methodology in Abnormal Psychology

Segment 5 MRI Scan: Comparison of schizophrenic and nonschizophrenic twins
(Tape I, Real Time Counter 0:18.39, Digital Counter 1437)
Source: Madness: In Two Minds, 1991 (BBC-Lionheart Television International)
Description: In this segment, Dr. Daniel Weinberger compares the MRI scan of a schizophrenic person to that of his nonschizophrenic identical twin and points out that the ventricles of the schizophrenic twin are bigger than those of his nonschizophrenic identical twin.
Relevant Lecture Topics: 1. Clinical Assessment; 2. Schizophrenia; 3. Biological View of Schizophrenia; 4. Research Designs and Methodology in Abnormal Psychology

Segments 6 & 7 Dr. Aaron Beck Conducts Cognitive Therapy
#6: Client and therapist examine thoughts leading to depression
#7: Client and therapist identify automatic thoughts, illogical thinking, and basic assumptions leading to depression
(Tape I, Real Time Counter 0:19.57, Digital Counter 1518)
Source: Cognitive Therapy of Depression, 1977 (Dr. Aaron Beck, The Beck Institute for Cognitive Therapy and Research)
Description: In these two segments Dr. Aaron Beck, originator of cognitive therapy, treats a depressed woman. In the first segment (#6), Dr. Beck helps the client carefully examine her thinking and pinpoints those thoughts that are making her depressed. In the second segment (#7), Dr. Beck helps the client identify the precise thoughts, illogical thinking processes, and maladaptive attitudes that are causing her depression, and he actively challenges these thoughts and interpretations.
Relevant Lecture Topics: 1. Cognitive Explanations of Depression; 2. Cognitive Therapy for Depression; 3. Clinical Picture of Depression; 4. Cognitive Model (General); 5. Cognitive Therapy (General)

Segment 8 Client-Centered Therapy by Dr. Carl Rogers
(Tape I, Real Time Counter 0:30.46, Digital Counter 2150)
Source: Client-Centered Therapy, Part II (Reuben H. Segel)
Description: In this session of client-centered therapy, Dr. Carl Rogers tries to show unconditional positive regard, empathy, and genuineness to a woman who first came to see him because of concerns about her relationships with family members. In this segment from the 32nd therapy session, Rogers's warm acceptance and his continual restatements and reflections of what the client is saying help her become more in touch with and embrace her deepest private feelings of hurt.
Relevant Lecture Topics: 1. Client-Centered Therapy; 2. Humanistic Therapy; 3. Humanistic Model; 4. History of Abnormal Psychology; 5. Clinical Picture of Depression

Segment 9 (*Version available on CD-ROM) **Psychoanalytic Therapy Session**
(Tape I, Real Time Counter 0:36.30, Digital Counter 2458)
Source: The Royal Road: Psychoanalytic Approaches to the Dream, 1988, Producer: Dr. Glenn Gabbard (Menninger Video)
Description: This sometimes humorous reenactment of a psychoanalytic therapy session, based on an actual case, effectively shows the principles of free association, transference, resistance, and dream interpretation in action.
Relevant Lecture Topics: 1. Psychoanalytic Therapy; 2. Psychodynamic Model; 3. Dreams

Segment 10 Multimodal Therapy by Dr. Arnold Lazarus
(Tape I, Real Time Counter 0:41.33, Digital Counter 2702)
Source: Multimodal Therapy Conducted by Arnold A. Lazarus, Ph.D. (This videotape is part of the 12-program "APA Psychotherapy Videotape Series," produced by the American Psychological Association. Information about the APA Psychotherapy Videotape Series can be obtained from the APA Order Department: 1-800-374-2721.)
Description: Dr. Arnold Lazarus, originator of the eclectic approach "Multimodal Therapy," uses the acronym B.A.S.I.C. I.D. to identify seven areas of client functioning that multimodal therapists assess and treat—a client's Behavior, Affect, Sensations, Imagery, Cognition, Interpersonal Relationships, and Drug/Biology. In this Segment, Dr. Lazarus goes over each of these areas with a client who has previously filled out a multimodal life history survey.
Relevant Lecture Topics: 1. Multimodal Therapy; 2. Eclectic Therapy; 3. Clinical Picture of Anxiety and Depression; 4. Current Trends in Abnormal Psychology; 5. History of Abnormal Psychology

Segment 11 Elevator Phobia
(Tape I, Real Time Counter 0:47.20, Digital Counter 2980)
Source: Phobias . . . Overcoming the Fear, 1991 (Producer, Lalia Gilmore-Madriguera; Connecticut Public Television)
Description: This video segment centers on a man who has a phobic fear of riding on elevators. It reveals various aspects of his phobia, and highlights behavioral exposure therapy for phobias, as conducted within a self-help supportive group program.
Relevant Lecture Topics: 1. Clinical Picture of Phobias; 2. Behavioral Exposure Treatment; 3. Self-Help Support Groups; 4. Cognitive-Behavioral Explanations of Phobias; 5. Current Trends in Abnormal Psychology; 6. Problems in Diagnosis

Segments 12 & 13 Anxiety Disorders
#12: Multiple Fears
#13: Homeopathic Approach to Anxiety Disorders
(Tape I, Real Time Counter 0:51.36, Digital Counter 3173)
Source: Phobias . . . Overcoming the Fear, 1991 (Producer, Lalia Gilmore-Madriguera; Connecticut Public Television)

Description: These two segments center on two individuals with multiple fears. In the first segment (#12), they describe in powerful terms the symptoms and origins of their fears and their effects on them. The second segment (#13) describes their treatment by homeopathy, an alternative treatment approach that uses drugs made from natural substances.
Relevant Lecture Topics: 1. Clinical Picture of Anxiety Disorders; 2. Clinical Picture of Specific Phobias; 3. Social Phobias, Agoraphobia, Panic Disorders, and Generalized Anxiety Disorders; 4. Comorbidity of Disorders; 5. Origins of Anxiety Disorders; 6. Biological Explanations of Anxiety Disorders; 7. Biological Treatment for Anxiety Disorders; 8. Biological Model; 9. Biological Treatments

Segment 14 Fear of Airplane Travel: Clinical Features and Special Exposure Treatment Program
(Tape I, Real Time Counter 0:57.42, Digital Counter 3442)
Source: Phobias . . . Overcoming the Fear, 1991 (Producer, Lalia Gilmore-Madriguera; Connecticut Public Television)
Description: This segment centers on a woman with a phobic fear of airplane travel. It reveals various aspects of her phobia, including the origins, and observes a special exposure treatment program developed for this problem.
Relevant Lecture Topics: 1. Behavioral Exposure Treatment for Phobias; 2. Cognitive-Behavioral Treatment for Phobias; 3. Relaxation Training; 4. Clinical Picture of Specific Phobias; 5. Origins of Phobias; 6. Behavioral and Cognitive Models; 7. Behavioral and Cognitive Treatments

Segment 15 Informal Exposure Treatment for a Dog Phobia
(Tape I, Real Time Counter 1:04.12, Digital Counter 3717)
Source: "Annie," 1990 (Ronald Comer)
Description: Often, desensitization occurs in real life. In a lighthearted video, Professor Comer describes how he recently overcame his fear of dogs after being increasingly exposed to his family's dog, Annie, and then demonstrates how "comfortably" he now interacts with the dog.
Relevant Lecture Topics: 1. Behavioral Exposure Treatment for Phobias; 2. Clinical Picture of Animal Phobias

Segments 16 & 17 Major Depressive Disorder
#16: Person with Major Depressive Disorder with Psychotic Symptoms
#17: Person after Electroconvulsive Therapy
(Tape I, Real Time Counter 1:09.46, Digital Counter 3941)
Source: The Mind: Depression, 1988 (Thirteen, WNET, New York Educational Broadcasting Corporation)
Description: These two segments focus on a woman with a major depressive disorder, who also displays psychotic symptoms as part of her depressive episode. The first segment (#16) finds her being interviewed during the height of her depressive episode, with strong suicidal ideation among other symptoms. In the second segment (#17) she is interviewed after recovery as a result of electroconvulsive therapy. The contrast is striking.
Relevant Lecture Topics: 1. Clinical Picture of Depression; 2. Self-Concept in Depression; 3. Suicide; 4. Mood Disorders and Psychosis; 5. Diagnosis of Mood Disorders; 6. Recovery from Depression; 7. Treatment for Depression; 8. Electroconvulsive Therapy; 9. Biological Treatment; 10. Biological Model

Segment 18 Person with Extreme Symptoms of Mania, Including Rushed Speech
(Tape I, Real Time Counter 1:14.10, Digital Counter 4113)
Source: The Mind: Depression, 1988 (Thirteen, WNET, New York Educational Broadcasting Corporation)
Description: In this segment a woman is interviewed during a manic episode. Her symptoms include rushed speech and grandiosity.
Relevant Lecture Topics: 1. Clinical Picture of Mania; 2. Mood Disorders and Psychosis; 3. Diagnosis of Mood Disorders; 4. Biological Treatment; 5. Biological Model

Segment 19 (*Version available on CD-ROM) **Early Electroconvulsive Therapies**
(Tape I, Real Time Counter 1:16.02, Digital Counter 4184)
Sources: Courtesy: History of Medicine Division, National Library of Medicine
Recent Modifications of Convulsive Shock Therapy, 1941 (A. E. Bennett, Bishop Clarkson Memorial Hospital, Psychiatric Department); *Metrazol, Electric, and Insulin Treatment of the Functional Psychoses,* 1934 (James G. Sheedy)
Description: In the 1930s, electroconvulsive therapy was developed in the belief that inducing a convulsion in patients with severe mental disorders would bring improvement. This segment shows the early versions of this therapy. The footage is very graphic and hard to take.
Relevant Lecture Topics: 1. Electroconvulsive Therapy; 2. History of Abnormal Psychology; 3. Biological Treatment; 4. Biological Model

Segment 20 Modern Electroconvulsive Therapy, by Dr. Max Fink
(Tape I, Real Time Counter 1:20.17, Digital Counter 4347)
Source: Madness: Brainwaves, 1991 (BBC-Lionheart Television International)

Description: In this segment, Dr. Max Fink applies and discusses electroconvulsive therapy. The segment illustrates what ECT is like today, including the use of medication to help persons sleep through the procedure, muscle relaxants to reduce thrashing, and oxygen, and the consequent reduction of the overt symptoms of the grand mal seizure. Dr. Fink also tries to explain ECT's effectiveness and describes the use of "maintenance" ECT.
Relevant Lecture Topics: 1. Electroconvulsive Therapy; 2. Biological Treatment for Mood Disorders; 3. Biological Treatment (General); 4. Biological Model; 5. History of Abnormal Psychology; 6. Current Trends in Abnormal Psychology

Segment 21 Experiment Linking Placebo Effects to Endorphins
(Tape I, Real Time Counter 1:23.50, Digital Counter 4479)
Source: The Keys of Paradise, 1979 (BBC-Lionheart Television International)
Description: This segment shows an experiment with human subjects whose findings suggest that the effectiveness of placebo drugs is partly a result of the patients' release of endorphins, their natural opioids. The implication is that, for some people, the expectation that a given treatment will soon be helpful causes them, without awareness, to release endorphins throughout their brain and body. In turn, the endorphins reduce their pain or help them to feel better in other ways.
Relevant Lecture Topics: 1. Research Designs and Methodology in Abnormal Psychology; 2. Treatment; 3. Placebo Effects; 4. Endorphins; 5. Psychological Factors and Physical Disorders; 6. Pain Disorders; 7. Opioids; 8. Substance-Related Disorders; 9. Cognitive Model; 10. Biological Model; 11. Cognitive and Biological Treatment

Segment 22 Survey of Dieting and Body Image Among 33,000 Women, by Drs. Susan Wooley and Wayne Wooley
(Tape I, Real Time Counter 1:28.35, Digital Counter 4651)
Source: The Waist Land: Eating Disorders in America, 1985 (Coronet/MTI)
Description: This segment brings to life the well-known 1984 *Glamour* magazine survey of 33,000 women revealing that most women in our society, even underweight women, consider themselves overweight, particularly in body parts from the waist down, and diet regularly.
Relevant Lecture Topics: 1. Eating Disorders; 2. Sociocultural Explanations of Eating Disorders; 3. Gender Differences in Abnormal Psychology; 4. Sociocultural Model

Segment 23 Woman with Anorexia Nervosa
(Tape I, Real Time Counter 1:31.01, Digital Counter 4739)
Source: The Waist Land: Eating Disorders in America, 1985 (Coronet/MTI)
Description: This segment focuses on a young woman with anorexia nervosa, including the issues of control and power in her disorder, origins of the disorder, cognitive and other features, and the impact of the disorder.
Relevant Lecture Topics: 1. Clinical Picture of Anorexia Nervosa; 2. Eating Disorders; 3. Origins of Eating Disorders; 4. Cognitive Explanations of Eating Disorders; 5. Gender Issues in Abnormal Psychology; 6. Projective Tests

Segment 24 (*Version available on CD-ROM)
Woman with Bulimia Nervosa
(Tape I, Real Time Counter 1:34.25, Digital Counter 4858)
Source: The Waist Land: Eating Disorders in America, 1985 (Coronet/MTI)
Description: This segment focuses on a young woman with bulimia nervosa, including her binge behaviors and purge behaviors, origins of her disorder, cognitive and other features, and impact of the disorder.
Relevant Lecture Topics: 1. Clinical Picture of Bulimia Nervosa; 2. Binge Eating; 3. Purge Behavior; 4. Eating Disorders; 5. Origins of Eating Disorders; 6. Gender Issues in Abnormal Psychology

Segment 25 Lateral Hypothalamus Stimulation Leads to Hunger and Eating Behavior
(Tape I, Real Time Counter 1:37.44, Digital Counter 4972)
Source: Hypothalamic Reward in Feeding, Running and Mating Behavior (Bart Hoebel, Alan C. Rosenquist, & Anthony R. Caggiula)
Description: Biological researchers have determined that the hypothalamus helps control eating behavior and may play a key role in eating disorders, as indicated in Segments #25, #26, and #27. One area of the hypothalamus that appears to help control hunger and eating behavior is the *lateral hypothalamus*, a brain area that produces hunger when it is activated or stimulated. If a person or animal has not eaten or has eaten too little, this part of the brain activates and the person experiences hunger and wants to eat. When researchers in this segment electronically stimulate the lateral hypothalamus in animal subjects, the subjects keep eating and eating, even when they have eaten recently and are biologically full.
Relevant Lecture Topics: 1. Eating Disorders; 2. Biological Explanations of Eating Disorders; 3. Dieting; Dieting and Binge Eating; 4. Body Weight Set Point; 5. Research Designs and Methodology in Abnormal Psychology (Analogue Studies); 6. Biological Model

Segment 26 Subjects Get Pleasure from Experiencing Hunger and Food Thoughts
(Tape I, Real Time Counter 1:40.49, Digital Counter 5077)
Source: Hypothalamic Reward in Feeding, Running and Mating Behavior (Bart Hoebel, Alan C. Rosenquist, & Anthony R. Caggiula)
Description: Apparently, not only is food itself rewarding, but so are having desires and thoughts about eating. Thus, people enjoy and actively seek out the smell or sight of a favorite pastry, enjoy magazine and television ads about food, or fantasize about favorite meals. In this segment, experimenters find that animal subjects will keep pressing a bar if the bar-pressing is rewarded with stimulation of their lateral hypothalamus, that part of the brain that triggers hunger and desire to eat. In short, the animal subjects seem to get pleasure from the feeling of hunger and desire for food and are willing to work purposefully to experience that feeling.
Relevant Lecture Topics: 1. Eating Disorders; 2. Dieting; 3. Anorexia Nervosa and Preoccupation with Food; 4. Biological Explanations of Eating Disorders; 5. Research Designs and Methodology in Abnormal Psychology (Analogue Studies); 6. Biological Model

Segment 27 Medial Hypothalamus Anesthetization and Eating Behavior
(Tape I, Real Time Counter 1:43.06, Digital Counter 5154)
Source: Hypothalamic Reward in Feeding, Running and Mating Behavior (Bart Hoebel, Alan C. Rosenquist, & Anthony R. Caggiula)
Description: A second area of the hypothalamus that helps to control eating and hunger is the *ventromedial hypothalamus,* an area that *reduces* hunger and eating when activated or stimulated. When subjects are full from eating, their ventromedial hypothalamus activates, and they no longer desire food or seek it. If, conversely, the ventromedial hypothalamus is destroyed or anesthetized, hunger and eating will increase, even if a subject has eaten recently and is biologically full, as shown in the animal study in this segment.
Relevant Lecture Topics: 1. Eating Disorders; 2. Biological Explanations of Eating Disorders; 3. Research Designs and Methodology in Abnormal Psychology (Analogue Studies); 4. Biological Model

Video Segments for Abnormal Psychology—Tape II

Segment 28 Therapy Reaction Tapes A-J: Overview
(Tape II, Real Time Counter 0:00.36, Digital Counter 0056)
Source: Ronald Comer, 1995
Description: The 10 brief videos in this segment are each *reaction tapes*—brief videos designed to place students into the mind-set of a therapist or client so that they may experience how it feels when addressed in a certain manner or when certain issues emerge in therapy. These videos help students appreciate issues such as personal reactions of therapists or clients, power issues in therapy, boundary issues, and limits of confidentiality. The segments also help students consider various choices that may be available to therapists or clients and the implications of each of these.

In each reaction tape, students should take the role of a therapist (or client) on the receiving end of a particular communication and consider how the communication in question makes them feel, what issues it raises, and how they might respond.
Relevant Lecture Topics: 1. General Treatment; Clients; 2. Therapists; 3. Law, Society, and the Mental Health Profession; 4. Power Issues in Therapy; 5. Boundary Issues in Therapy; 6. Patients' Rights; 7. Transference; 8. Counter-transference; 9. Problems of Aging; 10. Adolescents and Therapy; 11. Suicide; 12. Confidentiality; 13. Duty to Protect
Reaction Tape A—Elderly client questions value of therapy
Description: This reaction segment shows an actress looking into the camera as if she were an elderly client talking to a therapist and questioning the value of therapy for her very real problems of aging.
Reaction Tape B—Teenage client questions value of therapy
Description: This reaction segment shows an actor looking into the camera as if he were an adolescent client talking to his therapist and questioning whether therapy has been helping him.
Reaction Tape C—Client flatters therapist
Description: This reaction segment shows an actress looking into the camera as if she were a client talking to her therapist and praising or flattering the therapist.
Reaction Tape D—Teenage client expresses anger at therapist
Description: This reaction segment shows an actor looking into the camera as if he were a teenage client talking to his therapist and strongly expressing his anger at the therapist.
Reaction Tape E—Young adult client expresses suicidal thinking
Description: This reaction segment shows an actor looking into the camera as if he were a young adult client talking to his therapist and unveiling suicidal thoughts or wishes.
Reaction Tape F—Young adult hints at desire to hurt someone
Description: This reaction segment shows an actor

looking into the camera as if he were a young adult client talking to his therapist and hinting at a desire to hurt someone.
Reaction Tape G—Therapist questions termination
Description: This reaction segment shows Professor Comer looking into the camera as if he is a therapist talking to a client and subtly raising doubts about whether the client is ready to terminate therapy.
Reaction Tape H—Therapist criticizes client
Description: This reaction segment shows Professor Comer looking into the camera as if he is a therapist talking to a client and raising questions about the client's level of motivation in therapy.
Reaction Tape I—Therapist flatters client
Description: This reaction segment shows Professor Comer looking into the camera as if he is a therapist talking to a client, flattering the client's attire and appearance.
Extended Reaction Tape J—Therapist addresses a client's anger, by Dr. Arnold Lazarus
Source: Clinical Choice Points in Psychotherapy, 1992 (Lazarus, Fay, & Lazarus)
Description: In this reaction segment, Dr. Arnold Lazarus responds to a patient's anger during a therapy session. Students should consider Dr. Lazarus's handling of the situation. They might also consider how they, as a therapist, might react to the client's expression of anger and how they, as the client, might react to Dr. Lazarus's responses.

Segment 29 (*Version available on CD-ROM) **Family Dynamics Reaction Tape**
(Tape II, Real Time Counter 0:12.23, Digital Counter 1025)
Source: Alzheimer's: Coping with Catastrophic Reaction, 1993 (University of California, Davis, Alzheimer's Center, Maxine Verma)
Description: This reaction segment shows an accelerating interaction between a wife and her husband, who has Alzheimer's disease. Students should take the role of the wife and then of the husband and consider how each of them may be feeling during the interaction. Also, is there a different way that the wife might consider handling the interaction? In addition, what issues does this segment raise about persons with Alzheimer's disease and caretaker spouses or children?
Relevant Lecture Topics: 1. Problems of Aging; 2. Alzheimer's Disease; 3. Dementia; 4. Family Systems Theory; 5. Family Therapy; 6. Loss of Control and Depression

Segment 30 Onset and Etiology of Opioid Dependence
(Tape II, Real Time Counter 0:15.04, Digital Counter 1214)
Source: Methadone: An American Way of Dealing, 1973, 1978 (James Klein & Julia Reichert; WJCT—Jacksonville, Florida)
Description: In this segment several persons reveal the factors that contributed to their dependence on opioids, including recreational use, physical seduction of the drug, self-medication, and modeling.
Relevant Lecture Topics: 1. Origins of Opioid (Heroin) Dependence; 2. Clinical Picture of Opioid (Heroin) Dependence; 3. Substance-Related Disorders; 4. Biological Explanation of Opioid Dependence; 5. Behavioral Explanation of Opioid Dependence; 6. Family Systems Explanation of Opioid Dependence; 7. Biological Model; 8. Behavioral Model; 9. Family Systems Model

Segment 31 Sociocultural Overview of Opioid Dependence
(Tape II, Real Time Counter 0:17.56, Digital Counter 1406)
Source: Methadone: An American Way of Dealing, 1973, 1978 (James Klein & Julia Reichert; WJCT—Jacksonville, Florida)
Description: This segment presents the emergence and increase in cases of substance dependence as largely a sociocultural phenomenon. Its avid and provocative sociocultural position offers an opportunity for discussion of the strengths, limitations, validity, and possible inaccuracies of a sociocultural model of substance dependence.
Relevant Lecture Topics: 1. Sociocultural Explanation of Opioid Dependence; 2. Methadone; Biological Treatment of Opioid Dependence; 3. History of Abnormal Psychology; 4. Issues of Gender and Race in Abnormal Psychology; 5. Sociocultural Model; 6. Biological Treatment

Segment 32 Methadone Treatment Program, 1973
(Tape II, Real Time Counter 0:22.18, Digital Counter 1685)
Source: Methadone: An American Way of Dealing, 1973, 1978 (James Klein & Julia Reichert; WJCT—Jacksonville, Florida)
Description: This segment looks at a methadone program during the rise of such treatment programs in the 1970s, and raises many questions about the philosophy, effectiveness, and impact of methadone treatment. At the end of the segment, even Dr. William Dobbs, a leading researcher in methadone treatment, raises questions about its effectiveness.
Relevant Lecture Topics: 1. Methadone; 2. Biological Treatment of Opioid Dependence (Drug Maintenance Therapy and Detoxification); 3. Effectiveness of Biological Treatment of Opioid Dependence; 4. Biological Treatment

Segment 33 Group Therapy for Substance Dependence
(Tape II, Real Time Counter 0:28.07, Digital Counter 2035)

Source: Methadone: An American Way of Dealing, 1973, 1978 (James Klein & Julia Reichert; WJCT—Jacksonville, Florida)
Description: This group therapy session for persons with substance dependence, conducted at a self-help residential treatment program in Washington, D.C., in the 1970s, demonstrates the mixture of confrontation and support and the requirements of self-honesty that characterize many such programs. It also reveals the streetwise approach often used in treatment programs in urban settings.
Relevant Lecture Topics: 1. Group Therapy for Substance Dependence; 2. Residential Treatment Programs (Therapeutic Communities) for Substance Dependence; 3. Clinical Picture of Substance Dependence; 4. Group Therapy; 5. Self-Help Groups; 6. Treatment

Segment 34 Persons After Recovery From Substance Dependence
(Tape II, Real Time Counter 0:32.51, Digital Counter 2301)
Source: Methadone: An American Way of Dealing, 1973, 1978 (James Klein & Julia Reichert; WJCT—Jacksonville, Florida)
Description: In this segment two men are interviewed several years after recovery from substance dependence. These men, shown in previous segments while they were still dependent on substances, look and sound like different people. Their memories of their substance dependence and accompanying life style, and the road that led to their recovery, highlight the difficulties of recovery from substance abuse.
Relevant Lecture Topics: 1. Recovery from Substance Dependence; 2. Clinical Picture of Substance Dependence; 3. Treatments for Substance Dependence; 4. Methadone Treatment; 5. Residential Treatment Programs for Substance Dependence; 6. Self-Help Groups; 7. Sociocultural View

Segment 35 Person With Hallucinations
(Tape II, Real Time Counter 0:38.20, Digital Counter 2594)
Source: Madness: In Two Minds, 1991 (BBC-Lionheart Television International)
Description: In this segment, a woman with schizophrenia experiences and describes in detail hallucinations and their powerful impact upon her life.
Relevant Lecture Topics: 1. Clinical Picture of Schizophrenia; 2. Hallucinations; 3. Biological Model

Segment 36 Home Visit by Person with Schizophrenia
(Tape II, Real Time Counter 0:41.42, Digital Counter 2770)
Source: The Brain: Madness, 1984 (Thirteen, WNET, New York Educational Broadcasting Corporation)
Description: In this segment, a young man with schizophrenia, a former police officer, sits down and talks to his father during a visit home from a mental hospital. During this interaction certain symptoms are apparent, including loose associations and inappropriate affect.
Relevant Lecture Topics: 1. Clinical Picture of Schizophrenia; 2. Loose Associations; 3. Inappropriate Affect; 4. Schizophrenia and Family Impact; 5. Parents of Persons with Schizophrenia; 6. Treatments for Schizophrenia; 7. Institutionalization; 8. Treatment

Segment 37 Parent's Reaction to Her Adult Child's Schizophrenia
(Tape II, Real Time Counter 0:45.19, Digital Counter 2949)
Source: The Brain: Madness, 1984 (Thirteen, WNET, New York Educational Broadcasting Corporation)
Description: In this segment, a woman movingly describes her thoughts about and reactions to her son's psychotic symptoms. Her reaction, common to many such parents, contradicts the notions of a schizophrenogenic mother or double bind family communications, which were once the leading explanations for this disorder.
Relevant Lecture Topics: 1. Schizophrenia and Family Impact; 2. Parents of Persons with Schizophrenia; 3. Assessment and Diagnosis; 4. Genetic and Biological Views of Schizophrenia; 5. Family View of Schizophrenia; 6. Thought and Perceptual Dysfunctions in Schizophrenia; 7. History of Abnormal Psychology

Segments 38 & 39 Antipsychotic Drugs
#38: Person Before and During Antipsychotic Drug Therapy
#39: Undesired Effects of Antipsychotic Drugs
(Tape II, Real Time Counter 0:49.15, Digital Counter 3139)
Source: The Brain: Madness, 1984 (Thirteen, WNET, New York Educational Broadcasting Corporation); *Madness: Brainwaves,* 1991 (BBC-Lionheart Television International)
Description: These two segments demonstrate both the good and the bad features of antipsychotic drugs. The first segment (#38) demonstrates the near-miraculous turnaround that occurs for some schizophrenic persons when they take antipsychotic medication. The man in this segment is seen as extremely confused and unable to verbalize effectively prior to taking a new drug. A month later, after the introduction of the drug, he is clear, coherent, and planning for a return to work. The second segment (#39) reveals the undesired effects that may be brought about by these drugs, including extrapyramidal effects.
Relevant Lecture Topics: 1. Effects of Antipsychotic Drugs; 2. Clinical Picture of Schizophrenia; 3. Biological Treatment; 4. Biological Model; 5. Deinstitutionalization; 6. History of Abnormal Psychology

Segment 40 Deinstitutionalization and Homelessness
(Tape II, Real Time Counter 0:53.22, Digital Counter 3331)
Source: Madness: Brainwaves, 1991 (BBC-Lionheart Television International)
Description: This segment, centered in New York City's Grand Central Station, shows the failure of deinstitutionalization for many people with schizophrenia who have become homeless without proper community treatment and care.
Relevant Lecture Topics: 1. Treatments for Schizophrenia; 2. Deinstitutionalization; 3. Homelessness and Schizophrenia; 4. Community Mental Health; 5. Aftercare; 6. Law, Society and the Mental Health Profession; 7. Current Trends in Abnormal Psychology; 8. Sociocultural Model; 9. Institutionalization; 10. History of Abnormal Psychology; 11. General Treatment

Segment 41 Therapy Discussion Group: Patients with Severe Mental Disorders
(Tape II, Real Time Counter 0:55.22, Digital Counter 3422)
Source: Madness: In Two Minds, 1991 (BBC-Lionheart Television International)
Description: In this segment, people with chronic cases of schizophrenia and other disorders hold a therapy discussion group. The segment reveals their symptoms (including delusions, hallucinations, and loose associations), as well as their views of their disorders and their personal reactions to drug treatments.
Relevant Lecture Topics: 1. Clinical Picture of Schizophrenia; 2. Impact of Schizophrenia; 3. Treatments for Schizophrenia; 4. Group Therapy for People with Schizophrenia; 5. Antipsychotic Drug Treatment for Schizophrenia; 6. Group Therapy; 7. General Treatment; 8. Cognitive and Biological Views of Schizophrenia; 9. Cognitive View; 10. Biological Model

Segment 42 Prefrontal Lobotomy Procedure, 1942
(Tape II, Real Time Counter 0:59.55, Digital Counter 3626)
Source: "Prefrontal Lobotomy in the Treatment of Mental Disorders," 1942 (Producers: Walter Freeman and James Watts). Courtesy: History of Medicine Division, National Library of Medicine.
Description: In the late 1930s, the neuropsychiatrist Egas Moniz developed the lobotomy, a brain operation in which a surgeon would cut the connections between the cortex of the brain's frontal lobes and the lower centers of the brain. This segment from 1942 shows excerpts from a lobotomy procedure, done by the American neuropsychiatrist Walter Freeman. Parts of this segment are quite unpleasant to view.
Relevant Lecture Topics: 1. Lobotomy; 2. Biological Treatments for Schizophrenia; 3. History of Abnormal Psychology; 4. Biological Treatment; 5. Biological Model

Segment 43 Patients Before and After Prefrontal Lobotomy, 1944
(Tape II, Real Time Counter 1:03.26, Digital Counter 3780)
Source: Prefrontal Lobotomy in Chronic Schizophrenia, 1944 (A. E. Bennett, Bishop Clarkson Memorial Hospital, Psychiatric Department). Courtesy: History of Medicine Division, National Library of Medicine.
Description: This segment shows historical footage of patients before and shortly after their lobotomies. Although each case was pointed to as a success, it is obvious, looking back, that their postoperative behavior and functioning was hardly ideal or problem-free.
Relevant Lecture Topics: 1. Lobotomy; 2. Biological Treatments for Schizophrenia; 3. History of Abnormal Psychology; 4. Clinical Picture of Schizophrenia; 5. Institutionalization; 6. Patients' Rights; 7. Law, Ethics, and Abnormal Psychology; 8. Biological Treatment; 9. Biological Model

Segment 44 Lobotomized Persons at a State Hospital Today
(Tape II, Real Time Counter 1:09.48, Digital Counter 4048)
Source: Madness: Brainwaves, 1991 (BBC-Lionheart Television International)
Description: This segment shows the current state of some hospitalized patients who received a lobotomy in the past. It quickly reveals the lack of independence, loss of initiative, and other undesired effects often brought about by this procedure.
Relevant Lecture Topics: 1. Lobotomy; 2. Biological Treatments for Schizophrenia; 3. History of Abnormal Psychology; 4. Institutionalization; 5. Patients' Rights; 6. Law, Ethics, and Abnormal Psychology; 7. Biological Treatment; 8. Biological Model

Segment 45 Early Case of Multiple Personality Disorder
(Tape II, Real Time Counter 1:11.04, Digital Counter 4101)
Source: Case Study of Multiple Personality, 1923 (C.C. Wholey). Courtesy: History of Medicine Division, National Library of Medicine.
Description: Recently, there have been increases in the number of reported cases of multiple personality disorder, raising questions about whether it may sometimes be an iatrogenic phenomenon. But reports of the disorder are not new. The case presented in this segment was filmed very early in this century.
Relevant Lecture Topics: 1. Clinical Picture of Multiple Personality Disorder; 2. Dissociative Disorders; 3. History of Abnormal Psychology; 4. Memory; 5. Self-Hypnosis

Segment 46 Clinical Picture of Autism
(Tape II, Real Time Counter 1:17.44, Digital Counter 4368)
Source: Behavioral Treatment of Autistic Children, 1988 (Focus International, Inc.)
Description: This segment displays features of autism, including early onset, social unresponsiveness, language and communication deficits, limited imaginative play, and self-stimulatory behaviors.
Relevant Lecture Topics: 1. Clinical Picture of Autism; 2. Problems of Childhood; 3. Life-Span Disorders; 4. Treatments for Autism

Segment 47 Dr. Ivar Lovaas Treats Young Autistic Child with Behavioral Intervention
(Tape II, Real Time Counter 1:20.00, Digital Counter 4458)
Source: Behavioral Treatment of Autistic Children, 1988 (Focus International, Inc.)
Description: In this segment, Dr. Ivar Lovaas, a leader in the application of behavioral treatments for people with autism, treats a young child with the disorder, and relatively quickly helps change some of her dysfunctional patterns of behavior.
Relevant Lecture Topics: 1. Behavioral Treatment for Autism; 2. Clinical Picture of Autism; 3. Treatments for Autism; 4. Problems of Childhood; 5. Life-Span Disorders; 6. Early Intervention; 7. Behavioral Treatment

Segment 48 Adult with Autism
(Tape II, Real Time Counter 1:23.39, Digital Counter 4600)
Source: Behavioral Treatment of Autistic Children, 1988 (Focus International, Inc.)
Description: This segment first shows Ricky, a child with autism, learning to communicate in a behavioral treatment program 20 years ago. Then it shows Ricky today. During the intervening years, his treatment program, in which he had been making considerable progress, was stopped due to a lack of funding; thus, his adult functioning is considerably less than it might otherwise have been.
Relevant Lecture Topics: 1. Clinical Picture of Autism; 2. Problems of Childhood; 3. Life Span Disorders; 4. Behavioral Treatment for Autism; 5. Group Homes for People with Autism; 6. Treatments for Autism; 7. Behavioral Treatment

Segments 49 & 50 Patients' Rights
#49: Preparation of Patient for Commitment Hearing
#50: The Right to Have Delusions
(Tape II, Real Time Counter 1:26.26, Digital Counter 4708)
Source: Madness: In Two Minds, 1991 (BBC-Lionheart Television International)
Description: These segments focus on the rights of mental patients. In the first segment (#49), a patients' rights advocate prepares a patient for the next day's commitment hearing, to help ensure that the patient's legal and civil rights are upheld and that the patient's view is considered and his concerns addressed. In the second segment (#50), a patients' rights advocate goes still further and raises the general notion that people have a right to hold false ideas without being labeled and without being forced into treatment.
Relevant Lecture Topics: 1. Patients' Rights; 2. Civil Commitment; 3. Predicting Dangerousness; 4. Law, Society, and the Mental Health Profession; 5. Labeling and Mental Disorders; 6. Myth of Mental Illness; 7. Sociocultural View

Video Segments for Abnormal Psychology—Tape III

Segment 101 Postpartum Psychological Disorder
(Tape III, Real Time Counter 0:00.25, Digital Counter 0013)
Source: Obsessive-Compulsive Disorder, 1993 (University of California Regents, Behavioral Sciences Media Laboratory, Neuropsychiatric Institute and Hospital, UCLA)
Description: A number of psychological disorders may be triggered by giving birth, including *postpartum depression* and *postpartum psychosis.* In this segment, a woman describes her postpartum problems which, after several incorrect diagnoses, were assessed as obsessive-compulsive disorder. The segment clarifies both the difficulties and the importance of making a correct diagnosis. It also illustrates some obsessive-compulsive symptoms.
Relevant Lecture Topics: 1. Obsessive-Compulsive Disorder; 2. Postpartum Depression; 3. Postpartum Psychosis; 4. Assessment and Diagnosis; 5. Treatments For Obsessive-Compulsive Disorder; 6. General Treatment; 7. Biological Treatment

Segment 102 Obsessive-Compulsive Disorder in Childhood and Adolescence
(Tape III, Real Time Counter 0:05.25, Digital Counter 0156)
Source: Obsessive-Compulsive Disorder, 1993 (University of California Regents, Behavioral Sciences Media Laboratory, Neuropsychiatric Institute and Hospital, UCLA)
Description: Obsessive-compulsive disorder often begins in childhood or adolescence. In this segment, a 14 year old describes her disorder, which began at age 9. Her symptoms consisted largely of obsessive thoughts and doubts, and checking and counting rituals. Her significant improvement demonstrates the effectiveness of treatment for many people with this disorder.

Relevant Lecture Topics: 1. Clinical Picture of Obsessive-Compulsive Disorder; 2. Obsessive Doubts; 3. Checking Compulsions; 4. Counting Compulsions; 5. Relationship Between Obsessions and Compulsions; 6. Treatments for Obsessive-Compulsive Disorders; 7. General Treatment; 8. Disorders of Childhood and Adolescence

Segment 103 (*Version available on CD-ROM) **Compulsive Hoarding and Compulsive Symmetry, Order, and Balance**
(Tape III, Real Time Counter 0:08.06, Digital Counter 0225)
Source: Obsessive-Compulsive Disorder, 1993 (University of California Regents, Behavioral Sciences Media Laboratory, Neuropsychiatric Institute and Hospital, UCLA)
Description: The man in this segment, which is also presented in the student CD-ROM, displays compulsive collecting (hoarding) of items, such as napkins, rubber bands, and pennies, and a compulsive need to arrange certain items in perfect order or symmetry. His discussion illustrates the rise in anxiety and obsessing that may occur if persons with obsessive compulsive disorder try to resist performing their compulsions.
Relevant Lecture Topics: 1. Obsessive-Compulsive Disorder; 2. Compulsive Collecting or Hoarding; 3. Compulsive Need For Symmetry or Order; 4. Relationship Between Obsessions and Compulsions; 5. Relationship Between Compulsions and Anxiety; 6. Distinguishing Obsessive-Compulsive Disorder From Obsessive-Compulsive Personality Disorder

Segment 104 (*Short version available on CD-ROM) **Perfectionism: Obsessive-Compulsive Disorder Versus Obsessive-Compulsive Personality Disorder**
(Tape III, Real Time Counter 0:13.14, Digital Counter 0348)
Source: Obsessive-Compulsive Disorder, 1993 (University of California Regents, Behavioral Sciences Media Laboratory, Neuropsychiatric Institute and Hospital, UCLA)
Description: In this segment, part of which is also presented in the student CD-ROM, a young woman discusses and demonstrates how she is driven to perfectionism, and the powerful impact this has on her life. Her compulsive rituals, including her compulsive checking, touching, and need for order and symmetry suggest an obsessive-compulsive disorder. At the same time, her preoccupation with perfectionism and orderliness also may fit a pattern of obsessive-compulsive personality disorder. This segment thus raises questions about the possible comorbidity of the two disorders, how to distinguish the two, and the difference between "normal" perfectionism and psychopathology.
Relevant Lecture Topics: 1. Obsessive-Compulsive Disorder; 2. Compulsive Rituals; 3. Compulsive Checking; 4. Compulsive Touching; 5. Compulsive Need for Order; 6. Perfectionism; 7. Obsessive-Compulsive Personality Disorder; 8. Comorbidity; 9. Distinguishing Obsessive-Compulsive Disorder From Obsessive-Compulsive Personality Disorder; 10. Assessment and Diagnosis; 11. Defining Abnormality

Segment 105 Compulsive Vocalizations (Noise-Making) by a Child with Obsessive-Compulsive Disorder
(Tape III, Real Time Counter 0:17.26, Digital Counter 0441)
Source: Obsessive-Compulsive Disorder, 1993 (University of California Regents, Behavioral Sciences Media Laboratory, Neuropsychiatric Institute and Hospital, UCLA)
Description: This segment shows a child's compulsive behavior of making certain sounds throughout the day. Discussions with the child and his mother reveal that his extreme compulsion is, in part, a way of trying to "control" "bad" thoughts or attitudes. Cognitive theorists would suggest that they represent efforts to "neutralize" the bad thoughts. Segment 106 will later reveal that the child responds very successfully to treatment with an antidepressant medication. Note the similarities between the sounds that the child utters and those uttered by persons supposedly possessed by the Devil in centuries past, as portrayed in movies such as "The Exorcist." Such similarities indicate that at least some persons who were, in past times, thought to be possessed and to be speaking the words of the Devil, were actually suffering from a similar form of obsessive-compulsive disorder.
Relevant Lecture Topics: 1. Obsessive Compulsive Disorder; 2. Relationship Between Obsessions and Compulsions; 3. Cognitive Theory of Obsessive-Compulsive Disorder; 4. Verbal Rituals; 5. Past Views and Treatments; 6. Demonology; 7. Exorcism

Segment 106 Treatment for Obsessive-Compulsive Disorder
(Tape III, Real Time Counter 0:23.38, Digital Counter 0568)
Source: Obsessive-Compulsive Disorder, 1993 (University of California Regents, Behavioral Sciences Media Laboratory, Neuropsychiatric Institute and Hospital, UCLA)
Description: Two highly effective treatments for obsessive-compulsive disorder are the behavioral treatment of "exposure and response prevention" and the biological treatment of antidepressant medications that raise the activity of serotonin. In this segment, two individuals describe their improvement after having taken antidepressant medications. The treatment almost totally eliminated the symptoms of the child in

the segment (who was first observed on Segment 105). It brought more moderate improvement to the man in the segment—improvement that was nevertheless enough to make an enormous difference in the quality of his life.
Relevant Lecture Topics: 1. Obsessive-Compulsive Disorder; 2. Antidepressant Drug Treatment for Obsessive-Compulsive Disorder; 3. Obsessive Doubts; 4. Verbal Rituals; 5. Compulsive Touching; 6. Disorders of Childhood and Old Age

Segment 107 Young Man with Tourette Syndrome
(Tape III, Real Time Counter 0:28.17, Digital Counter 0657)
Source: Tourette Syndrome: The Sudden Intruder, 1972 (Regents of the University of California, Behavioral Sciences Media Laboratory, Neuropsychiatric Institute Center for the Health Sciences, UCLA)
Description: This segment shows a young man with Tourette syndrome, a neurological disorder in which individuals make unpredictable and involuntary sounds and movements, including swearing in some cases. Some researchers believe that the disorder's biological causes are related to those that underlie obsessive-compulsive disorder. Filmed before effective medications for this disorder were developed, the segment also shows that the acceptance of the young man's symptoms by his college classmates clearly helped him adapt more successfully to his disorder.
Relevant Lecture Topics: 1. Tourette Syndrome; 2. Neurological Disorders; 3. Sociocultural Model; 4. Biological Model; 5. Obsessive-Compulsive Disorder

Segment 108 (*Short version available on CD-ROM)
Assessment Interview with Depressed Man: by Dr. Max Hamilton
(Tape III, Real Time Counter 0:31.45, Digital Counter 0720)
Source: The Hamilton Depression Scale: Patient Interviews and Assessments by Max Hamilton, M.D., 1987 (University of California Regents, Behavioral Sciences Media Laboratory, Neuropsychiatric Institute and Hospital, UCLA, and The Pharmacology Research Institute, Long Beach, California)
Description: Two leading assessment tools for depression are the Beck Depression Inventory and the Hamilton Rating Scale for Depression. In this segment, part of which is also presented on the student CD-ROM, Dr. Max Hamilton helps assess the depression of an unemployed man. As these excerpts from the interview indicate, much of Hamilton's interview is structured, but it also allows for unstructured, open-ended questions at certain points. Over the course of the assessment interview, the man reveals a number of emotional, motivational, cognitive, and physical symptoms, along with information about the history, recurrences, and triggers of his depression.
Relevant Lecture Topics: 1. Depression; 2. Clinical Assessment; 3. The Clinical Interview; 4. Precipitants of Depression; 5. Explanations of Depression

Segment 109 (*Short version available on CD-ROM)
Woman Discusses a Suicide Attempt and Her Present Positive State of Mind
(Tape III, Real Time Counter 0:42.24, Digital Counter 0901)
Source: Suicides, 1987 (Barnett Addis, Ph.D., University of California Regents, Behavioral Sciences Media Laboratory, Neuropsychiatric Institute and Hospital, UCLA)
Description: In this segment, part of which is also presented on the student CD-ROM, a woman discusses a past suicide attempt and, in contrast, her positive present state of mind. Prior to her attempt, the woman had gone through a divorce, sent her 2 sons to live with her mother, and lived alone for 6 years, and she was feeling enormous guilt over not raising her sons.
Relevant Lecture Topics: 1. Suicide; 2. Depression; 3. Triggers of Suicide; 4. Dichotomous Thinking in Suicide; 5. Anger and Suicide; 6. Explanations of Suicide; 7. Impact of Suicide on Relatives and Friends; 8. Treatment After Suicide

Segment 110 (*Short version available on CD-ROM)
Suicide's Impact on Family Members
(Tape III, Real Time Counter 0:47.56, Digital Counter 0989)
Source: Suicides, 1987 (University of California Regents, Behavioral Sciences Media Laboratory, Neuropsychiatric Institute and Hospital, UCLA)
Description: Eight months after a woman committed suicide, her family members discuss their view of the suicide, their attitudes toward the lost relative, their grief and sense of loss, and the suicide's effect on family dynamics. A portion of this segment is also presented on the student CD-ROM.
Relevant Lecture Topics: 1. Suicide; 2. Impact of Suicide on Relatives; 3. Emotional Reaction of Relatives After Suicide; 4. Grief and Bereavement; 5. Depression and Loss; 6. Family Dynamics; 7. Family Theory; 8. Family Therapy

Segment 111 Sister's Reaction to Brother's Schizophrenia
(Tape III, Real Time Counter 0:54.10, Digital Counter 1083)
Source: Schizophrenic, 1989 (University of California Regents, Behavioral Sciences Media Laboratory, Neuropsychiatric Institute and Hospital, UCLA)
Description: In this segment a sister describes and shows the range of feelings, from fear to love to sadness, that she experiences as a result of her brother's struggle with schizophrenia. Her reactions illustrate the powerful impact that this disorder also has on family members and family dynamics.

Relevant Lecture Topics: 1. Schizophrenia; 2. Family Theories of Schizophrenia; 3. Family Dynamics; 4. Family Theory; 5. Family Therapy; 6. Sociocultural Model; 7. Hallucinations; 8. Delusions

Segment 112 (*Short version available on CD-ROM)
Hallucinations by a Man with Schizophrenia
(Tape III, Real Time Counter 0:57.07, Digital Counter 1126)
Source: Schizophrenic, 1989 (University of California Regents, Behavioral Sciences Media Laboratory, Neuropsychiatric Institute and Hospital, UCLA)
Description: In this segment, part of which is also presented on the student CD-ROM, a man who has suffered from schizophrenia for nine years experiences and describes his hallucinations. In the first part of the video segment, he is actually experiencing hallucinations while he is interviewed. In the second part, filmed three years later, he discusses the intervening three years and the impact that hallucinations periodically have had on his daily functioning, and the enormous stress the hallucinations have caused him. He also gives a detailed description of certain hallucinations.
Relevant Lecture Topics: 1. Schizophrenia; 2. Hallucinations; 3. Hospitalization/Institutionalization; 4. Antipsychotic Medications; 5. Biological Treatment

Segment 113 Recovery from Schizophrenia
(Tape III, Real Time Counter 1:02.10, Digital Counter 1198)
Source: Schizophrenic, 1989 (University of California Regents, Behavioral Sciences Media Laboratory, Neuropsychiatric Institute and Hospital, UCLA)
Description: The man with schizophrenia who is presented in Segment 112 eventually improved greatly. In this segment, filmed 6 years later, he looks back on his past symptoms, and also discusses his past and present emotions. Although he still has feelings of anxiety and distrust, and perhaps some continuing problems, he is clearly improved as he now tries to recover fully and make his way in the community.
Relevant Lecture Topics: 1. Schizophrenia; 2. Treatment for Schizophrenia; 3. Recovery from Schizophrenia; 4. Community Treatment; 5. Hallucinations; 6. Symptoms of Schizophrenia

Segment 114 Schizophrenia and Social Relationships
(Tape III, Real Time Counter 1:06.12, Digital Counter 1253)
Source: Schizophrenic, 1989 (University of California Regents, Behavioral Sciences Media Laboratory, Neuropsychiatric Institute and Hospital, UCLA)
Description: The man recovering from schizophrenia, also presented in Segments 112 and 113, looks back on the friendships he has lost and formed over the many years of his disorder. His statement that he has usually lost friends who were normal and made friends only with persons who themselves have significant psychological disorders reflects the sociocultural position that one's social context may help produce and/or maintain the symptoms of a disorder and that the social context must always be considered and addressed.
Relevant Lecture Topics: 1. Schizophrenia; 2. Sociocultural View of Schizophrenia; 3. Recovery from Schizophrenia; 4. Community Treatment for Schizophrenia; 5. Sociocultural Model

Segment 115 (*Short version available on CD-ROM)
Children with Attention-Deficit Hyperactivity Disorder (ADHD)
(Tape III, Real Time Counter 1:08.12, Digital Counter 1281)
Source: Attention-Deficit Disorder, 1994 (University of California Regents, Behavioral Sciences Media Laboratory, Neuropsychiatric Institute and Hospital, UCLA)
Description: In this segment, part of which is also presented on the student CD-ROM, the parents of two boys with ADHD describe the boys, and the children also react to various situations, revealing some of the features of this disorder, its impact at home and at school, and efforts by parents and teachers to address it. In addition, one of the boys himself describes how he feels about the disorder, its impact on his life, and his self-concept.
Relevant Lecture Topics: 1. ADHD; 2. Impact of ADHD on Parents and Family Life; 3. Impact of ADHD on Self-Image and Emotions; 4. Problems of Childhood; 5. Interventions for ADHD; 6. ADHD at School; 7. Explanations of ADHD

Segment 116 Adult with Attention-Deficit Disorder (ADD)
(Tape III, Real Time Counter 1:15.40, Digital Counter 1379)
Source: Attention-Deficit Disorder, 1994 (University of California Regents, Behavioral Sciences Media Laboratory, Neuropsychiatric Institute and Hospital, UCLA)
Description: A successful television director describes the Attention-Deficit Disorder which dominated his functioning throughout his childhood and adult years. For many individuals, the symptoms of this disorder persist into adulthood, although in somewhat modified form. Nevertheless, as this interview reveals, the symptoms may continue to be significant and to cause significant problems. The individual also describes the dramatic positive effect that treatment has had on his functioning and on his self-image.
Relevant Lecture Topics: 1. Adult Attention-Deficit Disorder; 2. Features of Attention-Deficit Disorder; 3. Effect of ADD on Self-concept; 4. Treatment of ADD; 5. Effect of Treatment on ADD; 6. Biological Treatment

Segment 117 Desire for Isolation by Person with Autism: Parent and Family Interactions
(Tape III, Real Time Counter 1:21.56, Digital Counter 1459)
Source: Portrait of an Autistic Young Man, 1986 (University of California Regents, Behavioral Sciences Media Laboratory, Neuropsychiatric Institute and Hospital, UCLA)
Description: When Dr. Leo Kanner first identified autism in the 1940s, he believed that the parents of individuals with this disorder were cold, "refrigerator" parents whose behavior helped cause their child's disorder. Research and clinical observations have strongly challenged this notion, and Kanner himself later completely changed his mind. If parents sometimes distance themselves from the child, it is often the result of the child's desire for isolation, rather than the cause of it. This segment highlights the parent-child interactions of a very high functioning, verbal 26-year-old man with autism, an individual who is also seen on Segments 118 and 119. In the first part of this segment, filmed 19 years earlier, his mother describes her 7-year-old child's desire for isolation. Next, his mother and father describe the same desires in their young adult son. Finally, the young man is seen interacting with his family at a kitchen table. His questions and comments at the table indicate that this is not a comfortable or usual experience for him, although he does rise to the occasion.
Relevant Lecture Topics: 1. Autism; 2. Explanations of Autism; 3. Family Theory; 4. Disorders of Childhood

Segment 118 Peer-Mediated Interventions for Person with Autism
(Tape III, Real Time Counter 1:26.33, Digital Counter 1516)
Source: Portrait of an Autistic Young Man, 1986 (University of California Regents, Behavioral Sciences Media Laboratory, Neuropsychiatric Institute and Hospital, UCLA)
Description: An intervention for helping persons with autism to improve, especially in the social realm, is to have a companion accompany them, pointing out and stopping inappropriate behaviors, and encouraging and role-modeling appropriate behaviors—an approach called *peer-mediated interventions.* In this segment, a high-functioning young man with autism, also seen on Segments 117 and 119, is accompanied and guided by such a companion, who helps him to participate in everyday activities, to test the reality of his thoughts, and to notice the social impact of his behaviors.
Relevant Lecture Topics: 1. Autism; 2. Clinical Picture of Autism; 3. Treatment for Autism; 4. Sociocultural Treatments; 5. Behavioral Treatment; 6. Cognitive Views of Autism; 7. Disorders of Childhood

Segment 119 Music and Psychological Functioning: A Case Study in Autism
(Tape III, Real Time Counter 1:30.12, Digital Counter 1560)
Source: Portrait of an Autistic Young Man, 1986 (University of California Regents, Behavioral Sciences Media Laboratory, Neuropsychiatric Institute and Hospital, UCLA)
Description: In the textbook, Dr. Oliver Sacks makes the point that individuals with various psychological disorders, including those with neurological disorders, brain damage, severe memory loss, or dementia, can nevertheless appreciate, remember, and be "reached" by music. In this segment, music has a mesmerizing and calming impact on a young man with autism, also seen on Segments 117 and 118. The segment indicates that his responsiveness to music has been life-long, and at one point in the segment, his mother is seen commenting on it 19 years earlier, when he was seven years old.
Relevant Lecture Topics: 1. Music and Psychological Disorders; 2. Music Therapy; 3. Autism; 4. Clinical Picture of Autism; 5. Cognitive-Perceptual Views of Autism; 6. Treatment for Autism; 7. Cognitive Model; 8. Biological Model

Segment 120 Impact of Autism on the Family
(Tape III, Real Time Counter 1:34.06, Digital Counter 1606)
Source: Parent to Parent: A Different Journey, Program One: The Families, 1996 (University of California Regents, Behavioral Sciences Media Laboratory, Neuropsychiatric Institute and Hospital, UCLA)
Description: Few disorders have as great an impact on a family's life as a child's autism, largely because of autism's unique, dramatic, and broad symptoms. In this segment, several sets of parents describe the impact of their child's disorder on their own state of mind and on family functioning. They cover such issues as difficulties arriving at an accurate diagnosis, the power of the child's diagnostic label, the stress of the child's disorder on their marriage and family, effects of the child's autism on their own friendships with others, personal pain, and positive feelings and experiences as well.
Relevant Lecture Topics: 1. Autism; 2. Family Theory; 3. Couple Therapy; 4. Family Therapy; 5. Diagnosis and Classification; 6. Labeling; 7. Adjustment; 8. Sociocultural Model

Segment 121 (*Short version available on CD-ROM) **The Savant Syndrome**
(Tape III, Real Time Counter 1:42.16, Digital Counter 1701)
Source: July 19, 132, 470 A.D. Is a Saturday, 1967 (The Behavioral Sciences Audio Visual Laboratory of the Department of Psychiatry, Neurology and Behavioral

Sciences, University of Oklahoma Medical Center)
Description: Some persons with mental retardation, autism, or other disorders manifest the savant syndrome—spectacular abilities in one special area, beyond anything they would otherwise seem capable of. In this segment, 28-year-old identical twins with mild mental retardation display the skill of near perfect calendar calculating and very detailed memories of events that are important to them. Their savant functioning contrasts sharply in the segment with their incorrect responses to seemingly simpler questions involving math or other areas of functioning. Part of this segment is also presented on the student CD-ROM, but this longer segment demonstrates more fully their special areas of functioning, along with their cognitive limitations.
Relevant Lecture Topics: 1. Savant Syndrome; 2. Explanations of Savant Skills; 3. Mental Retardation; 4. Autism; 5. Memory Peculiarities; 6. Disorders of Memory; 7. Disorders of Childhood and Old Age; 8. Cognitive Explanations of Mental Retardation; 9. Cognitive Explanations of Autism; 10. Biological Explanations of Mental Retardation; 11. Biological Explanations of Autism; 12. Cognitive Model; 13. Biological Model

Segment 122 Adapting to One's Symptoms
(Tape III, Real Time Counter 1:48.56, Digital Counter 1776)
Source: Tourette Syndrome: The Sudden Intruder, 1972 (Regents of the University of California, Behavioral Sciences Media Laboratory, Neuropsychiatric Institute Center for the Health Sciences, UCLA)
Description: In certain cases, particularly when psychological disorders or symptoms are relatively mild, persons may "work around" their symptoms in their social relationships and jobs. This segment observes how one man was able to help limit the negative impact and adapt to the symptoms of Tourette syndrome, a neurological disorder in which individuals make unpredictable and involuntary sounds and movements. He in fact managed to achieve great success in his work. Not only did he adapt to his symptoms; he says that he even missed them in some ways after they were later eliminated by treatment. This last issue is worth particular note, not only with regard to this disorder, but to a wide range of psychological disorders and symptoms.
Relevant Lecture Topics: 1. Tourette Syndrome; 2. Adjustment; 3. Coping; 4. What is Abnormality?

Video Segments for Abnormal Psychology—Tape IV

Segment 201 (*Version available on CD-ROM under title *Mood Disorders: Hereditary Factors*) **Studies Link Mood Disorders to Hereditary Factors**
(Tape IV, 4:04)
Source: The Mind, Second Edition, 1999 (Thirteen, WNET and Worth Publishers)
Description: This segment, which is also presented on the student CD-ROM, shows how researchers have linked mood disorders to certain genes by conducting genetic linkage studies. Such studies examine patterns of inheritance across the generations of large, closely-linked families which experience little intermarriage. The work of researcher Janice Egeland with large Amish families is highlighted.
Relevant Lecture Topics: 1. Research Designs and Methodology; 2. Mood Disorders; 3. Bipolar Disorders; 4. Genetic Factors in Abnormal Behavior; 5. Biological Model

Segment 202 (*Short version available on CD-ROM under title *"Mark"—Aggression, Violence, and the Brain*) **Aggression, Violence, and the Brain**
(Tape IV, 7:00)
Source: The Brain, Second Edition, 1997 (The Annenberg/CPB Projects)
Description: This segment, part of which is also presented on the student CD-ROM, demonstrates how the activation of certain regions in the brain can lead to increases or decreases in violent and aggressive behavior. Starting with animal studies on a bull and a cat and continuing with the real life case of a man with a brain tumor, the segment powerfully demonstrates that violence sometimes has clear biological roots and can sometimes be controlled by biological interventions.
Relevant Lecture Topics: 1. Clinical Assessment and Diagnosis; 2. Violence and Dangerousness; 3. Law, Society, and the Mental Health Profession; 4. Research Designs and Methodology; 5. Neurological Disorders; 6. Personality Disorders; 7. Biological Model; 8. Biological Treatment; 9. Media and Psychological Disorders

Segment 203 (*Short version available on CD-ROM under title *"Jim"—Treating Drug Addiction: A Behavioral Approach*) **Craving for Cocaine: Triggers and Treatment**
(Tape IV, 4:46)
Source: The Mind, Second Edition, 1999 (Thirteen, WNET and Worth Publishers)
Description: This segment, part of which is also presented on the student CD-ROM, demonstrates how various cues trigger cravings for cocaine in a regular user of the substance. It also shows an experimental treatment program in which reinforcements for such cues are systematically stopped, resulting in fewer and less intense physiological reactions and, in turn, a reduction in the person's cravings. Unlike aversion therapy, this behavioral treatment does not pair drug cues with negative reinforcements; it simply eliminates positive reinforcements for the drug cues.
Relevant Lecture Topics: 1. Cocaine Use and Abuse; 2. Substance-Related Disorders; 3. Treatment for Sub-

stance Related Disorders; 4. Classical Conditioning; 5. Behavioral Therapy; 6. Behavioral Model; 7. Research Designs and Methodology in Abnormal Psychology

Segment 204 (*Version available on CD-ROM under title *The Mind of the Psychopath*) **Assessing Psychopathy**
(Tape IV, 3:55)
Source: *The Mind, Second Edition,* 1999 (Thirteen, WNET and Worth Publishers)
Description: This segment, which is also presented on the student CD-ROM, offers a clinical picture of psychopathy and demonstrates a leading tool for assessing this antisocial pattern. The segment focuses on the work of Robert Hare and on the "Hare Psychopathy Checklist," and considers how well clinicians can predict criminal behavior or violent behavior.
Relevant Lecture Topics: 1. Psychopathy; 2. Sociopathy; 3. Antisocial Personality Disorder; 4. Clinical Assessment and Diagnosis; 5. Dangerousness and Violence; 6. Personality Disorders; 7. Law, Society, and the Mental Health Profession

Segment 205 (*Short Version available on CD-ROM under title *"Claude & Claude"—Emotion, Stress, and Health*) **Stress on the Job: Psychological and Physical Effects**
(Tape IV, 5:34)
Source: *The Brain, Second Edition,* 1997 (The Annenberg/CPB Projects)
Description: This segment, part of which is also available on the student CD-ROM, demonstrates the psychological and physical impact of occupational stress by focusing on two men in the high stress job of air traffic controller. The segment powerfully demonstrates the role of the environment in stress reactions, shows the brain's and body's reactions to stress, and ties stress to both physical illness and psychological disorders.
Relevant Lecture Topics: 1. Stress; 2. Occupational Stress; 3. Anxiety; 4. Stress and Anxiety; 5. Anxiety Disorders; 6. Psychophysiological Disorders; 7. Psychosocial Factors and Physical Disorders; 8. Sociocultural Model; 9. Brain and Biochemical Reactions; 10. Biological Model

Segment 206 People with Bipolar Disorder
(Tape IV, 6:54)
Source: *The Mind, Second Edition,* 1999 (Thirteen, WNET and Worth Publishers)
Description: A variety of people with mood disorders, particularly bipolar disorder, describe their problems in this segment. They discuss how their moods dominate their lives and, over time, may wear them down. Several clinicians also discuss bipolar disorder, including its symptoms, impact, and distinction from unipolar depression.
Relevant Lecture Topics: 1. Mood Disorders; 2. Bipolar Disorder; 3. Depression; 4. Mania; 5. Treatments for Mood Disorders; 6. Suicidal Thinking; 7. Biological Factors

Segment 207 Woman with Major Depressive Disorder Improves with Electroconvulsive Therapy
(Tape IV, 5:04)
Source: *The Mind, Second Edition,* 1999 (Thirteen, WNET and Worth Publishers)
Description: Segments 16 and 17 focused on a woman with major depressive disorder (including psychotic symptoms) prior to and after treatment with electroconvulsive therapy. Her manner before and after ECT illustrated the positive impact that this procedure may have. The present segment not only shows this same woman's demeanor before and after treatment, but follows her as she undergoes the ECT procedure, thus offering a more comprehensive, case-history-like presentation of her disorder, her treatment, and her recovery.
Relevant Lecture Topics: 1. Clinical Picture of Depression; 2. Mood Disorders with Psychotic Features; 3. Electroconvulsive Therapy; 4. Treatment for Depression; 5. Biological Treatment; 6. Recovery from Depression; 7. Biological Model; 8. Suicidal Thoughts and Actions

Segment 208 (*Version available on CD-ROM under title *"Meredith"—Mood Disorders: Medication and Talk Therapy*) **Woman with Depression Receiving Antidepressant Drug Treatment**
(Tape IV, 3:46)
Source: *The Mind, Second Edition,* 1999 (Thirteen, WNET and Worth Publishers)
Description: This segment, which is also available on the student CD-ROM, offers a dramatization of a patient receiving antidepressant drug treatment and improving significantly over time. The physician-like treatment contrasts sharply with Beck's cognitive therapy approach shown in Segments 6 and 7, as well as with other verbal therapies such as Rogers' client-centered therapy (Segment 8), psychoanalytic therapy (Segment 9), and Lazarus's multimodal therapy (Segment 10). At the same time, the segment emphasizes the value of combining medication treatment with psychotherapy, often with two different clinicians. Finally, the segment demonstrates the features of depression and shows how symptoms subside and give way to positive perceptions, thoughts, outlook, and feelings as the depression improves.
Relevant Lecture Topics: 1. Treatment for Depression; 2. Antidepressant Medications; 3. Integrated Treatments for Depression; 4. Clinical Picture of Depression; 5. Recovering from Depression; 6. Clinical Assessment and Diagnosis; 7. Biological Model and Treatment; 8. Suicidal Thinking; 9. Issues of Gender in Abnormal Psychology

Segment 209 (*Short Version available on CD-ROM under title *"Doug"—Mood Disorders: Medication and Talk Therapy*) **Patients with Mood Disorders Respond to Treatment**
(Tape IV, 4:00)
Source: The Mind, Second Edition, 1999 (Thirteen, WNET and Worth Publishers)
Description: In this segment, part of which is also available on the student CD-ROM, a variety of people with mood disorders, particularly bipolar disorder, discuss the impact of their treatment—antidepressant drugs, lithium, psychotherapy, or group therapy. The segment emphasizes the importance of support, in combination with any form of intervention, and clarifies why psychotherapy may be needed even when medication is helpful. The segment further illustrates the biochemical activity that accompanies mood disorders and the biological operation of antidepressant medications and lithium treatment.
Relevant Lecture Topics: 1. Treatments for Mood Disorders; 2. Antidepressant Medications; 3. Lithium Treatment; 4. Group Therapy for Mood Disorders; 5. Integrated Treatments for Mood Disorders; 6. Self-Esteem and Mood Disorders; 7. Biological Explanation of Mood Disorders; 8. Biological Model and Treatment; 9. Sociocultural Model and Treatment

Segment 210 (*Version available on CD-ROM under title *"Fran"—Treating Chronic Pain*) **Woman Receives Treatment for Chronic Pain**
(Tape IV, 5:00)
Source: The Mind, Second Edition, 1999 (Thirteen, WNET and Worth Publishers)
Description: This segment, which is also available on the student CD-ROM, follows a woman as she successfully undergoes a treatment program for her chronic pain. The segment also demonstrates the influence that pain typically has over the lives of people with chronic pain, and it highlights the contributions that expectation, anxiety, generalized suffering, reinforcement, and sociocultural factors may make to the experience of pain.
Relevant Lecture Topics: 1. Pain; 2. Psychosocial Factors and Physical Disorders; 3. Psychosocial Treatments for Physical Disorders; 4. Integrated Treatments; 5. Behavioral Medicine; 6. Stress and Health; 7. Comorbidity of Symptoms; 8. Current Trends in Abnormal Psychology

Segment 211 (*Version available on CD-ROM under title *"Al"—Alcoholic Disorders: Hereditary Factors*) **Man with History of Alcohol Dependence Is Tested for Genetic Predisposition**
(Tape IV, 5:10)
Source: The Mind, Second Edition, 1999 (Thirteen, WNET and Worth Publishers)
Description: This segment, which is also available on the student CD-ROM, examines the case of a man who had previously been dependent on alcohol. His recollection of his drinking history suggests a possible biological predisposition to alcohol dependence. Furthermore, EEG testing conducted on him as part of a research study demonstrates brain wave differences which may reflect a genetic predisposition to develop alcohol dependence.
Relevant Research Topics: 1. Alcohol Abuse and Dependence; 2. Substance-Related Disorders; 3. EEG; 4. Clinical Assessment and Diagnosis; 5. Research Designs and Methodology; 6. Genetic Theories of Abnormal Functioning; 7. Biological Model

Segment 212 The Effects of Alcohol and Other Depressants on the Brain
(Tape IV, 3:42)
Source: The Mind, Second Edition, 1999 (Thirteen, WNET and Worth Publishers)
Description: This segment illustrates the similar effects on brain functioning brought about by the use of alcohol, benzodiazapines, and other depressants. Research into the suppressing effect of these substances on calcium channels is highlighted in particular. The segment also includes some powerful patient recollections of their reactions to long-term use of depressants.
Relevant Lecture Topics: 1. Substance-Related Disorders; 2. Alcohol; 3. Benzodiazapines; 4. Depressants; 5. Research Designs and Methodology in Abnormal Psychology; 6. Biological Explanations of Substance-Related Disorders; 7. Biological Model

Segment 213 (*Version available on CD-ROM under title *"Brad"—Gender Identity Disorder*) **Man with Gender Identity Disorder Describes His Feelings and His Body Image**
(Tape IV, 4:00)
Source: The World of Abnormal Psychology, 1992 (The Annenberg/CPB Projects)
Description: In this segment, which is also available on the student CD-ROM, an individual recalls his past life with gender identity disorder (including past feelings, body-image, and interactions) after he has undergone sex-change surgery to become a man. He also discusses the changes in his outlook brought about by the surgery. In addition, a specialist in gender identity disorder highlights the expectations held by candidates for sex change surgery, the pros and cons of such surgery, and alternative forms of treatment.
Relevant Lecture Topics: 1. Gender Identity Disorder; 2. Sexual Disorders; 3. Sexual Dysphoria; 4. Sexual Confusion; 5. Clinical Assessment; 6. Comorbidity of Symptoms; 7. Problems of Childhood; 8. Life Span Disorder; 9. Biological Model and Treatments

Segment 214 Young Man with Symptoms of Schizophrenia
(Tape IV, 5:48)

Source: The Brain, Second Edition, 1997 (The Annenberg/CPB Projects)
Description: This segment illustrates some of the symptoms of schizophrenia by focusing on a hospital interview with a young man with the disorder, the same man who was seen during a home visit in Segment 36. In the present segment, the man reveals delusions of persecution and grandiosity, disorganized thinking, loose associations (derailment), and motor symptoms. Several experts on schizophrenia also offer their thoughts on the disorder in the segment.
Relevant Lecture Topics: 1. Schizophrenia; 2. Psychosis; 3. Delusions; 4. Loose Associations (Derailment); 5. Disorganized Thinking; 6. Course of Schizophrenia; 7. Medical (Disease) Model of Abnormal Functioning; 8. Biological Model of Abnormal Functioning

Segment 215 Woman with Alzheimer's Disease
(Tape IV, 6:38)
Source: The Brain, Second Edition, 1997 (The Annenberg/CPB Projects)
Description: This segment provides an overview of Alzheimer's disease, focusing on interviews with a woman who has the disease, discussions by a clinical researcher who worked with and studied her, and pictures of changes in the brain. The segment reveals the progression of the disease, brain changes that accompany it, current research directions, and future treatments.
Relevant Lecture Topics: 1. Alzheimer's Disease; 2. Dementia; 3. Organic Memory Disorders; 4. Memory; 5. Biological Factors in Alzheimer's Disease; 6. Problems of Aging; 7. Biological Model and Treatments; 8. Research Designs and Methodology; 9. Assessment and Diagnosis

Segment 216 Man with Severe Amnestic Disorder: Anterograde Amnesia
(Tape IV, 5:53)
Source: The Mind, Second Edition, 1999 (Thirteen, WNET and Worth Publishers)
Description: This powerful segment demonstrates the amnestic disorder of Clive Wearing, a former world-renowned choir director and musical arranger whose 15 years of anterograde memory problems are the result of his having contracted viral encephalitis. The segment shows that although Wearing maintains his fundamental abilities in intellect, speech, recognition of his wife Deborah, reading music, and the like, he is unable to form new memories. With each new day or interaction, he is virtually starting over, forgetting the events and learning of previous experiences or interactions. The segment also indicates the impact of amnestic disorders on family members.
Relevant Lecture Topics: 1. Memory; 2. Memory Disorders; 3. Amnestic Disorders; 4. Organic Memory Disorders; 5. Anterograde Memory; 6. Biological Causes of Abnormal Functioning; 7. Biological Model; 8. Sociocultural Model

Segment 217 (*Short version available on CD-ROM under title *"Tony"—Multiple Personality Disorder*) **Man with Multiple Personality Disorder (Dissociative Identity Disorder)**
(Tape IV, 4:21)
Source: The Brain, Second Edition, 1997 (The Annenberg/CPB Projects)
Description: This segment, part of which is also available on the student CD-ROM, focuses on Tony, a man who manifests multiple personality disorder, including at least 53 subpersonalities. The segment includes a powerful therapy session in which the individual "switches" from subpersonality to subpersonality, demonstrating his range of personalities. It also focuses on the memory difficulties produced by the disorder and the impact of this disorder on the individual and on family members.
Relevant Lecture Topics: 1. Multiple Personality Disorder (Dissociative Identity Disorder); 2. Subpersonalities; 3. Dissociative Disorders; 4. Memory Disorders; 5. Memory; 6. Treatment for Multiple Personality Disorder; 7. Identity; 8. Personality; 9. Family Dynamics; 10. Sociocultural Effects

Segment 218 Temple Grandin, An Extremely High-Functioning and High-Achieving Person with Autism, and Research on Autism
(Tape IV, 9:04)
Source: The Brain, Second Edition, 1997 (The Annenberg/CPB Projects)
Description: This segment focuses on autism from two different perspectives. First, it examines the brain tissue research of Dr. Margaret Bauman which points to the brain's limbic system and cerebellar system as key factors in autism. Second, it focuses on the life and functioning of Dr. Temple Grandin, an extremely high-functioning individual with autism who has achieved enormous academic and professional success, and who applies an autistic perspective to her work designing facilities for cattle and other animals.
Relevant Lecture Topics: 1. Autism; 2. Pervasive Developmental Disorder; 3. Impact of Labeling; 4. Research Designs and Methodology; 5. Life Span Disorders; 6. Childhood Disorders; 7. Brain Activity and Regions; 8. Biological Explanations of Autism; 9. Biological Model

Segment 219 (*Different version available on CD-ROM under title *"Pat"—Psychopathy*) **Psychopathy**
(Tape IV, 2:59)
Source: The Mind, Second Edition, 1999 (Thirteen, WNET and Worth Publishers)
Description: This segment, which is also available on the student CD-ROM in a different version, focuses

on people with psychopathy who commit criminal behavior. One such individual discusses his behavior and the changes he has experienced. In addition, Robert Hare, an expert on this pattern, discusses the issue of whether psychopathy can be changed or treated, focusing on the ways in which most treatments available for prisoners do not address the symptoms and functioning of those prisoners with psychopathy.
Relevant Lecture Topics: 1. Psychopathy; 2. Sociopathy; 3. Antisocial Personality Disorder; 4. Treatment for Psychopathy; 5. Law, Society, and the Mental Health Profession; 6. Clinical Assessment and Diagnosis; 7. Predicting Dangerousness and Violence

VIDEO SEGMENTS ORDERED TOPICALLY

Organized by Lecture Topic

Defining Psychological Abnormality
Segments 1, 11, 22, 28A, 28G, 31, 40, 41, *50, 122

History of Abnormal Psychology
Segments 1, 2, 3, 8, 19, 20, 31, 32, 37, 40, 42, 43, 44, 45, 49, 52, 105

Current Trends in Abnormal Psychology
Segments 1, 3, 4, 5, 10, 11, 13, 14, 20, 38, 39, 40, 47, 49

Research Designs and Methodology in Abnormal Psychology
Segments 4, 5, 21, 25, 26, 27, 201, 202, 203, 211, 215, 218

Clinical Assessment, Interpretation, and Diagnosis
Segments 4, 5, 23, 37, 101, 103, 104, 115, 122, 202, 204, 208, 211, 213, 215, 219

Anxiety Disorders and Treatments for Anxiety Disorders
Segments 10, 11, 12, 13, 14, 15, 101, 102, 103, 104, 105, 106, 205

Mood Disorders and Treatments for Mood Disorders
Segments 6, 7, 8, 10, 16, 17, 18, 19, 20, 28A, 29, 101, 106, 108, 109, 110, 201, 206, 207, 208, 209

Suicide
Segments 16, 17, 28E, 101, 109, 110, 206, 207, 208

Psychological Factors and Physical Disorders; Psychological Treatments for Physical Disorders
Segments 21, 205, 210

Eating Disorders and Treatments for Eating Disorders
Segments 22, 23, 24, 25, 26, 27

Substance-Related Disorders and Treatments for Substance-Related Disorders
Segments 21, 30, 31, 32, 33, 34, 203, 211, 212

Sexual Disorders and Gender Identity Disorder
Segment 213

Schizophrenia and Treatments for Schizophrenia
Segments 3, 4, 5, 35, 36, 37, 38, 39, 40, 41, 42, 43, 44, 111, 112, 113, 114, 115, 214

Disorders of Memory and Treatments for Disorders of Memory
Segments 45, 121, 215, 216, 217

Personality Disorders
Segments 103, 104, 202, 204, 219

Problems of Childhood, Adolescence, and Life-Span Disorders and Treatments
Segments 28B, 28D, 46, 47, 48, 102, 105, 115, 116, 117, 118, 119, 120, 121, 218

Autism and Treatments for Autism
Segments 46, 47, 48, 117, 118, 119, 120, 218

Savant Syndrome
Segment 121

Problems of Aging and Treatments for Problems of Aging
Segments 28A, 29, 215

Tourette Syndrome
Segments 107, 122

Law, Society, and the Mental Health Profession
Segments 1, 2, 19, 28E, 28F, 31, 32, 39, 40, 42, 43, 44, 49, 50, 202, 204, 219

Gender Issues in Abnormal Psychology
Segments 22, 23, 24, 28A–J, 30, 31, 101, 208

Comorbidity of Symptoms
Segments 12, 101, 104, 110, 210, 213

Psychodynamic Model
Explanations: Segments 9, 12, 14, 28G, 28H, 28I, 29
Treatment: Segments 9, 28A–J

RECOMMENDATIONS FOR PURCHASE OR RENTAL

Video Segments for Abnormal Psychology includes excerpts from many superb clinical documentaries. While the segments alone are ideal for use in lectures, it is often useful to assign the entire documentary for special class screenings or library use by students. Thus, the following videos are heartily recommended for purchase or rental. Collectively, they represent a veritable course in abnormal psychology.

General Interest

Madness by Jonathan Miller (5 one-hour programs)
Lionheart Television International, Inc.
630 Fifth Avenue, Suite 2220
New York, NY 10111
(212) 373-4100

General Treatment

Demonstration of the Cognitive Therapy of Depression
Aaron T. Beck, M.D., Director
The Beck Institute for Cognitive Therapy and Research
GSB Building, Suite 700
1 Belmont Avenue
Bala Cynwyd, PA 19004-1610
(610) 664-3020

The Royal Road—Psychoanalytic Approaches to the Dream
Menninger Video
Box 829
Topeka, KS 66601-0829
(913) 273-7500

Clinical Choice Points
Arnold Lazarus
56 Herrontown Circle
Princeton, NJ 08540

Multimodal Therapy Conducted by Arnold A. Lazarus, Ph.D.
APA Psychotherapy Videotape Series
American Psychological Association
(This videotape is part of the 12-program "APA Psychotherapy Videotape Series," produced by the American Psychological Association. Information about the APA Psychotherapy Videotape Series can be obtained from the APA Order Department: (800)374-2721.)

Client-Centered Therapy: Part II—Therapy in Process: The 32nd Interview (Carl Rogers and Reuben H. Segel)
Distributor: Penn State Audio-Visual Services
University Division of Media and Learning Resources
The Pennsylvania State University
University Park, PA 16802
(800) 826-0132

Anxiety Disorders and Treatments for Anxiety Disorders

Phobias: Overcoming the Fear
Filmmakers Library, Inc.
122 E. 58th Street, Suite 703A
New York, NY 10022
(212) 889-3820

Mood Disorders and Treatments for Mood Disorders

The Mind: Depression
PBS Video
1320 Braddock Place
Alexandria, VA 22314-1698
(800) 344-3337

Psychological Factors and Physical Disorders

Mysteries of the Mind
National Geographic Society
1145 17th Street, N.W.
Washington, D. C. 20036-4688
(800) 638-7337

The Keys of Paradise
Lionheart Television International, Inc.
630 Fifth Avenue, Suite 2220
New York, NY 10111
(212) 373-4100

Eating Disorders

The Waist Land: Eating Disorders in America
Coronet/MTI Film & Video
4350 Equity Drive
Columbus, OH 43228
(800) 777-8100

Schizophrenia and Treatments for Schizophrenia

The Brain: Madness
Annenberg/CPB Project
P. O. Box 2345
South Burlington, VT 05407-2345
(800)-LEARNER

Problems of Childhood and Adolescence

Behavioral Treatment of Autistic Children
Focus International
1160 E. Jericho Turnpike
Huntington, NY 11743
(516) 549-5320

Problems of Aging

Alzheimer's: Coping with Catastrophic Reaction
Health Sciences Consortium
201 Silver Cedar Court
Chapel Hill, NC 27514-1517
(919) 942-8731

Historical Films

Available through: National Library of Medicine
History of Medicine Division
National Institutes of Health
8600 Rockville Pike
Bethesda, Maryland
(800) 272-4787

"Treatments in Mental Disorders," 1949
"Recent Modification of Convulsive Shock Therapy," 1941
"Metrazol, Electric, and Insulin Treatment of the Functional Psychoses," 1934
"Prefrontal Lobotomy in the Treatment of Mental Disorders," 1942
"Prefrontal Lobotomy in Chronic Schizophrenia," 1944
"Case Study of Multiple Personality," 1923